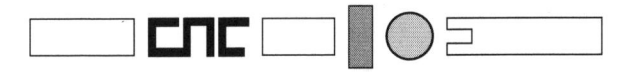

MAXIMUM POWER!

THE COMPLETE UNAUTHORISED
GUIDE TO ALL 64 EPISODES
OF **BLAKE'S 7**

MATTHEW WEST, ANDY DAVIDSON,
ROBERT HAMMOND, ANDREW ORTON,
CHRIS ORTON, PHIL WARE

TEN ACRE FILMS

MAXIMUM POWER!

First published January 2012 by Miwk Publishing Ltd.

This edition published August 2021 by Ten Acre Films Ltd.
by arrangement with Miwk Publishing Ltd.

ISBN 978-1-908630-00-1

Copyright © 2021 Ten Acre Films Ltd.

The rights of Matthew West, Robert Hammond, Chris Orton, Andy Davidson, Phil Ware and Andrew Orton to be identified as the authors of this work have been asserted in accordance with the Copyright, Designs and Patents Act 1988.

All rights reserved. No part of this publication may be reproduced, stored in or introduced into a retrieval system, or transmitted, in any form or by any means (electronic, mechanical, photocopying, recording or otherwise) without the prior written permission of the publisher. Any person who does any unauthorised act in relation to this publication may be liable to criminal prosecution and civil claim for damages.

A CIP catalogue record for this book is available from the British Library.

Internal illustration/book design and layout by Robert Hammond.
Typeset in Utopia and Aquarius Medium.

Printed in Great Britain by 4Edge Ltd.

This book is sold subject to the condition that it shall be not, by way of trade or otherwise, be lent, re-sold, hired out, or otherwise circulated without the publisher's pr ior consent in any form of binding or cover other than that in which it is published and without a similar condition including this condition being imposed on the subsequent purchaser.

MAXIMUM POWER! is a work of parody, poking affectionate fun at a series we all love. No insults to persons living, dead, real or fictional are intended (except to Tarrant – we all hate him). All author profits from this book are being donated to benefit Motor Neurone Disease, so by turning a blind eye to any perceived infringement or nastiness you're ensuring that several worthy causes benefit from our stupidity. Which is really nice of you. Thanks!

CONTENTS

Foreword 7
Introduction 9

EPISODE GUIDE

SEASON M 11
SEASON N 65
SEASON P 117
SEASON R 181

OTHER WORLDS

BLAKE'S 7 FILM TREATMENT #1 242
BLAKE'S 7 FILM TREATMENT #2 247
THE JAPANESE REMAKE 253
TRAVIS SPIN-OFF 258
THE MOLOCH AND GOLOCH CHRISTMAS CAVALCADE 262
THE BLAKE'S 7 COMIC STRIPS 266
THE ADVENTURES OF FSR-1 270

OTHER OTHER WORLDS

MATHSCENE 276
BLAKE'S 7 COMPUTER GAME 280
ROAD SAFETY 284
FOODSTUFF STUFF 287

ADDENDA

NUMBER CRUNCHING 292

A to Z 297
Acknowledgements 336

FOREWORD

by HARRY 'Aitch' FIELDER

Hello *Blake's 7* fans everywhere,

My name is Harry 'Aitch' Fielder and I spent most of my working life between the years of 1966 - 1998 as a supporting artist or 'extra' in films and TV. I worked on almost 800 productions and it was an absolute joy to go to work each day.

I remember my time working on ten episodes of *Blake's 7* with great fondness – they were always lovely, fun days and with a good, friendly cast and excellent BBC crew.

I remember one episode in particular, "Space Fall", where Olag Gan, played by David Jackson, had to lift me up by the throat and force me to open a door for him. In another episode, however, I managed to get my own back when I had to fight some of Blake's crew! The full list of my appearances is available on IMDb and there are plenty of clips to watch on YouTube.

There are also some photographs and some further memories on my website *www.harryfielder.co.uk* and I will be going into more details of all my work, including my time on *Blake's 7* in my upcoming book *Extra, Extra, Read All About It...*

You never know how something will be received by the viewing public when you are actually working on it, so it's always nice when, like *Blake's 7* has during the past thirty-odd years, the show develops something of a cult following and is enjoyed over and over again by future generations.

I am delighted to be able to make a small contribution to this wonderful book and very much hope it helps the publisher's determination to use the proceeds from its sale to aid their chosen charities.

As always, my best wishes to you all.
Aitch.

INTRODUCTION

We've gone to the effort of watching every episode of *Blake's 7* to save you the bother. Listed below are all the episodes in broadcast sequence. Any discrepancies you find are due entirely to mistakes other people have made elsewhere.

Fan lore has it that the seasons were lettered A, B, C and D. However, having studied the original BBC paperwork at length, we can confirm that this is actually not the case and that the BBC started further down the alphabet at M.

So Season M is the first broadcast season, N the second, P the third and R the fourth. The omission of O and Q is because of their similarity to the numeral '0', much in the same way that car registration numbers are handled.

We considered adding much more thorough information, such as locations used for filming and complete production credits, but frankly it's very boring and you're never going to need it. If you do, buy a different guide.

Information is provided for each episode. This is best read as a commentary to the action, so sit yourself down with the book and the story in question. Alternatively, you can skip the whole section but please bear in mind that it forms the main thrust of the book. You may feel a little cheated if you do skip it, and then you'll tell your friends 'Oh that book was rubbish, just a couple of pages! What a rip off!' and because they're better, cleverer and more brilliant than you, they'll say 'What?! Are you an idiot? It was great, that massive episode guide!' and you'll be all like 'Uh? What? Eh?' and they'll turn round to you and say 'Uhhhh ... did you skip it?' and you'll be like 'Yeah' and they'll be like 'Div' and you'll be like 'Why are we friends exactly?' and they'll say 'We're not, this is a hypothetical conversation.'

6.0-6.50 *New series*
Blake's Seven

The first of a new space adventure series in 14 episodes
The Way Back by TERRY NATION
starring **Gareth Thomas,
Sally Knyvette, Michael Keaton**.

Life in a domed city of the future is secure and comfortable but Roj Blake, a loyal citizen of the Federation, commits a Category 4 crime by venturing outside it. What he discovers is a nightmare that contradicts everything he knows and threatens an end to his life on Earth …

Blake	GARETH THOMAS
Jenna	SALLY KNYVETTE
Vila	MICHAEL KEATON
Bran Foster	ROBERT BEATTY
Glynd	ROBERT JAMES
Tarrant	JEREMY WILKIN
Varon	MICHAEL HALSEY
Maja	PIPPA STEEL
Ravella	GILLIAN BAILEY
Richie	ALAN BUTLER
Arbiter	MARGARET JOHN
Dr Havant	PETER WILLIAMS
Dr Have	JAMES LENTON
Alta Morag	SUSAN FIELD
Clerk of Court	RODNEY FIGARO
Computer Operator	NIGEL LAMBERT
Guard	GARRY MCDERMOTT

Series created by TERRY NATION
Script editor CHRIS BOUCHER
Designer MARTIN COLLINS
Producer DAVID MALONEY
Director MICHAEL E. BRIANT

FEATURE p114

SEASON M 1978

Regular Cast

Gareth Thomas	*Roj Blake*
Michael Keating	*Vila Restal*
Paul Darrow	*Kerr Avon*
Sally Knyvette	*Jenna Stannis*
Jan Chappell	*Cally the Psychic Terrorist*
David Jackson	*Ol' Gan*
Peter Tuddenham	*Zen / Orac*
Jacqueline Pearce	*Servalan*
Stephen Greif	*James Travis*
Aitch	*Everyone else*

Episodes

The Way Back
Space Fall
Cygnus Alpha
Cygnus Beta
Time Squad
The Web
Seek-Locate-Destroy
Mission to Destiny
Duel
Project Avalon
Breakdown
Bounty
Deliverance
Orac

01 THE WAY BACK

Writer: Terry Nation   **Director**: Michael E. Briant

Guest Stars: Robert Beatty (Bran Foster), Michael Halsey (Tel Varon), Pippa Steel (Maja Varon), Jeremy Wilkin (Dev Tarrant), Robert James (Ven Glynd), Gillian Bailey (Ravella), Alan Butler (Richie), Susan Field (Alta Morag), Peter Williams (Dr. Havant), James Lenton (Dr. Have) Margaret John (Arbiter), Rodney Figaro (Clerk of Court), Nigel Lambert (Computer operator), Garry McDermott (Guard)

Opening Shot: A Federation security camera watching a white BBC corridor, then a pan across to Blake standing next to some polystyrene. A taste of things to come.

You Just Described the Story:
Dr Havant: Try not to think.

Random Insult: Can't think of anything worse than Blake's rap sheet.

In A Nutshell: Grim, future dystopia. Bleak's 7.

Story: Roj Blake finds his world turned inside out when an old friend reveals to him that his family have been murdered by the Terran Federation and that Blake himself is a former rebel leader whose memory has been erased. Rocked by these discoveries, Blake agrees to meet with other rebels, but they are betrayed and wiped out by Federation troops. Blake is arrested on a false charge of child molestation and put on public trial in order to discredit him and quash the rebellion. Convicted and tried for murder, Blake is sentenced to life on the Federation penal colony Cygnus Alpha.

Information:
According to the title, Blake's 7, but he's clearly nearer 40.

Terry Nation sets his stall out early with all of his 'Dev' and 'Tarrant' nonsense.

Tarrant doesn't even SOUND like Terry Nation.

Varon appears to be both a solicitor and a barrister. He also seems genuinely surprised that there might be corruption in the Federation. Where's he been?

Going outside is a category four crime! That's up there with punching babies. That said, it's not the worst crime Blake's going to have to his name.

Weather Report: it's 16mm outside.

When Varon goes on a dangerous mission outside the dome to find evidence of corruption, he takes his wife. This is fortunate for the administration, who want them both dead.

Blake's charges including 'assault on a miner' and 'attempting to corrupt a miner'. Of course, it could be 'minor' but it's not made clear. Since Blake's reaction is to fly off the handle somewhat, we have to assume that one or the other has touched a nerve.

Despite the stories of tranquilisers being placed in food and drinking water, none of the main characters act remotely drugged. That's probably right for Ven Glynd and Dr Havant, but shouldn't the Varons be affected at least?

Blake's conditioning sequence is shown three times.

Dudley Simpson's score twinkles annoyingly when the prosecution and defence globes flash during the judgement sequence. Unfortunately, the globes don't flash in time, leaving the music in a time signature never before heard by human ears.

It comes as a surprise to no one (except Blake) that Jeremy Wilkin is the traitor.

Michael Keating plays Vila completely differently in this episode to the other 63. Here, he's a wily, sneaky, weasely thief; elsewhere he's a witty, idle, comic relief figure, and often the one character able to speak the truth. Both work.

Nigel Lambert, as the bored computer records chap, is brilliant. When he's dancing with his musical sunspecs on, he's the only person in the episode enjoying himself. Lambert went on to narrate *Look Around You*. Thanks Nigel. Thigel.

Blake really doesn't like the light bulb in his cell.

Leesal Renor was inspected by Dr A.J. Globbs, Deca Carl by Dr Painter Hamer and Fen Payter by Dr Caen Wen. Did they really think that Globbs sounded like a futuristic name?

We can't help thinking that the Federation made a bit of a blunder by appointing a free-thinking, investigative barrister as Blake's defence.

This justice computer thingy is a bit like the National Lottery draw: 'Justice Machine – Guinevere! Justice Balls – set number 12! And here's Terence Trent D'Arby to press the button.'

We get to see lots of the studio floor in this episode. It should really have had a credit.

The couches in Ven Glynd's Justice Department office were previously used in the *Doctor Who* story "The Robots of Death", also directed by Michael Briant. They belonged to Briant personally and were of a type made by his brother James, who sold them around the Birmingham area.

There's some fine model work at this stage of the series. The matte shots of the dome exterior are magnificent. The *London* take-off sequences are nice too. We love the two chaps standing in the bottom right corner of the screen, watching the ship take off. Brilliantly, they're not there in the preceding shot. Apparently, the money ran out quite quickly.

The prisoners make their way to the *London* very slowly to ensure the guard can say all his lines before they reach the other end of the set.

Given that the 'confinement mode' for the chairs on the *London* is essentially a seatbelt, why not 'confine' the prisoners on the ship rather than wait for them to put seatbelts on?

In the final panning shot across the interior of the prison ship, you can catch sight of actor Paul Darrow. The producers were so impressed with his performance as 'Non-speaking Prisoner' that they gave him a speaking part the following week. His canny agent negotiated a deal which ensured Darrow would take over the lead should the series run for more than 2 years – much to the annoyance of Gareth Thomas, who had to slum it at the National after the second series.

Vila's still got Blake's wallet.

Closing Shot: Blake's coming again.

Delightful Dialogue:

Vila: I hate personal violence, especially when I'm the person.

Jenna: I was trading round the free worlds. I'm a free trader.
And we all know what that means, you dirty minx.

Ravella (to Blake): Doesn't it bother you that you spend your life in a state of drug-induced tranquillity?
It's unlikely. You see, he's in a state of drug-induced tranquillity.

Guard: Take a long look. It's the last you'll ever see of it.
Blake: No, I'm coming back.
He does too, in "Pressure Point". He'll wish he hadn't bothered.

Amateur Hour:
The first wobbly set in the series – in the Sub-43 dome exit tunnel, a guard knocks the set as he comes down the stairs to arrest Blake.

Additional Scraps of Knowledge:
Blake's charges:
1 ML583 (unreadable)
2 ML583/MIN ATTEMPT TO CORRUPT
3 ML583/MIN CONSPIRE TO CORRUPT
4 ML583/MIN INCITE CORRUPT ACTS
5 ML583/MIN COMMIT CORRUPT ACTS
6 CR326/PER KIDNAPPING
7 CR193/PER ASSAULT
8 CR193/PER INTENT TO INJURE

9 CR193/PER CAUSE ACTUAL INJURY
10 CR333/SEC RESIST ARREST
11 ML100/DEV MORAL DEVIATION
12 RPOB/COK REVISE AND REPRINT AN OLD BOOK

We can assume 'MIN' means crimes committed against minors, 'PER' is crimes against persons. 'DEV' must be Tarrant's brother or something. Blake really did a number on him.

Important Fact: *The Way Back* is also the title of a 2010 film starring Colin Farrell, based on Sławomir Rawicz's claimed 1941 escape from a Siberian Gulag.

Planets: Earth.

Space-isms:
Vis-tapes, picture tapes.

Below: During May 1978 Timex released the B7-001, the first in a successful range of *Blake's 7* watches. B7-001 was closely modelled on the watch worn by Blake in the first episode and came cleverly packaged in a box that resembled Blake's prison cell. Highly desired by collectors, you can expect to pay up to £16 for a B7-001 in good condition.

02 SPACE FALL

Writer: Terry Nation **Director**: Pennant Roberts

Guest Stars: Glyn Owen (Leylan), Leslie Schofield (Raiker), Norman Tipton (Artix), Tom Kelly (Nova), David Hayward (Teague), Brett Forrest (Krell), Michael MacKenzie (Dainer), Bill Weston (Garton)

Opening Shot: Model shot of the *London*. Get used to it: you'll be seeing it a lot as the series wears on.

You Just Described the Story:
Avon: You've got an army of FIVE, Blake!

Random Insult:
Vila: I've got this problem with confined spaces. There's a medical name for it.
Jenna: Cowardice?

In A Nutshell: *Mutiny on the Buses.*

Story: The prison transport *London* is en route to the Federation penal colony on Cygnus Alpha. Following a failed attempt to seize control of the ship, Blake and fellow prisoners Avon and Jenna are forced to board a mysterious vessel found floating in the aftermath of a space battle. Blake succeeds in disabling the vessel's security protocol and escapes to freedom with his new crew.

Information:
If you're revising for an exam, shove a biro in your ear.

Vila must discover his ability to open any door later on, because he can't even comprehend how a simple palm-activated lock works. All he has to do is high-five the bloody thing.

'Nova' is 'Avon' backwards. Thankfully, we're spared Aliv, Nez and Nag.

The prisoners couldn't conspire more conspicuously if they tried.

Sevateem

This prison ship is quite cosy by Federation standards.

Blake's reputation as a kiddy-fiddler precedes him.

Nova is a promising crewmember.

Why does the security camera only bleep when Vila does magic tricks?

Nova enjoys a one-man foam party in some ducts. Maybe he's not so promising after all.

If you see a hole blown in a spaceship hull, just cover it with your hand.

Yay! It's Aitch! He's throttled by Gan when he realises the camera's stopped working.

Avon hand-claps the ears of his attacker. Wouldn't be allowed these days.

When about to run across the line of fire in a corridor, always remember to shout 'NOW!' at the top of your voice to ensure your attackers don't know what you're doing. Blake is such a div.

Vila drops his gun. The silly sod. Gan's so annoyed he calls him 'Veeeeeela'.

'Tarrant' in the last story and 'Dainer' in this story – are we watching a Season P episode here?

The execution of prisoners is... well, it's Destiny of the Bloody Daleks, isn't it.

Two David Bowie track titles are mentioned in quick succession: "Heroes" and "Sound & Vision". Weirdly, "Earthling" doesn't get a look in.

My God, but the *Liberator* is a sexy minx.

The transfer tube looks very naughty from the outside. From the inside, it's just some sort of bouncy castle filmed in the BBC car park.

Why was ~~Raper~~ Raiker wearing his seatbelt on the bridge? No one else is. They're just wandering around the place.

The *Liberator* flight deck is summed up brilliantly by Jenna of all people: 'Beautiful!'

Avon's brother is clearly mouthing his name as 'Avon'. This must make family get-togethers massively baffling: 'Hello, Avon.' 'Hello, Avon.' 'Hi, Avon.' 'You alright, Avon?'

Raiker being sucked out into space is rather well-realised.

Closing Shot: A cartoon *Liberator* flies through cartoon space.

Delightful Dialogue:
Avon: Have you ever met an honest man?
Jenna (looking at Blake): Perhaps.

Vila: Nervous? I'm not nervous, just... poised for action.

Avon: Listen to me. Wealth is the only reality. And the only way to obtain wealth is to take it away from somebody else. Wake up, Blake! You may not be tranquilised any longer, but you're still dreaming.

Leylan: I like 'em docile.
Course you do, darlin'.

Nova: I've not done anything yet.

Jenna: It goes solid in seconds.
There speaks a voice of experience.

Amateur Hour:
The seat that Blake is confined to at the start of this episode isn't the same one he was in at the end of "The Way Back".

The flight deck wobbles impressively as the ship enters turbulence; the corridor, as seen through the door of the flight deck, doesn't. The actors occasionally forget to knock their cups over, too.

How can the stray plasma bolts in space be heard from inside the ship?

The *London*'s thrusters fire out smoke. Which drifts upwards. In zero-gravity space.

Nova's cries as he gets covered in shaving foam aren't in synch with his lips.

Additional Scraps of Knowledge:
Jenna Rape-Threat:
Leylan: Mr Raiker, there's a female prisoner on our manifest.

Vila's Massive Sideburns: Absent

Planets: Earth.

Space-isms:
Artix says that they are 'five subsecs on the Hi-D grid'. Given the silence from all around him, this is clearly nonsense in the future as well as the 70s.

Geek facts: The backpack worn by the character Dave Bowman in Kubrick's *2001: A Space Odyssey* turns up as set-dressing on the ceiling of the *London*'s airlock.

Terry Nation came up with Jenna's surname during a visit to an elderly relative – Stannis is an corruption of Stannah stairlift.

The switches Jenna uses on her flight console would later become the main controls in the teleport room.

The Gamble with Time: During a lunchbreak in the BBC canteen *Doctor Who* star Tom Baker bet Gareth Thomas that he couldn't get the expression 'Spack off!' into an episode of *Blake's 7*. Thomas, always up for a challenge, bet £20 that he could and, in return, offered the same wager to Baker. Thomas won when he impressively got the phrase into the first scene filmed following that lunch break (the scene where Blake watches ~~Raper~~ Raiker shooting prisoners – go to 32m 12s and listen carefully). Baker duly coughed up the cash and then had to wait until a year later to win it back when he shouted 'Spack off!' during the filming of "Destiny of the Daleks" (episode 3, go to 11m 55s if you're interested). Thomas was so impressed with Baker's childishness that he upped the winnings to £50 and also paid for him to enjoy a weekend break in Ilfracombe.

03 CYGNUS ALPHA

Writer: Terry Nation   **Director**: Vere Lorrimer

Guest Stars: Brian Blessed (Vargas), Pamela Salem (Kara), Glyn Owen (Leylan), Norman Tipton (Artix), Robert Russell (Laran), Tony Selby (Sabalom Glitz), Peter Childs (Arco), David Ryall (Selman)

Opening Shot: Space: The Final Frontier. Then some fire.

You Just Described the Story:
Blake: I need a crew!

Random Insult:
Avon (to Zen): Don't philosophise with me, you electronic moron.

In A Nutshell: Bad religion.

Story: Blake, Jenna and Avon take the *Liberator* to the planet Cygnus Alpha, destination of the prison ship *London*. Planning to release the prisoners, Blake teleports down only to be captured by Vargas, head priest and ruler of Cygnus Alpha. Vargas wants to spread the word of his god among the planets and plans to force Blake into giving him the *Liberator*.

Information:
The *London* flies over the same rotating planet thing as in the last episode. Let's call it a flashback and have done with it.

Leslie Schofield doesn't appear in this episode because he died last week. Remember?

Hey look, Artix and Leylan have swapped seats. Anything to relieve the boredom of eight months in space.

Oh, no, hang on – now we get the flashback. Montage time.

Jenna accidentally presses the high-pressure air cannon face-blast button. Silly cow.

The *Liberator* handguns are fantastic, designed to represent miniature swords. Avon describes them as 'single-function isomorphic response'. 'I think he means it will only let us have one gun each' says Blake as he hands his gun to Jenna, who's already holding one. She's got two now!

God is apparently called Neil. We know this because Kara says 'I am the servant of your god, Neil.' (Look, we can use a joke twice in ten years, OK?)

Avon appears to be sticking hole-punch reinforcers to the teleport controls.

Pamela Salem and Brian Blessed – the sublime and the ridiculous.

The nice consistency of having Leylan and Artix appear from the previous episode is spoiled by having new prisoners appear from the *London*. Where did Arco and Selman come from? Arco was the name of a possible member of Blake's crew in one of Nation's early proposals for the series. Selman is just an anagram of Salem.

This was Pamela Salemn's favourite episode.

Robert Russell is a weird bloke, isn't he? He looks odd and his acting style is distinctly odd too.

Who exactly put the treasure on board the *Liberator*? Does it come as standard?

It's good to see that this episode features a good old-fashioned punch-up rather than just some of that nonsense with space guns.

The drugs the prisoners think they need are just Extra Strong Mints.

The last disciple to attack Vila appears to have a drawn-on beard.

Hang on – there are two teleport bays? And just where is it meant to be in relation to the rest of the room?

Closing Shot: Blake staring heroically at the upper left-hand corner of your telly.

Delightful Dialogue:

Blake: Handgun?
Avon: It's a bit elaborate for a toothpick.

Arco: Are you going to shut your mouth or have I got to do it for you?
Gan: Only if you're lying down, 'cause if you touch him again, I'm going to break your arms and legs off.

Vila: Cold as a corpse's armpit.

Zen: You require the remote visualisation unit?
Avon: Yes.
Zen: Please look at the screen.

Amateur Hour:

Some of the *London* shots are recycled from "Space Fall". This only becomes a problem when they re-use the shot of the ship speeding away from the Earth and the Moon as it approaches Cygnus Alpha. Perhaps the penal planet is in our solar system and they've been flying in circles for eight months.

Though more a consequence of BBC production methods than amateur hour, it's a very odd design to have the *Liberator*'s main screen placed off to the port side of the flight deck. It's necessary for the cameras to get in but you'd expect it to be right at the front instead of the gun rack.

And then there's the Extra Strong Mints...

Watch the scene where Vargas walks backwards into the teleport bay – he's wearing trainers!

ADDITIONAL SCRAPS OF KNOWLEDGE

Terrynation Street: This is Nation's second barbarous prison planet, following Desperus in *Doctor Who*'s "The Daleks' Masterplan", another title with potential apostrophe confusion. The word 'Vargas' appears in the same story, although it's a plural there.

In Zen, Dalek creator Terry Nation has invented an intelligent machine which has lights flashing in time with its speech. Can't think where he got that idea from.

Planets: None. Oh, except Cygnus Alpha.

Space-isms: Single-function isomorphic response, negative hyperspace, aquatar.

Page Filler: In order to fill a mostly blank page in any book, sometimes it's necessary to just type a load of old waffle that doesn't really mean anything purely for the hell of it. This same approach was followed by the BBC when it came to commissioning *Blake's 7* to fill fifty minutes in the schedules.

Below: The cover of the first - and only - Junior *Blake's 7* novelisation.

04 CYGNUS BETA

Writer: Gerry Davis   **Director**: Derek Martinus

Guest Stars: John Brandon (American Captain), David Dodimead (Darclay), Dudley Jones (Tyson), Robert Beatty (General Butler), Barry Crooks (Tang), Cameron Williams (Earl), Matthew Christopher (Technician), Roy Skelton, Peter Hawkins (Cyborgpeople voices)

Opening Shot: A three minute cross-fade of snowdrifts accompanied by some light lunchtime jazz from the Dudley Simpson Quintet.

You Just Described the Story:

Jenna: They're almost like real people. But they've got metal parts.

Random Insult:

Avon: If that's the best you have to offer, I'm sure you'll forgive us if we decline, Tang.

Bin Liner: Red Tangs! Red Tangs! Red Tangs are best!

In A Nutshell: Cyborgspeople!

Story: As it tries to leave Cygnus Alpha, the *Liberator* is drawn off course by a mysterious force. Blake, Avon and Vila teleport back down, infiltrating a Federation Space Tracking Station to try to find the cause. The station, under the command of General Butler, has been invaded by aliens – Cyborgspeople – from a new planet that has appeared in the solar system. The new planet, Cygnus Beta, is draining energy from Cygnus Alpha and its gravitational pull is the force affecting both the *Liberator* and an incoming prison ship piloted by Butler's son. The Cyborgspeople explain they were once flesh and blood but gradually replaced their bodies with mechanical parts and eliminated emotion from their brains. The station crew attempt to fight back with a deadly X-bomb. Avon, realising the bomb will annihilate the helpless *Liberator*, attempts sabotage but absorbs a high dose of radiation in the process. Meanwhile, Cygnus Beta has drawn too much energy and disintegrates, as do the invading Cyborgspeople. Blake, Avon and Vila teleport back to the *Liberator*. As it speeds away, Avon is affected by his exposure to the radiation. He collapses on the flight deck, unmoving.

Information:

When Cygnus Beta first appears it looks the same as Cygnus Alpha but back-to-front.

Special computer printout-style opening and closing credits were created for this story by graphic designer Bernard Lodge.

Avon's snow outfit doesn't suit him one little bit.

Watch closely the scene in which Vila takes down his hood – he gets a mouthful of polystyrene snow.

Avon doesn't appear for twenty minutes in the middle of the episode, as Paul Darrow had the squits during one of the studio recording days. Vila only speaks two lines in this episode, preferring to look slightly askance for most of the time instead.

Paul Darrow's request to perform all of his scenes in this story on a motorbike was declined on health and safety grounds.

The BBC 'forgot' to transmit this episode during the original run of *Blake's 7* and only remembered to put it out in 1987.

The idea of Cyborgspeople isn't exactly an original one. For example, *The Avengers* had already featured a similar idea several times.

Surely *something* could have been done to try and cover up the sound of squeaking polystyrene when the cast walk across the 'snow'? It's dreadfully off-putting.

We genuinely can't remember if Gan was still in the series at this point or not.

Production paperwork reveals that Derek Martinus attempted to secure the services of horror veteran Peter Cushing for the role of the lead Cyborgsperson.

Closing Shot: Avon lying unconscious on the floor of the *Liberator* flight deck.

Delightful Dialogue:

Blake: I don't like your tone, sir.
Butler: And I don't like your face, nor your hair.

Tang: You must come and live with us.
Jenna: But we cannot live with you! You're different. You've got no feelings.
Tang: Feelings? I do not understand that word.
Blake: Emotions – love, pride, hate, fear! Have you no emotions, Tang?
Tang: Come to Cygnus Beta and you will have no need of emotions. You will become like us.

Jenna: What's happened to you, Avon?
Avon: Oh, I'm not sure. Comes from an outside influence. Unless this old body of mine is wearing a bit thin.

Amateur Hour:

Sometimes, the Cyborgspeople start to talk before their mouths open.

When one of the Cyborgspeople is shot, his 'ears' flap about.

When Tyson has to crawl into the ducting at 17m 53s the snowy landscape outside the window moves and billows as though it is painted onto an old bedsheet; this is because it was.

The script requires the Cyborgspeople to pass for human in their parkas, an effect ruined by the lamps on their heads.

The Cyborgspeople's helmets are held together with clear sticky tape.

Planets: Cygnus Alpha, Cygnus Beta.

Dumb Guard Alert: All of the Federation troopers at the tracking station, for letting the Cyborgspeople in so easily.

Space-isms: X-bomb, space plague.

05 TIME SQUAD

Writer: Terry Nations   **Director**: Pennant Robert

Guest Stars: Edward Peel (San Diego), Tony Smart, Mark McBride, Frank Henson (Aliens)

Opening Shot: Paper *Liberator*, paper stars, yada, yada, yada.

You Just Described the Story:

Blake: They've built a vast transceiver complex there. All Federation signals and navigation controls are beamed into Saurian Major, boosted and redirected. It's a vital nerve centre in the Federation space control system. Destroy that and you blind, deafen and silence them. That's what we're going to do.

Random Insult:

Vila (to Avon): Listen, fingers. Computers are yours, doors are mine.

In A Nutshell: You know you're in trouble when the high point of an episode is recognising a familiar nuclear power station.

Story: Blake and his crew plan to attack the Federation outpost on Saurian Major. En route, they come across a derelict spaceship with three cryogenically frozen bodies on board. Gan and Jenna attempt to resuscitate the bodies while Blake and the others teleport to the planet below. There, they join forces with Cally, a telepath from the planet Auron. Meanwhile, aboard the *Liberator*, the frozen aliens are revived, and there's murder on their minds.

Information:

This story marks the debut of a much-loved *Blake's 7* tradition: swanning around an industrial complex on 16mm film.

Blake, when you are in space you don't need to call vehicles 'space vehicles'. They're just vehicles. It would be like us travelling down the motorway and pointing out 'land vehicles'.

Is Zen off his head on crack in this episode?

Blake tells Zen to conduct a 'three-six' degree survey. He's not going to find much with that.

Blake's hands-in-pockets acting is unfortunate, since it just looks like he's playing with himself under his tunic. Which he probably is, if his Federation charge sheet is anything to go by.

Unlike every other industrial complex we'll see as the hours drag by, this one is nestled in a sea of candy floss. Yum.

The reason there are no artificial satellites to be seen is because Blake hasn't turned the screen on.

The accepted stance for freedom fighters is hands on hips, legs akimbo.

Wow. There's nearly ten teleport bracelets missing already.

Avon uses an entirely different set of controls for the teleport from last week.

Those plants on the surface of Saurian Major are called Trumpet Flowers.

The capsule prop turns up in at least two other episodes throughout the series.

Avon is stroking an invisible cat when he should be flying the ship.

Zen is being a shirty little cow and sulking.

Isn't it rather hasty of Avon to activate the defrost on the two aliens?

In these earlier stories, Avon's indifference to the rest of the crew and the mission at hand is very satisfying.

Gan packs ten bracelets into Vila's box of tricks before they teleport down to Saurian Major. Perhaps that's why they were missing in the earlier shot?

Where's Orac?

Gan explains he killed the security guard who 'killed my woman'. Where Gan comes from, your closest, dearest love doesn't need a name. Presumably Terry ran out of corruptions and anagrams that week. We're lucky she wasn't called Shegirlady.

Cally's voice, demeanour and attitude are completely at opposites to how she would be written later. You can see why Chappell was miffed. The tragedy is that she was ultimately replaced with Soolin, who's basically the same except for the telepathy.

Not wishing to bang on about this, but Chappell's putting in a really good performance here. These initial scenes for Cally on location are really well-played.

Cally's telepathy works well but Blake's diplomacy is woeful.

Nation is managing to juggle all of his characters rather well, proving that a story doesn't need to focus on two or three of the regulars as happens later in the series. That said, there's more to reveal and learn about them at this stage.

Gan has an implant. A limiter. An implant. A limiter.

San Diego's comedy lighting of his pipe spoils the rather effective mood created by Pennant Roberts.

Reactor goes Kablooey-Fwoom! Shame, because San Diego was good fun. It would've been better to keep him than introduce Travis.

Jenna questions the wisdom of bringing aliens aboard when Cally has just joined the crew. RACIST!

Where was the Time Squid?

Closing Shot: Avon looking moody.

Delightful Dialogue:

Vila: I plan to live forever – or die trying.

Cally: May you die alone… and silent.

Dirty

Avon: Well, hooray for us.

Vila (to Blake): I don't follow you.
Avon: Oh, but you do! And that's the problem!

Gan: Deaf, dumb and blind, how are they going to catch us?
Avon: I'm sure Blake will manage it somehow.

Amateur Hour:
David Jackson's footwork hammers over the dialogue when he's not even in shot.

San Diego's hat is science fiction gone stupid.

Jenna's hair is almost too big for her neck to support.

One of the alien attackers throws a tool at Jenna, hitting her squarely in the back. When we see the bruise, it's on her arm.

The broken cryogenic pod mysteriously disappears from the capsule.

Jenna's gun accidentally lights up three times as she stalks along the *Liberator*'s corridors on her way to the hold.

During the fight in the teleport room, the console rocks every time Gan or the alien falls against it. It also gains visible damage. In future episodes you can see some of the control panels are actually stuck down with black gaffer tape.

ADDITIONAL SCRAPS OF KNOWLEDGE

Terrynation Street: Cryogenic capsules (that's ice cubes to you and me), carnivorous plants (which are probably radioactive too)

Planets: Saurian Major (it's much better than all the other Saurians), Auron, Centero.

Space-isms: Paraneutronic generators. In terms of power, we're improving week-on-week – it's standard by TWO now!

Nerd Fact: This is one of only two episodes where we hear Gan's name in full; on both occasions it is spoken by Zen.

06 THE WEB

Writer: Terry Nation **Director**: Michael E.Briant

Guest Stars: Richard Beale (Saymon), Ania Marson (Geela), Miles Fothergill (Novara), Janine Wood (Claire), Joan Sanderson (Eleanor), Jonathan Newth (Russell), Deep Roy, Marcus Powell, Gilda Cohen, Molly Parkin, Ismet Hassam, Molly Tweedley, Willie Sheara, Tessa Peake-Jones (Decimas)

Opening Shot: POV of a hedgehog running through a forest. They haven't dusted in a while. Then ... a bouncy castle.

You Just Described the Story:
Jenna: It's getting worse all the time.

Random Insult:
Vila: Everyone's an alien to Avon.

In A Nutshell: Psychic Malus in a fish tank breaks the *Liberator*.

Story: The *Liberator* is trapped in a web like substance, controlled by a gestalt creature on the planet below. Blake teleports down to negotiate their release but learns that the natives have other plans, including genocide.

Information:
No idea why, but there's a monkey with a balloon head in a jar.

Cartoon *Liberator*, cartoon space.

There's a lovely high-angle shot of Jenna on the bridge of *Liberator*, the second good shot in less than a minute.

Everyone's got new clothes. Jenna looks pretty hot in her new dress but Cally doesn't seem to fancy Vila's outfit, as she clonks him round the head with a flippin' great spanner.

Avon's playing with his magic wand again.

Darrow's reaction to Cally's detector link question is absolutely terrific. His timing is impeccable.

Gan has a lot to do as usual. Here he must wake up and ask a question.

The monkey in the jar's pretty damn disturbing if you catch it in the right light. And squint.

Cally's still telepathic in this one.

If the auto repair can fix the teleport in 5 seconds, why have they got to wait so long for the forward navigation sensors?

Jenna's possessed face is *much* scarier than Cally's. Her eyes are rolling like a bovine mental case.

They'd probably be able to get out of the web if they didn't stop the ship every time Vila wants to fire the neutron blasters.

A moment ago we were worried that the ship was going too fast; now we're worried it's slowing down. We're only 20 minutes in and a lot has happened.

Avon out-and-out insults Gan for no readily apparent reason.

Blake patronises Cally to the point where anyone else would've smashed his stupid curly Welsh face in.

There's an interesting series of crossfades here as Jenna info dumps the situation. Nice try by the director but it's pretty clear he's just as bored with the speech as we are.

Are these little fellas on the planet meant to be people in costumes or tiny monster things?

It makes us happy that we can hear Deep Roy's fantastic voice among those of the other Decimas.

When the Decimas start banging on the windows (for real this time), Blake exclaims 'Dwarves!'

Ooh, sad-eyed Decima, I love you, with your seaweed underpants.

The monkey in the jar is where Vic & Bob got the idea for little Marvin Gaye & Otis Redding.

Gareth Thomas must have really given his agent an earful the day he saw The Lost in the fish tank.

Good grief, the Decima attack is a bit of a racket. Their yells are even creating microphony.

The Lost is inexcusably terrible. How can a director make several very good decisions and one majorly bad call?

It takes Avon an age to suggest 'Let's get out of here' as he and Blake watch the Decimas trash the place.

Blake could sit anywhere on the flight deck but opts to sit in the tiny little gap between Cally and Gan. Just typical of his sort. Oh, and listen out for the *Reggie Perrin* chair noise as Blake plonks his girthy frame down.

Closing Shot: No idea – we fell asleep and woke up on the director's credit.

Delightful Dialogue:

Blake (to Zen): If the ship's blown up, lofty disinterest won't save you.

Avon (to Gan): It's slow. You should appreciate that problem.

Amateur Hour:

When your only way of writing for aliens is to say things like 'Come, I shall help' or 'No matter,' then frankly you should just shove the pencil or typewriter into the nearest sewage pipe and pick a new profession.

The water sound effect for The Lost probably had much of the audience getting up to go to the toilet mid-episode.

Gan's control console wobbles alarmingly when he gets up to go and help Avon.

As Cally runs to her control panel to track the beacon, there's a bad case of boom shadow.

Monkey-in-a-jar becomes quite evidently man-in-polystyrene. His head's not even joined to his body.

ADDITIONAL SCRAPS OF KNOWLEDGE

Terrynation Street: Nation's still exploring his favourite themes: here we have genetic mutation and the creation turning against the creator.

Planets: Terry's script probably calls it Webulon or Web Prime or something.

Space-isms: Neutron blasters – where would we be without them? Up to our eyeballs in neutrons, presumably.

Below: A page from Deep Roy's original script; note how he has highlighted his lines as an aid to memorising them.

```
BLAKE     So you want me to provide fully charged
          energy cells. And in return ...

GEELA     We provide clear passage out of orbit.

BLAKE     (Examining the unit) I don't know that we
          have this type of cell. I dare say we have something
          that can be adapted.

NOVARA    Then you agree?

DECIMA    Squuuuueeeeeeee! Sqqquuueeeee! Sqqquuuuee!

BLAKE     Dwarves?

GEELA     Decimas.

(Geela and Novara move to one side of the lab. Blake
moves to the other side of the lab and looks out the
door. He sees a circle of Decimas removing their dead
comrade. A few moments later, Geela and Novara join
him.

NOVARA    The attack was a diversion so they could
move their dead.

GEELA     Stupid creatures. Taking of life seems to
affect them. Almost as if they had emotions.

DECIMA    Squuuuueeeeeeee! Sqqquuueeeee! Sqqquuuuee!

NOVARA    The changes in them are astonishing.
```

15

07 SEEK-LOCATE-DESTROY

Writer: Guess   **Director**: Vere Lorrimer

Guest Stars: Peter Craze (Prell), Peter Miles (Rontane), Jonathan Pryce (Mr Dark), John Bryans (Bercol), Ian Cullen (Escon), Ian Oliver (Rai), Astley Jones (Eldon)

Opening Shot: A zoom-in on a planet, followed by a shot of an oil refinery or something.

You Just Described the Story:

Servalan: I am appointing a space commander to take control of this matter. He will be exclusively concerned to seek, locate, and destroy Blake.

Random Insult:

Servalan (to Travis): You're certainly not decorative.

In A Nutshell: SEEK-LOCATE-THE-STORY.

Story: Blake and his crew destroy a communications outpost on the planet Centero, but Cally is left behind, presumed dead. With Blake's notoriety growing with every successful attack, Supreme Commander Servalan appoints Space Commander Travis to eliminate Blake and his freedom fighters.

Information:

Whoah. That robot looks like it could have been really good if they'd had the money to make it properly. As it is, it just looks stupid beyond words.

Its head even wobbles and, oh, what's that? It's a flame thrower in a cupboard. Brilliant.

And a grippy claw!

This episode has TWO actors called Ian in it.

And it is also the first episode with Travis in it. Oh, and Servalan.

Travis has an eyepatch (with working eye underneath, 'cos you can see it moving), a robotic arm and a crusty yellow ring.

Servalan is at her most Thatcher-esque here. If you can imagine Margaret Thatcher in a Princess Leia costume. We can. We're doing it now.

Vila's opening gambit to the Federation security guards, funny though it is, has no place in a drama.

It's almost as if Terry's forgotten his own brief by this episode. In "The Way Back", Vila's a thief, though not much more than a common pickpocket; here, he's a wisecracking Houdini who can open any lock simply by waggling a bit of clothes hanger at it.

Now *that's* a space station.

Servalan's building this Travis chap up to be some kind of warmongering psychopath. This guy's going to be badass.

Throat-cancer vocalisers are the communications device du jour.

Travis is watching a montage of Blake's 'o' face. It's not a pretty sight.

Whose job is it to move the flight deck coffee table when Blake wants to have storytime? We're betting it's Gan.

Budget constraints mean it's time for Jenna to wear an old costume this week.

Closing Shot: Close up on tough-talking Travis. He's a bit camp isn't he?

Delightful Dialogue:

Servalan: Oh, don't be afraid of the words, Secretary: ruthless; committed. He does his duty as he sees it, and he sees it clearly. He has no time for the dirty grey areas of your politics.

Servalan: Travis is an advocate of total war. He carries out his orders with meticulous thoroughness. An enemy does not cease to be an enemy simply because it has surrendered.

Vila (to guards): I've come to blow something up – what do you think would be most suitable?

Amateur Hour:

The security robot. Where do you want to start? The head, arms, body and bits you can't even see all wobble at various times. But that's the least of its problems.

ADDITIONAL SCRAPS OF KNOWLEDGE

Terrynation Street: The entire explanation of how the cypher machine works – where to begin? Travis' hand has a laseron destroyer built into it. That's Nationese for 'gun'.

Planets: Centero, Auros, K14.

Space-isms: Federation Space Control, spaceway, space commander, space watch reports, space station – it's all about the space in this one.

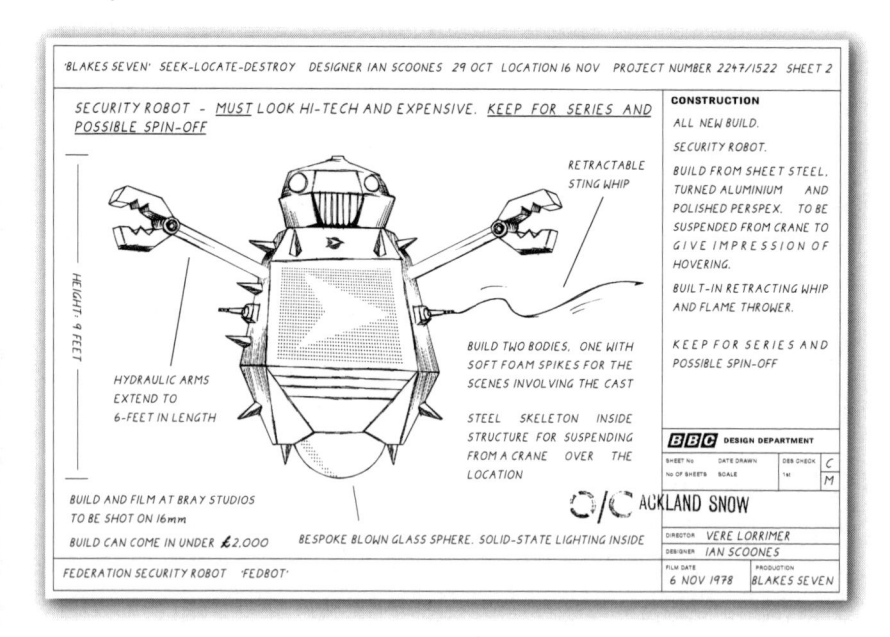

Above: Ian Scoones' original design sheet for the security robot. The short reply from the Head of Drama read 'There is £4.00 left in the kitty and a tin of grey paint. Think again.'

Dirty Eight

08 MISSION TO DESTINY

Writer: Kingsley Amis (not really)   **Director**: Pennant Roberts

Guest Stars: Barry Jackson (Kendall), Beth Morris (Sara), Stephen Tate (Mandrian), Nigel Humphreys (Sonheim), John Leeson (Pasco), Betty Driver (Red Kang), Kate Coleridge (Levett), Carl Forgione (Grovane), Brian Capron (Rafford), Stuart Fell (Dortmunn)

Opening Shot: A spaceship heading towards us. Oh no! Get out of the way, quick!

You Just Described the Story:

Kendall: We've got the neutrotope now, nothing else matters.

Random Insult:

Avon: Not a very expert job.

In A Nutshell: Murder on the Ortega Express.

Story: The freighter Ortega is circling in space. The *Liberator* investigates and finds the freighter's controls destroyed, most of the crew unconscious and one of them murdered. When the survivors are woken, their leader Doctor Kendall informs Blake that they were on a mission to bring a valuable energy device, a neutrotope, to the agricultural planet Destiny. Blake agrees to take the neutrotope to Destiny himself, leaving Avon and Cally to repair the ship and uncover the killer.

Information:

Martin Bower built a 26-inch model of the spaceship Ortega from Ian Scoones' design and they only film the thing in long shot for the whole episode! Madness. Yet, in "Children of Auron", you get a useless balsa wood traffic control model that they zoom in on so closely you can smell the flippin' Bostik.

John Leeson makes his first of three appearances in the series. He filmed his scenes during lunch breaks from *Doctor Who*, where he played The K-Nine.

Sonovapour – the sleepy gas drug stuff – makes it debut, returning again in "Pressure Point".

Everyone goes to great lengths to mention their names in the introduction scene with the exception of 54124 – sorry – Sara. Not suspicious.

Half of the Ortega is on video, half is on film.

You can't be 'very' dead, Blake. You either are or you aren't.

We don't like Levett. She's very sour. We don't like Sonheim either – he's got one of THOSE faces. And he's a sex pest.

Gan hands around what look like glasses of ORANGE.

No character called Rebec, Terry?

BBC documentation officially logs this as 'the dullest episode since "The Way Back"'.

Avon's explanation of the difficulty in moving Dortmunn's corpse to a life-rocket is *piffle* – hefting the corpse up onto a seven-foot-high filing cabinet is surely harder work, especially when it eventually transpires the murderer is five-foot-nothing weedy nutbag Sara 54124.

Despite a murder on the Ortega and the overwhelming urgency of getting the neutrotope to Destiny, Sonheim is still thinking with his trousers when he follows Cally to the storage hold.

An anagram of 'Carl Forgione' is 'Orange Frolic '– coincidentally the full name of the drink Gan was serving earlier.

The recording of this episode was severely disrupted by a union dispute. However, nobody on either side of the incident actually knew what the dispute was over.

This is the 800th time Terry Nation used the name Dortmunn. It appears in everything he ever wrote, including shopping lists.

Paul Darrow throws the greatest punch in the entire series when he decks 54124.

Toyah was inspired to write her hit song 'It's a Mystery' immediately after watching this episode, stating it was the most gripping and dramatic whodunnit she had seen outside the work of Agatha Christie.

Closing Shot: A zoom in on Vila's smirking head.

Delightful Dialogue:

Cally: We must help these people.
Avon: Must we? Personally, I don't care if their whole planet turns into a mushroom.

Cally: My people have a saying – a man who trusts can never be betrayed, only mistaken.
Avon: Life expectancy must be fairly short among your people.

Avon: It is frequently easier to be honest when you have nothing to lose.

Amateur Hour:

The Ortega has to be the cheapest, emptiest spaceship set ever – the Nostromo it ain't.

Blake turns off the ventilator in Mandrian's room by pulling half the controls off the wall.

Look at the circuit that Avon pulls out of the wrecked computer at 13m 56s – it's got a set of dominoes glued to it!

Cally says 'The answer is here. If only we could see it...' You can! LOOK! The word SARA is written in BLOOD five inches from your right arm. Idiot.

The mix of film and video is very jarring in this episode.

ADDITIONAL SCRAPS OF KNOWLEDGE

Terrynation Street: Dortmunn, fungal diseases.

Planets: Destiny.

Space-isms: Sonovapour, ison crystal, neutrotope, laser transfer linkage, laser knife.

09 DUEL

Writer: Him again   **Director**: Douglas Camfield

Guest Stars: Carol Royle (Mutoid), Isla Blair (Sinofar), Patsy Smart (Giroc)

Opening Shot: The camera zooms in on a painting of a planet – imagine a low budget version of *Doctor Who*'s "Rose" – then on to a gloomy cave full of Village People statues, before settling on a priestess in a see-through dress who's feeling the cold.

You Just Described the Story:

Travis: A duel, is that what you're suggesting?

Random (Failed) Insult:

Avon: He was calling me a machine. And since he undoubtedly defines himself as a human being, I shall choose to accept that as a compliment more than anything else.

In A Nutshell: A duel.

Story: Travis has tracked the *Liberator* to an uncharted planet where it lies powerless in orbit, recharging its cells. Blake, Jenna and Gan discover the remains of an ancient civilisation on the planet below, but before they can investigate, the *Liberator* is attacked by Travis and his pursuit ships. The ensuing battle is halted by the mysterious Sinofar, who transports Blake, Jenna, Travis and a Mutoid to the planet below where they are forced to fight a duel in the hope that they will come to understand the true meaning of death.

Information:

Mutoids are augmented humans who require regular top-ups of blood to survive.

This episode is one of only three known cases where the part of 'Crone' isn't taken by Eileen Way – she was already booked to play a decaying ship's figurehead in an episode of *The Onedin Line*.

Vila appears to be wearing a KKK armband. So much hate.

Despite being given a machete, Blake favours a pointy stick as his weapon of choice. Travis goes all-out and builds an elaborate multi-pointy-stick device, and it doesn't even work.

The *Liberator* crew are forced to watch the action on the planet below, commentating on the struggle like spaced-up Jimmy Hills.

There is no 16mm on the area of the planet where Sinofar and that hag live.

Travis' Mutoid friend is called Kiera, a name which translates as 'useless cow' in Polish.

Blake is really good at climbing trees. *Really* good.

The efficiency of Travis' fiendish plan to capture Blake is hampered by the Mutoid's inability to cut a rope with a bloody great machete.

Mutoids are easily dispached with a blow to their novelty headgear.

Carol Royle, playing the mutoid Kiera, was well-known to TV audiences at the time as Laura Collins in *The Cedar Tree*. So, the production team made her unrecognisable by encasing her head in an awesome-sized eraser.

The thing that Blake draws on the screen with his little pen looks like a crude picture of Travis' face.

Travis is a SPACE commander. Not just any old commander, remember – a SPACE commander.

Sinofar must smoke around 60 cigs a day – have you seen the staining on her outfit?

We keep on getting Patsy Smart mixed up with Patsy Rowlands.

'Patsy Smart' is an anagram of 'Ratty Spasm'. And 'Pastry Mast'. There are some for 'Sinofar' too: 'Afro Sin' and 'Insofar'. Can you tell that we're bored by this episode yet?

Blake clearly states that there are SIX members of the *Liberator* crew. SIX, not SEVEN, SIX. Blake's Six.

We reckon the BBC must have bought a new video effects machine around this time.

Closing Shot: Close-up on Travis as he points out Blake's error: 'He should have killed me.'

Delightful Dialogue:
Avon: Blake is sitting up in a tree. Travis is sitting up in another tree. Unless they're planning to throw nuts at one another, I don't see much of a fight developing before it gets light.

Amateur Hour:
Isla Blair's CSO hair.

Blake refers to Travis' happy band as 'purshoot sips'.

Sally Knyvette fluffs the line where she explains her presence on the planet to Blake.

At the start of the episode Gan is the only one to see Sinofar. So why at the end of the episode does he ask Blake what she looked like? And why does Blake reply 'Of course. You never saw her'. HE DID! He was the one who told you about her! Gan's line 'They were here! Two women, watching us' is something of a clue!

ADDITIONAL SCRAPS OF KNOWLEDGE
Terrynation Street: Radiation.

Planets: The planet's unnamed, so we're going to call it Lindberg 69.

Space-isms: Blake's space stick.

Jenna Rape-Threat: Well, she gets tied up. Worse is to come.

IMPORTANT FACT: Blake's a smug fool. He tells the priestess that as long as Travis is alive, he knows who'll be chasing him. There's more than one person in the Federation, *idiot*. There's 8.

10 PROJECT AVALON

Writer: Terry bloody Nation   **Director**: Michael E. Briant

Guest Stars: Julia Vidler (Avalon), David Bailie (Taren Capel), Glynis Barber (Mutoid), John Rolfe (Terloc), June Chadwick (Lydia), Jane Badler (Diana), Burn Gorman (Rapie Owen), John Baker (Scientist), David Sterne, Mark Holmes (Guards)

Opening Shot: Stock footage of snow with snow superimposed over it.

You Just Described the Story:

Travis: Couple of hours and it should all be over.

He means about fifty minutes.

Random Needless Aspersion:

Avon: There are humanoid creatures called Subterrons. They live in caves. Quite what that does for their intelligence I really wouldn't know.

In A Nutshell: Needlessly complicated trap. (Sprung.)

Story: The *Liberator* crew set down on a frozen planet, planning to locate and rescue renowned resistance leader Avalon, but Travis gets to her first. He uses Avalon as bait in his plan to wipe out Blake and his gang and take control of the *Liberator*.

Information:

David Bailie is a well-known photographer, but we don't see him take any pictures here. He's also a very good actor, so it's a shame that he doesn't get a few more lines.

Glynis Barber. We predict a bright future for that young lady. And by crikey, she looks fine.

Travis seems to be wearing one of Servalan's coats. I can just picture him swiping it on the way out of her office.

Does Travis really need those goggles in the snow? A monocle would be better.

Vila's sideburns are really starting to find their feet now.

Avon's look of bemusement as he watches Vila trying to get his coat on is terrific.

Costume designers do seem to put more effort into Jenna's outfits than Cally's. Once again, she looks like she's pegged a sheet to her shoulder blades.

Gan does not appear in this story except in scenes where he's required.

Servalan and Travis have iPads.

We have another bloodbath slaughter of innocent rebels by nasty Federation types dressed in black.

It's tough not to adore Blake's big fur collar.

Patronising Cally is a new game among the *Liberator* crew. This time it's Jenna's go.

We're missing more than half of the teleport bracelets from the rack this week.

Darrow is meticulous when it comes to teleport operation. He hits the same combination of buttons every week. Sometimes.

For some reason, the Mutoids left Taren Capel alive and well.

The medical team must be Space Medics because in addition to the green in their uniforms they also have silver.

When Blake confronts the Federation trooper, the trooper says 'I was sez posted here by the Security Commander.'

We never thought that Blake would be the type to snap a man's neck but he does it here.

The prisoners (and the cells holding them) are: Istar, A-12; Hend, S-7; Raiker, N-15; Kalor, T-5; Pelar, G-1; Avalon F-2. Wasn't Raiker used as a character name the other week, Terry?

The original title of this script was "Project Arkon". However, it was changed at a late stage owing to the discovery of a comic book series by the same name. As some of the location footage had already been shot, look closely and you'll see several characters mouth the word 'Arkon' with 'Avalon' overdubbed.

Avon has turned into the guy in the control tower from *Airplane!* who keeps leaning into shot with camp one-liners – 'The tower? RAPUNZEL!'

The *Liberator* teleport dispenses big red mittens.

The direction is very plodding and lifeless. There's no sense of urgency.

When Blake shoots the metal cup with his gun we hear a 'clang', which we shouldn't, given that the gun is an energy discharge weapon and not one with a bullet in it.

Something's up with Gan's implant, as he starts behaving a bit queer towards Avalon.

Closing Shot: Pursuit ships wobble off in pursuit (of the *Liberator*).

Delightful Dialogue:

Blake: Does it support any intelligent life?
Avon: Does the *Liberator*?

Avon: I think I shall contain my enthusiasm here in the warm.

Vila: I've got a weak chest.
Avon: The rest of you's not very impressive.

Amateur Hour:

The Federation virus has the unique ability to move scenery as well as destroy humans. Watch the chair in the interrogation centre.

Robot Avalon makes whirry noises when she moves only after she's been identified as a fake. Handy, that.

You can see Robot Avalon's mark on the studio floor.

ADDITIONAL SCRAPS OF KNOWLEDGE

Terrynation Street: Caves, ice, Subterrons (why are they called that, Terry?), slave labour forces, genocide, mutated viruses (the Phobon plague).

Planets: Unnamed. Cold though. We think Terry would've called it something like Frostfar.

Special Mention: Avalon strapped to the bed in the interrogation centre with naught but a couple of silver lamé belts to cover her modesty.

Below: Released by MB Games, *Blake's 7: Project Avalon* holds the title of being the most incomprehensible board game ever produced. The creators themselves struggled to understand the rules they had written and, with the deadline looming, they had no choice but to release it into the market without an instruction sheet. Confusion abounded, with many eventually throwing away the board game and 20-sided die and just keeping the rather natty little plastic figures of Blake and four Federation troopers.

11 BREAKDOWN

Writer: Terry Nation   **Director**: Vera Lorrimer

Guest Stars: Julian Glover (Kayn), Jason Robards (Cheyenne), Christian Roberts (Renor), Ian Thompson (Farren)

Opening Shot: Cartoon space, no cartoon *Liberator*.

You Just Described the Story:

Blake: We need a neurosurgeon.

Random Insult:

Kayn (to Farran): You pathetic little feeble-minded bureaucrat.

In A Nutshell: Gan goes *mental*.

Story: Gan's behavioural limiter malfunctions, leading to a series of increasingly violent attacks on his fellow crew members. Kayn is the only surgeon who can successfully repair the limiter, and Blake recklessly endangers the rest of the crew in order to get to him. Kayn isn't happy about saving a traitor to the Federation and alerts the authorities.

Information:

In a surprising move, this episode begins with the *Blake's 7* title sequence.

This is 'the Gan episode'. Count his lines.

Blake is in his Robin Hood costume again, first seen in "The Web". Will he ever get to his fancy dress party?

The Gan/Blake fight at the start of the episode provides both some great handheld camerawork and, when the cameraman slips, a shot of the top of the studio wall. Seconds later, he shoots off-set to the left, exposing the exterior of the *Liberator* corridor. Twice.

Talking of camerawork, in a rare move, the camera comes round the other side of the flight deck, near Zen, and shoots back across the console positions. It's a bit different.

The *Liberator* medical computer is apparently voiced by David Jackson. Suppose they had to give him something to do after the first scene.

Avon spends much of the episode fiddling with Zen's innards.

Though certain other guidebooks may suggest Gan was a sexual pervert who had a limiter placed in his brain to stop him attacking women, we think he just fancies Jenna a bit and was annoyed Blake got there first.

The main indication of Gan's instability is that he squeezes his hand together a few times while lying on a medical bed. Incidentally, this was the week the Blood Donation Service came to the BBC.

David Jackson does his pig impression when he tries to escape the secure bed. Oink.

Thanks to a conversation over a few pints in the BBC bar, this was to have been the episode in which Tom Baker appeared in full *Doctor Who* outfit, nonchalantly passing Blake in a corridor. Or maybe it was one of the other episodes.

The flight deck has a secondary screen near the gun rack, seen here for the first time. There's a third one in "Redemption". Collect them all!

At one point, Jenna stands next to the secondary screen with her hand on her hip like a camp mariner on shore leave in Portsmouth.

Nice bit of foreshadowing from Avon when he says that one day he will find out who programmed Zen. We know, we know!

That star chart they wheel onto the flight deck must be a bugger to set up every time they move to a different system.

The *Liberator* entering the gravitational vortex is somewhat spoiled by the cartoon plughole noise.

The crew go to extreme lengths to find a specialist capable of saving Gan's life, putting themselves at great risk to do so. Given events in

Season N, they probably shouldn't have bothered.

Vila's at his best – he works out Kayn's up to no good and pulls a gun on him without telling the others. Great stuff.

XK-72 is a decent design for a modular space-station, one of those you could believe might follow from today's technology. If today's technology was based around toilet roll tubes and Airfix paint, that is.

Christian Roberts was interviewed for the roles of both Blake and Tarrant. He might've worked. Tru dat.

JULIAN GLOVER! Oh, Julian Glover. We love Julian Glover. We'd just like to say that Julian Glover has been a *Doctor Who* villain, a *Blake's 7* villain, a *Star Wars* villain, an *Indiana Jones* villain and a James Bond villain. We love Julian Glover. He's married to Sinofar, too. We think David Maloney got them both in a job lot. It's a travesty that he turns up 31 minutes into the episode.

Renor is named for John Louis Renor, a French agent and git during the Second World War. Actually, this isn't true. It's a blatant attempt at finding something interesting to say.

The limiter, which is implanted in Gan's brain and cruelly renders him unable to function as a normal human being, is fictional.

Zen goes to sleep for a bit in the middle of this one.

The character called Kayn turns out to be a baddie. Despite that, Nation attempts no Biblical subtext whatsoever.

Closing Shot: Blake, Jenna and Gan laughing heartily after the death of hundreds of people on that space station.

Delightful Dialogue:

Jenna: Five, four, three, two, one – THRUST!

Blake: How soon will you complete?
Kayn: Thirty-five minutes.
Blake: Do it in twenty.

Kayn: Or you'll kill me?
Blake: Oh, no, no, no. In twenty-five minutes, I'm returning you to your station. If you haven't completed your work –
Kayn: Your threats don't bother me in the least, you know.
Blake: – I shall destroy your hands. Twenty minutes.

Something Boucher this way comes...

Amateur Hour:

Look closely at the left side of the frame when Blake says 'We've made it – we are through' over the shot of space on the secondary screen: the stars can be seen passing over the edge of the set. (That same vista is also used behind the closing titles. We haven't checked how many episodes though. There's a limit to our idiocy.)

Considering the ship is meant to be static the model of the *Liberator* is wobbling *very* strangely at 31m 45s.

Blake tells Kayn that the *Liberator*'s surgical unit is very well equipped. Well, we saw that earlier in the episode and to be honest it looked like the contents of a kitchen drawer sprayed silver.

ADDITIONAL SCRAPS OF KNOWLEDGE

Planets: Kainnessos, Cassiona, Overon, Epinal, XK-72.

Space-isms: Voray scan, space laboratory.

In-Action Figure: Trying to get a slice of the money raked in by merchandise for *Star Wars*, UK toy manufacturers Denys Fisher planned to release a playset based on "Breakdown". It comprised of an Action Man-sized Gan doll and a hospital-style trolley for the figure to lay on, along with two folded cardboard sheets that resembled a corridor from the *Liberator*. Unfortunately the mould to create the head of David Jackson was damaged during a test run and no further budget could be allocated to make a new one – so the head from an unreleased action figure of boxer Henry Cooper was used instead. Production ended up being delayed by over a year and when the ghastly thing was finally ready for the toy shops "Pressure Point" had been broadcast and the project was abandoned at great expense.

12 BOUNTY

Writer: Mr Terry Nation   **Director**: Mr Pennant Roberts

Guest Stars: T. P. McKenna (Sarkoff), Carinthia West (Tyce), Marc Zuber (Tarvin), Mark York (Cheney), Terry Kaiser (Bernie), Derrick Branche (Amagon guard)

Opening Shot: Cally having a wee in the woods.

You Just Described the Story:

Blake: I came here to take President Sarkoff back to his people. My name is Blake.

Random Insult:
Terry Nation thinking this was acceptable is insult enough.

In A Nutshell: Blake's jail-break escapade leads to the *Liberator* being taken over. Again.

Story: Blake locates President Sarkoff, deposed leader of the planet Lindor, who is exiled on a remote Federation outpost. Hoping to avert a civil war on Lindor which would end with the Federation in control, Blake tries to persuade Sarkoff to return home and resume leadership of his planet. Meanwhile, the *Liberator* receives a distress call and hurries to respond. Waiting for them is notorious bounty hunter Tarvin, a former colleague of Jenna, who hijacks the *Liberator* and tries to claim the bounty on the crew.

Information:
Blake and Cally take their packed lunch with them down to the planet. They had sandwiches, crisps, Scotch eggs and fizzy pop.

There are lots of different Federation colour-coded commands in this episode. Do you think that Federation personnel have a full rainbow of command codes that they have to learn before being able to pass their Federation Trooper exam? Like cabbies with the Knowledge.

The *Liberator* guns still look brilliant.

Gareth Thomas trying to climb a rope is the least heroic-looking thing in *Blake's 7* to date.

TP McKenna is dressed in the sort of bad *Doctor Who* outfit you sometimes see at fancy dress parties.

This episode is called "Bounty". We do all the chocolate jokes elsewhere in the book.

Gan's really good here – he's surprisingly moralistic and assertive.

The interior of Sarkoff's house is all pointed Gothic arches made of plastic bricks and painted silver, but he says 'This building is a replica of a typical residence of that period' (i.e. the 20th century). Do you think Nation was expecting them to shoot it in a real house somewhere?

Carinthia West has a massive mouth.

West was a model in the 70s and spent much time hanging out with Mick Jagger and David Bowie. She's a photographer now. None of the authors of this book are related to her.

Items in the grand collection of 20th-century Earth artefacts in Sarkoff's residence include a stuffed bird, a pipe, a desk fan, a packet of 20 Senior Service, a cutlery set, a microscope, a sieve, a flag, a gas mask, a Dutch Elm tree, an Evel Knievel stunt bike, a packet of Toffos, casual racism and one of those trimphones. It's not exactly the British Museum but he's tried his best.

Derrick Branche is best-known for playing the Indian porter Gupta in Yorkshire Television's hospital sitcom *Only When I Laugh*.

Servalan got the week off here. She went to Eastbourne apparently.

The plot goes in a completely different direction thirty minutes in. It's almost as if Mr Terry preferred writing half-hour telly…

Blake instantly suspects Jenna is behind the Amagon plot. She's his girlfriend!

At the last gasp, Nation tries an 'Aren't I President Sarkoff's daughter?' gambit in an attempt to make the episode interesting.

Although there's absolutely no chemistry between Tyce and Blake, the final joke of the episode is that she may have fancied him a bit.

In one scene, Zen falls out of his housing and rolls across the flight deck floor.

Closing Shot: Cally and Jenna laughing while Blake looks a bit grumpy.

Delightful Dialogue:

Blake: I'd forgotten how useful telepathy is.
Cally: I must practise that too.

See, even Nation has realised he keeps forgetting she's telepathic!

Vila: I'm entitled to my opinion.
Avon: It is your assumption that we are entitled to it as well that is irritating.

Avon: First sign of trouble, we get out, right?
Jenna: Goes without saying.
Avon: I only wish it did.

Tyce: You'd sell your grandmother, wouldn't you?
Tarvin: I did. She was going to sell me, I got in first.

Amateur Hour:

The restraining neck bracelet things are just a bit of plastic with the sort of shiny silver paper glued to them that you used to get on football stickers in Panini albums.

The teleport controls look as if they are coming loose from the control deck. The double-sided tape had obviously perished.

When Vila runs across the flight deck to grab a weapon before investigating the teleport bay, a camera drifts into shot.

The lock on the room Blake and the crew are being held in starts buzzing before the keycard goes in.

ADDITIONAL SCRAPS OF KNOWLEDGE

Planets: Lindor, Cadbury, Mars, Caramac 14.

Space-isms: Painful descriptions of the past in clichéd sci-fi dialogue.

Jenna Rape-Threat: Tarvin 'may decide to keep' Jenna.

Further Space-isms: There's a lot of space on this page, so why not use it to draw what you think Avon wears in bed.

MY BEST '**AVON IN HIS NIGHT TROUSERS**' DRAWING

13 DELIVERANCE

Writer: Terry Nation   **Director**: Michael E. Briant

Guest Stars: Tony Caunter (Ensor), Chuck Wagner (Automan), Dave E Wavy (Hiya), Suzan Farmer (Meegat), James Lister (Maryatt), Peter Davison (Dish of the Day)

Opening Shot: That "Time Squad" capsule is back.

You Just Described the Story:

Meegat: You have come. The waiting is over. As it was promised, the Lord Avon will save our race.

Random Insult:

Vila (to Avon): Counting yourself, that's two people who think you're wonderful.

In A Nutshell: Orac.

Story: Avon, Vila, Gan and Jenna teleport to Cephalon to rescue the crew of a ship which exploded in orbit around the planet. Jenna is kidnapped by the planet's Neanderthal-like inhabitants. While the others search for her, Blake and Cally are confronted by one of the survivors, who demands to be taken to the planet Aristo where his father requires urgent medical supplies. The man's father, Ensor, has invented a device known as Orac, which the Federation are desperate to acquire. Meanwhile, back on Cephalon, Avon becomes the unwitting saviour of a race who have waited hundreds of years for someone capable of launching the rocket which contains their genetic bank.

Information:

Just what is all of that crap on Servalan's desk?

And what are all of the buttons on the teleport console for, exactly? It's only a teleport – surely you just need 'Up' and 'Down'?

The chalk pit filming location looks rather good, especially when combined with the snow.

Oh God. Unconvincing Neanderthals. It's going to be one of those stories.

Why does Avon get his own special silver suit when the others have matching anoraks?

The jazz music played on the *Liberator* seems very out of place indeed.

Orac is worth 100 million credits. We reckon that this was probably around 100 million sterling (c.1978).

Posh woman in toga, scruffy men in animal suits. *Blake's 7* starts here.

Servalan pours a hefty slug of GREEN.

They've still got trimphones in the future.

Those cave men really aren't dressed for cold weather.

Vila's pig squeals are more convincing than Blake's, who sounds more like a concerned cat.

If Meegat was a plain, frumpy woman in a shapeless smock, Avon wouldn't be half as keen to entertain her bloody prophecy.

Servalan and Travis meet for a chat and do nothing else in this episode. It's a nice chat as chats go, but purely set-up for next week.

Closing Shot: Jenna saying 'Standard by six.'

Delightful Dialogue:
Vila: You're enjoying this, aren't you?
Avon: Probably.

Amateur Hour:
Ensor's spaceship doesn't look too great, and the shot of it crashing into Cephlon is woeful.

Tony Caunter's 'heart attack' acting is a little ripe.

Obvious stock footage is used for the rocket launch.

ADDITIONAL SCRAPS OF KNOWLEDGE

Planets: Cephlon, Aristo, Magdalen Alpha System.

Space-isms: The dead spaceman was a space surgeon, doing space operations and everything; sub-beam communications system.

Jenna Rape-Threat: She gets kidnapped by the natives for some nefarious purpose.

Below: The promotional wine given to visiting journalists in the mistaken belief it might help them find good things to write about "Deliverance". The Plan didn't work as the wine was terrible too.

14 ORAC

Writer: T. Nation (bored of typing 'Terry')   **Director**: Vere Lorrimer

Guest Stars: Derek Farr (Ensor), Livia Venturini (La Suorina), James Muir, Paul Kidd (Phibians)

Opening Shot: The *Liberator* flying through the stars, followed by Gan coming out of the bog.

You Just Described the Story:

Servalan: That box – Orac – that's what we came for.

Random Insult:
Vila: Orac, be a good junk heap and shut up.

In A Nutshell: The *Liberator* gains a new crew member. Are we up to seven yet?

Story: The *Liberator* is en route to Aristo, delivering medical supplies to the inventor, Ensor. But the mission becomes a race against time as Avon, Vila, Gan and Jenna begin to suffer from the radiation they were exposed to on Cephalon. Blake and Cally teleport down to Aristo and reach Ensor before Servalan and Travis, who are also on the trail of Orac. Ensor dies before he can reach the *Liberator* and bequeaths Orac to Blake along with the medicine needed to cure Blake's crew. Orac's first demonstration is a prediction – the destruction of the *Liberator*.

Information:

We're not sure if this episode is called "Orac" or "ORAC". It's not something we'll be examining in the book. Or even being consistent on, probably.

The opening scene with Gan having a drink seems to go on for ages.

Since when did Blake keep a captain's log?

'There is nothing that will counter radiation sickness.' Medically speaking, this isn't strictly true.

Radiation sickness in a Terry Nation story. Golly.

The ship which explodes is a Space Master 5000.

The micro power cells are extremely noisy.

Give 'em their dues – the make-up for Ensor's chest unit is pretty good.

In space, mushroom clouds still go up.

Let's be honest, it's a brave move to try to carry off a sentient fish tank. Blake carries him off mostly. Haha.

Terry Nation flexed his writing muscles when naming the marine life on the planet 'Phibians'.

Gan is in almost every scene for the first fifteen minutes but doesn't have a single line.

A Brilliant Scientist On Life Support in a Terry Nation story. Golly golly! Waiting for a rockfall.

There would appear to be only five teleport bracelets left by this stage in the series. The rack is pretty bare.

Skulking through dark tunnels infested with traps and creatures in a Terry Nation story. Golly golly gumdrops! Where's my rockfall?

Wikipedia states that this is the first episode in which Peter Tuddenham provides the voice of Ensor. We'd change it, but we'd probably change it to someone even less likely, like Gwyneth Paltrow or Jimmy Stewart.

You can do most of the stuff Orac does in this episode on your computer at home these days. Orac is in fact a perfectly ordinary computer that happens to have a wireless internet connection and thus appears intelligent.

Jenna does nothing in this episode.

Travis is using an explosive charge in a cave... this could be it ...

Wooooo hoo! Blake's plan to hold off Servalan and Travis is to try and bring the cave roof down. Here we go, here we go...

Suddenly, Travis appears only from the neck down. This is because Vere Lorrimer was trapped in the Land of Fiction at the time. He was forced to rebuild Travis' face and did it wrong.

Blake's method of creating a rockfall is dubious at best. He stands under the roof and pulls rocks down one at a time. Why not stand to one side and poke it?

Orac's first trick is to predict the future. Would've been useful if he'd kept it up.

Closing Shot: The *Liberator* blows up. Get used to it – it does this a lot.

Delightful Dialogue:
Vila: Die? I can't do that!
Avon: I'm afraid you can. It's the one talent we all share, even you.

Jenna: Well, for a hundred million credits you'd expect something a little more spectacular than that.
Vila: Try kicking it.

Servalan: You're in a lot of trouble, Travis.

Amateur Hour:
The camera hits a cable as it dollies in on Jenna feeling faint...

...and again as Cally and Blake enter Ensor's lab.

Vila's teleport bracelet drops off as they carry Ensor out of the teleport.

Servalan's map is bloody rubbish. A child using a broken Etch-A-Sketch could have done better.

The lizard creature that attacks Servalan is about as impressive as Davros' clam. So to speak.

ADDITIONAL SCRAPS OF KNOWLEDGE
Planets: Cephlon, Aristo (again).

Space-isms: Micro power cells, electronic anaesthesia.

Below: The cover of *The Adventures of Orac And Other Mechanical Creatures* paperback. Released the day after Season M finished, the book ran to a slim 26-pages as Orac, the Federation security robot and Ensor's drone were the only mechanical things to have appeared in the series up to that point. A revised version was released in 1980, where the inclusion of the robot from "Volcano" pushed the book up to a giddying 28-pages.

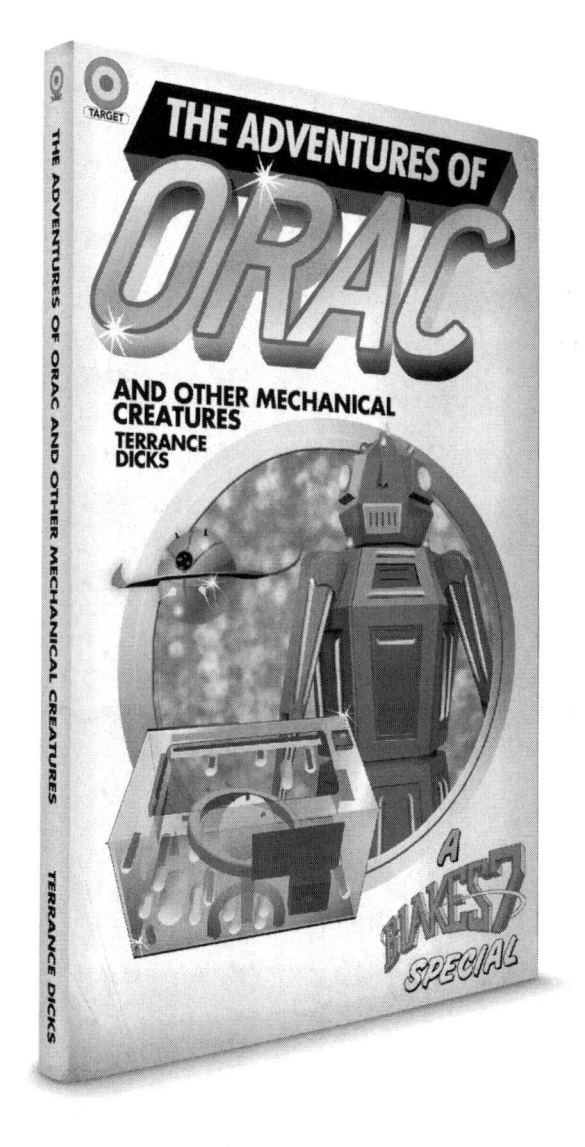

7.15-8.10 *New series*
Blake's Seven

The first of a new space adventure series in 14 episodes

Redemption by **TERRY NATION**
starring
Gareth Thomas, Sally Knyvette, Paul Darrow, Jan Chappell, Michael Keating, David Jackson

Blake and his crew witness a gigantic explosion that destroys their spaceship The Liberator. The event is shown to them by Orac, the super-computer. Orac confirms this prediction but refuses to say when it will happen - but it will happen soon.

Blake	GARETH THOMAS
Jenna	SALLY KNYVETTE
Vila	MICHAEL KEATING
Avon	PAUL DARROW
Gan	DAVID JACKSON
Cally	JAN CHAPPELL
Zen	PETER TUDDENHAM
Alta One	SHEILA RUSKIN
Alta Two	HARRIET PHILPIN
Alta Boy	ROY EVANS

Series created by TERRY NATION
Script editor CHRIS BOUCHER
Designer SALLY HULKE
Producer DAVID MALONEY
Director LERE VORRIMER

FEATURE p27

SEASON N 1979

Regular Cast

Gareth Thomas	*Roj Blake*
Michael Keating	*Vila Restal*
Paul Darrow	*Kerr Avon*
Sally Knyvette	*Jenna Stannis*
Jan Chappell	*Cally the Earth Mother*
David Jackson	*Bow-Legged Gan*
Peter Tuddenham	*Zen / Orac*
Jacqueline Pearce	*Servalan*
~~Stephen Greif~~ / Brian Croucher	*James Travis*
Aitch	*Everyone else*

Episodes

Redemption

Shadow

Weapon

Horizon

Pressure Point

Restitution

Trial

Killer

Hostage

Countdown

Voice from the Past

Gambit

The Keeper

Star One

15 REDEMPTION

Writer: Terry Nation **Director**: Leer Vorrimer

Guest Stars: Sheila Ruskin (Alta One), Harriet Philpin (Alta Two), Roy Evans (Alta Boy)

Opening Shot: A couple of pages from *Astronomy Now*.

You Just Described the Story:

Blake: Alright, Zen, standby to run it again – at half-speed.
Zzzzzz…

Random Insult:
Vila: I've got this shocking pain right behind the eyes.
Avon: Have you considered amputation?

In A Nutshell: Can we have our green pulsating ball back, please?

Story: Following Orac's grave foretelling of the destruction of the *Liberator*, the ship is attacked by the alien race who built it. Zen blocks all attempts at escape and the whole ship becomes hostile. It takes the crew back to the aliens' space station, where they are taken prisoner. No prizes for guessing they escape, but they are pursued by *Liberator*'s sister ship. Which one was it that Orac predicted would be destroyed?

Information:

Apparently there was a large increase to the show's budget between Season M and N. As far as we can tell most of it was spent on the leather used to make Blake's blouse.

Cally pokes some teleport bracelets with a stick.

Olag's started wearing his pregnancy gown.

There's more shooting off the top of set when Roj has a chat with Orac.

Kerr hides from Roj on the flight deck. Um … where on the flight deck?

Roj and Kerr do the 'slow-mo through a spaceship exploding' bit exactly like they did one episode earlier with Ensor's ship.

Avon's analogy about predictions being akin standing on a cliff edge has a beautiful logic. He then chucks it all away by saying if you chose not to stand there in the first place, none of it would matter.

Olag and Roj share the two channels of a pair of headphones like lovers.

Cally doesn't speak for the first eight minutes.

We like how Restal's job on the flight deck is to fire the guns, like a child with a spud shooter.

We get to see a lot more of the *Liberator* in this episode and even though it's mostly just passageways and struts it's all bloody cool. The differing film/video stock used for each section of the ship only adds to the effect.

There's a mysterious dining room set in the main control room which only appears when needed.

The designs for the super-duper beings – their hand weapons, pursuit ships, space station – is superb. Just beautiful. Their costumes, not so much.

Cally's waist is non-existent in this episode.

Terry has a habit of writing his episodes with 25 minutes of chatting on the *Liberator* and 25 minutes of actual plot. In his head, he's writing *Doctor Who* two-parters.

Nice to see Daft Punk turn up on the System space-station. We recommend 2001's "Discovery".

Ooh, the Altas are wearing teleport bracelets…

Roj is attacked by an electrical wire. It's a bit like "Death to the Daleks". By Terry Nation.

The wire is held up on wires.

Roj says 'Redemption' just to get the title of the episode into the script.

When Alta One tells Roj that asking questions is not permitted, he asks several anyway and gets very detailed answers.

We reckon Chris Boucher nicked the circular things on the forehead for "Death-Watch".

When Kerr says to Stannis 'You're looking at it', she isn't.

Another big fat door.

Oh yeah, it's the same big fat door as in "Time Squad". They filmed it in the same power station. And it turns up again in "Killer".

Even though they all escaped together, Roj and Stannis get to the flight deck by a different corridor to Kerr and Restal and arrive a few seconds after them. What were they up to?

If you have the DVD handy, spin forward to 44m 51s. There's a really odd shot of a control panel with the numbers 0, 1, 2, 3, 4, 5, 6 written across the bottom. It looks like someone has tried to turn them into weird space-age numbers with a felt tip.

The sister ship gag at the end works rather well.

This episode ends with Roj setting course for 'Earth sector'; in Terry's next script, "Pressure Point", the *Liberator* arrives at Earth. Boucher did tell him that other people were writing the three episodes in between, didn't he?

The closing titles on the BBC Video compilation release incorrectly credited John Nathan-Turner as producer.

Closing Shot: Blake moon-faces up at the camera. Look at him – he's a man of action!

Delightful Dialogue:

Blake: Avon – concentrate on Zen. Give priority to the detectors and the navigation systems. And then see if you can get us some scans.
Avon: Is that all? What shall I do with the other hand?

Amateur Hour:

The *Liberator* take-off shot is achieved by playing a shot of an aeroplane landing in reverse.

Accidentally or otherwise, when the first explosion throws Blake and Avon to the ground, Avon puts his arm around Blake.

"Redemption" is one of those episodes when the director remembered to add background noise to the *Liberator* interior shots. Because we're not used to it, it's horribly distracting.

The effect of the *Liberator* flying so fast that the stars whizz by is almost *Tom & Jerry*-like.

Paper cut-out planets!

There's absolutely no consistency between model shots of the *Liberator*: in some scenes it's white with a green orb; in others it's almost metallic. Then there's that bloody photographic blow-up rushing towards the camera again.

With five control stations full of knobs and buttons, couldn't the *Liberator*'s builders have put the force wall and internal comms controls on them somewhere? It's a bit of a faff having to run over to the comfy chairs every time you want to stop a missile or chat with Gan when he's gone for a stroll. Thinking about it, why is there a comfy seating area anyway? The Altas don't strike us as the sort of people who would say to the ship designer 'Five uncomfortable stand-up pilot pod things, great... hexagonal corridors – quirky, I *like* that. One last thing – can you bung a cream leather three-piece suite in front of the main view screen?' It's not as though the area beneath Zen has got a built-in Xbox or something. (That said, the circuit cubby hole that Avon checks is the ideal space to put one.)

This story breaks all previous records for Amateur Hour entries.

ADDITIONAL SCRAPS OF KNOWLEDGE
Vila's Massive Sideburns: Now massive.

Planets: Not really.

16 SHADOW

Writer: Chris Boucher (is that right? Not Terry?) **Director**: Jonathan Wright Miller

Guest Stars: Karl Howman (Jacko), Adrienne Burgess (Hanna), Derek Smith (Largo), Archie Tew (Enforcer), Vernon Dobtcheff (Chairman), Terry Nostra (Aur Tel), Raul Julia (Gomez)

Opening Shot: Space City, the biggest Fisher Price toy in the known universe.

You Just Described the Story:

Blake: Think, Gan, think what they've got: men, material, information… Think what we could do with a fraction of the resources they control.

Random Insult:

Gan: Can't find Orac. Even tried calling his name.
Avon: Oh, I'm sorry I missed that. It's the kind of natural stupidity no amount of training could ever hope to match.

In A Nutshell: Just Say No! NO! Just Say No…

Story: Blake identifies the Terra Nostra, a shady criminal organisation, as potential allies in their fight against the Federation. The crew arrive at Space City (a city in space) to seek an audience with Largo, but whose side is he on? And why is Orac sending Cally up the cuckoo creek without a paddle? Never mind, there's plenty of Shadow to go around.

Information:

I don't know much about art, but that's just a bowel movement in a box. A faecal Orac, if you will.

Gan, possible former rapist, is a little upset about visiting a 'dirty, degrading' place like Space City. We hate hypocrites.

Burgess and Jacko try their best as a drug addict and her brother, but they do come across a little … stage school. Though, you can see why the director didn't cast anyone who was actually on hard drugs. They could've turned up late for work or anything.

Dream Head – bet that's something to do with drugs.

Shadow is the Federation name for Karvol capsules.

Apparently, the Terra Nostra own the drug-addled fools.

Nobody steals from the Terra Nostra. This is likely to change.

Orac uses 'special communication waves' which pass through another dimension. Special communication waves? You're going to have to try harder than that, Mr Boucher.

Derek Smith spends the episode dressed as Jon Pertwee.

The plastic toy gun that Archie Tew uses appears again in the hands of Ronald Lacey in "Killer", which was shot immediately before this episode. The chap who catches Gan uses it too.

The great Vernon Dobtcheff, patron saint of actors, appears, feeding a spider.

Cally remembers she's telepathic again, but if I were Largo I'd be a bit suspicious that it takes her 20 seconds to remember how many shuttles the *Liberator*'s got.

Shadow is such a powerful drug that it can even affect computers; Zen does a scan of Hanna's Shadow and then says 'There are traces of an elephant.'

Cally's unique running style is why she never got caught, causing all pursuers to think she was a harmless mental.

Shadow comes from a plant resembling a cactus, which suggests it is could be a mescaline derivative and therefore psychedelic. Why is it Cally who gets all the mad, trippy, black void sequences then?

As far as we can tell, Largo dies from eating gold paint. He's probably a fan of *Goldfinger*, and was licking it off somebody. It is Space City, after all.

The moon discs look exactly the same as the shades that are beside them.

The sequences on the planet were sponsored by Mars. Viewers complained that they compulsively ate Galaxy Minstrels after watching this episode, but an internal BBC inquiry cleared the programme of any wrongdoing.

Avon kills for the first time on-screen. It's a guard.

Blake, meanwhile, decides to become a drug-dealer. He's changed a lot since we first met him. If you're watching the series in order accompanied by this book (the only way to view it), look out in upcoming episodes for Blake driving round in his blinged-up pimp-mobile, Blake getting a big purple fur coat and Blake piling on the pounds when he gives up smack.

Does anyone have the remotest idea what's going on in the Cally plot? Do write in and tell us.

The crew of the *Liberator* explain that the Terra Nostra was the Federation all along in three different ways. Ceefax spoilered this several days before transmission with their article "What else can we blame the Terra Nostra for?" It was rubbish.

Closing Shot: Mulberry presses a button.

Delightful Dialogue:

Vila (about Blake): Thinks of himself as a hard man. Hard? He's strictly a fluffy-cheeked amateur compared to those boys.

Largo: They're beautiful stones. I'm a bit of a collector, in a modest way. I could make you an offer.
Avon: They have a sentimental value for me.
Largo: Oh, family heirlooms?
Avon: No, I'm just sentimental about money.

Vila: Stop worrying, Cally, I'll be back soon. Tell you what, I'll bring you back a present! What would you like, Cally? Name it and it's yours.
Cally: A necklace, Vila. Made from your teeth.

Avon: Yes, of course. Law-makers, law-breakers, let us fight them all. Why not?

Amateur Hour:

Jump to 30m 35s and keep your eye on Karl Howman. Michael Keating says 'It's a complete blank...' only for Howman to come in with his own line far too early. He realises, stops himself, bites his lip and then waits for his cue proper to get the scene back on track.

The moving moon discs are clearly being pulled along on fishing wire. To be honest, that's probably how we'd have done it too. But better, obviously.

The hot red sun of the arid planet Zondar is a blob of red paint on some glass, shot against a very overcast sky.

The planet the *Liberator* arrives at isn't the same as the one it subsequently leaves.

When Cally teleports back up to the *Liberator* she isn't carrying a moon disc, just the key for Orac.

Considering one of the themes in this episode is isolation it doesn't seem very fair to separate one moon disc from all of the others and then keep it in what looks like a cat's litter tray. Where did the litter tray come from? Does Orac use it?

Between filming the first and last *Liberator* scenes for this episode, an ashtray was been built into the console between the back cushions of the flight deck sofa. You can even see a stubbed-out cigarette during the final scenes!

ADDITIONAL SCRAPS OF KNOWLEDGE

Planets: Zondar.

Space-isms: Neutron blasters? We fell asleep. Sorry. Oh, and Space City of course.

Important Fact: Cally may be telepathic, but she's so slow at it she may as well not bother.

17 WEAPON

Writer: Chris Boucher   **Director**: George Spenton-Foster

Guest Stars: John Bennett (Coser), Candace Glendenning (Rashell), Scott Fredericks (Carnell), Kathleen Byron (Clonemaster Fen), Terrance Stamp (Zod), Graham Simpson (Officer)

Opening Shot: Standard BBC shuttle prop exploding in slow motion.

You Just Described the Story:

Carnell: It's all as predictable as that very expensive chess machine.

Random Insult:
Servalan: Travis, you are pathetic... Of all the cripple-brained idiots...

In A Nutshell: Migraine-inducing gung-ho red-spot clone mayhem.

Story: Paranoid nutter Coser has done a runner from the Federation with his highly plausible invention IMIPAK (Induced Molecular Instability Projector and Key). It's a gun which marks its victim and can then kill them, at any time, by remote control. Naturally, Servalan wants it back, and employs a psycho-strategist named Carnell to assist her. Meanwhile, Orac has told Blake and the others about the gun, and they try to get to it before Servalan.

Information:

Blake's clone is just as good an actor as he is.

Lucky the Clonemasters manage to clone Blakes' clothes as well. And pick the same outfit he happens to be wearing in this story.

You'd never believe John Bennett is Chinese. The make-up is amazing.

Brian Croucher is clearly out to make an early impression, good or otherwise.

Gan is wearing a dress.

Hooray! Industrial complex time.

This episode takes place during Federation Collar Week. The height of a collar is in direct proportion to that character's competence – Travis has only got a little one, Servalan's is large and ornate (and oh-so feminine), and Coser's and Raschel's are so enormous they turn back on themselves for fear of breaking their owners' necks. These two are clearly the baddest of baddassery.

Travis has completed the transition from feared space bastard to Servalan's pet monkey on a rope.

Kathleen Byron's under the mistaken impression that Servalan's French.

Which came first? The acronym or the actual name? IMIPAK hardly trips off the tongue.

Carnell will go on to feature in the *Kaldor City* plays, also written by Boucher.

When Carnell dismisses the officer from Servalan's office, how does the door know to open before anyone's moved?

Servalan's wardrobe is a game of two halves, one moment an ill-fitting crop-top, the next moment all White Witch. She has no concept of subtlety.

IMIPAK is a wholly flawed concept on its own, but thrown into a medallion-man clone story it's taking science fiction to a ludicrous point.

If Travis can mark each *Liberator* crew member with IMIPAK then surely he can just shoot them? Note also how you can see Croucher closing his covered eye when he aims. Force of habit.

Blake's clone protects Reshal by grabbing her chest lumps.

If Coser's so brilliant, why does he dress like Evil Uncle Abanazar?

Carnell has no reason to act so smugly. His collar's fallen down.

Industrial complexes of the future have 20th-century British road markings. If it ain't broke, don't fix it.

The whole place is besieged by birds, too. We counted a blackbird, a thrush and a starling chirping away in the background. And a great tit every time Travis appeared.

Servalan marks Travis for death, so why doesn't he die when she uses IMIPAK on the trooper?

The filming location is the Lowcocks Lemonade factory in Goole.

Closing Shot: Servalan smirks into a plastic red flower. As usual.

Delightful Dialogue:

Travis: Contempt?
Servalan: Or respect. A man might see it as respect. You would have. Once.

Avon: Auron may be different, Cally, but on Earth it is considered ill-mannered to kill your friends while committing suicide.

Avon: We do not know what IMIPAK is.
Vila: I can live without it.
Blake: It's just conceivable that you can't.
Avon: Unless of course you want your last words to be 'So that's IMIPAK'?

Carnell (to Servalan): You are undoubtedly the sexiest officer I have ever known.

Amateur Hour:

Even Fred West's defence lawyer was more convincing than the creature that attacks Coser and Rachell.

ADDITIONAL SCRAPS OF KNOWLEDGE

Planets: Ursa Prime.

Space-isms: Maximum security space zone!

Important Facts: This story has a relatively short title but three vowels.

Pay Attention! We planted four incorrect spellings of 'Rashel' over the last three pages and you didn't even notice. Sigh.

18 HORIZON

Writer: Allan Prior **Director**: Jonathan Wright Miller

Guest Stars: William Squire (Kommissar), Darien Angadi (Ro), Souad Faress (Selma), Brian Miller (Assistant Kommissar), Michael Craze (Ben Jackson), Paul Haley (Chief Guard)

Opening Shot: The *London* again. Whatever that model shot cost, it was worth every penny.

You Just Described the Story:

Blake: Horizon?

Random Insult:

Avon: Wonderful. We have all the resources of Zen, Orac and the *Liberator* and you feel that they are in trouble. You do not feel it, you reason it. They have not called in, therefore they must be in trouble. You don't have to be telepathic to know that.

In A Nutshell: Bored, tired crew decide to relax by going to a tired, boring planet.

Story: The *Liberator* narrowly avoids a collision with a Federation freighter in the middle of nowhere. Following it, Blake and the crew discover it's headed for a planet called Horizon where a secret mining operation is taking place. While Blake tries to incite an uprising on the planet, Avon considers a rather different uprising aboard the *Liberator*.

Information:

This is the only story of Season N that Servalan doesn't appear in.

Gareth Thomas has his hand to his neck in order to hide a scratch he received from a cat during the crew's lunchtime visit to a nearby pub.

Cally is 18% thinner in this episode.

A ship with a demagnetised hull can pass through a magnetic barrier unharmed.

Almost everyone in this story declares an intention or requests permission to 'go down'.

Michael Piller, executive producer of *Star Trek: The Next Generation*, liked this story so much that he named his character Ensign Ro in honour of it.

In Prior's original script, Ro was female. She was a camp commandant on Horizon and kept a pack of hunting hounds called 'Razors'.

Among those short-listed for the part of Ro were Steven Pacey, who would later go on to play Space Pilot Del Tarrant in *Blake's 7*.

Monopasium 239. That's what we're mining, folks.

The lights on the disorientor would doubtless be more effective if they were in front of Blake and Jenna rather than behind them.

The *Blake's 7* Appreciation Society named themselves after this episode. One wonders what they saw in it. There's also an adult services website for like-minded fans called "Headhunter" and a crossover BDSM/*Blake's 7* club called "Powerplay" based in Grantham, if you're interested.

There are three drinks in this episode: Blake has some CLEAR at the start, Vila drinks some GREEN Buck-U-Uppo, and Jenna and Blake are given a wooden beaker of CLEAR during their chat with Ro. This is not the highest number of drinks seen in one episode. That honour belongs to "Gambit", which has something like nine.

Why, in *Blake's 7* world, have there been no technological advances in mining? It's always peasants with crude tools and wicker baskets.

Blake's patronising attitude toward the other miners as they gobble their lunch is infuriating. If any of us tried that, we'd been bludgeoned to death with pickaxes.

Why are Blake and Vila topless but Jenna's still fully clothed?

The swamp creature is an element from Prior's original script. Its inclusion in the scene with Gan seems costly, given that it doesn't appear again or have any significance to the plot.

Avon's near-treachery is terrific stuff for Darrow. It would've made for an almighty upheaval to the series if Avon had gone through with his plan to run away.

Why are we meant to care about what happens to Ro and his little lady? Prior's script makes them more important than the *Liberator* crew. The scenes with them both in peril aren't achieving anything, especially since the *Liberator* crew have already made it back to the ship alive.

Blake takes the time to have a bath and put on fresh clean clothes before saving the day. The others are still muddy. This is why Blake had to go.

Closing Shot: Vila, blacked up: 'It beats work.'

Delightful Dialogue:

Vila: Why don't you go?
Avon: You are expendable.
Vila: And you're not?
Avon: No, I am not. I am not expendable, I am not stupid, and I am not going.

Vila: What's the point of being famous if you can't get a last minute booking?

Amateur Hour:

Jenna's bracelet swaps from her left to her right arm in the teleport bay. When they land on Horizon it is back on her left arm.

Are we really expected to believe that Blake and Jenna don't hear the loud buzzy camera that emerges from the undergrowth right behind them?

The approaching Federation pursuit ships wobble even more unconvincingly than usual.

ADDITIONAL SCRAPS OF KNOWLEDGE

Planets: Horizon.

Space-isms: Gawd knows … um … hang on, hang on, space… pickaxes?

19 PRESSURE POINT

Writer: Terry Nation (is back!) **Director**: George Spenton-Foster

Guest Stars: Alan Halley (Arle), Jane Sherwin (Kasabi), Martin Connor (Berg), Sue Bishop (Mutoid), Joseph Cotten (Dr Vesalius), Yolande Palfrey (Veron)

Opening Shot: Two resistance fighters bicker like frightened girls about whether they should enter the Forbidden Zone.

You Just Described the Story:

Jenna: You're suggesting that we go into the Forbidden Zone and attack Control?

Random Insult:

Avon (referring to the Liberator crew): Not very bright, but loyal.

In A Nutshell: Pressure Pointless.

Story: In a desperate attempt to get themselves noticed, Blake decides the crew should return to Earth and attack Control, the central computer network for the whole of the Federation. Unfortunately, after a lot of to-ing and fro-ing, they find themselves in a big empty room because they're in the wrong place. Hot-footing it, they lose Gan to a slowly closing door.

Information:

The inside of the cottage doesn't really square with the outside.

Has Vila got a bad shoulder or something? He appears to be wearing a sling.

Who exactly are all of the other people who have been trying to attack Control?

Travis is a complete nutcase by now. He's probably some sort of monstrous sexual deviant too.

Kasabi's face is filthy. Get a wash, woman!

Blake: 'As far as I can see it's all clear.' No it isn't. It's full of trees.

It's nice to see Gan getting something to do at last. He's really starting to show a bit of potential as a character.

Setting part of the episode in an old church is an interesting touch. They borrowed the set from a guy called Alan, who swore it was used in *The Avengers*. At least, that's what the production documentation says.

What ARE those squeaking things that we hear every time that we are on location? We don't have any creatures on Earth that make that sort of noise do we?

Cally continues her character development by having nothing to do yet again.

We do wish that Avon wouldn't wear that horrid red leather uniform. It does nothing for him.

Heh, heh … look at what Servalan's chameleon is doing … heh, heh…

Sue Bishop's performance as the Mutoid is a bit off.

Blimey. Gan's dead.

Closing Shot: Gan's chair, followed by a picture of Earth.

Delightful Dialogue:
Avon: What's the matter Blake, don't you trust your friends?
Blake: Of course. I trust them in the same way I trust you.

Amateur Hour:
The dummies that represent Arle and Berg being blown up don't blow very up.

The homing beacon doesn't exactly look to be the height of technology, does it?

You might think that the ladders the team climb down are all the same ladder lit differently, but in fact Spenton-Foster spent as much as a small cottage would cost building a multi-floor set for these sequences and a powered lift to elevate the cameras for each individual set.

Nation was so proud of himself for coming up with the name 'Kasabi' that he wrote it into every line of dialogue, sometimes twice. On-set rewrites were hastily carried out when Spenton-Foster noticed that the cast were still saying it twenty minutes after her death.

David Jackson fluffs a line in his big episode when he tries to say 'The teleport will have to be precise.'

ADDITIONAL SCRAPS OF KNOWLEDGE

Terrynation Street: Terry's back! Radiation. Again. What is it with him and radiation? Did he have a bad experience with an x-ray machine or something?

Planets: Earth.

Space-isms: High-intensity radiation grid, sono gas, some stuff about 'repair mesh'.

THE Sun

Tuesday, February 6, 1979 — 10p — TODAY'S TV: PAGE 14

BBC AXE HERO GAN

Sad... Blakes Seven star David Jackson

By CHARLES CATCHPOLE

BBC BOSSES WERE PREPARED for their

Jackson, aged 45, was unavailable for comment. The producer of the show, David Maloney, said that the BBC switchboard had been jammed for three hours after the show was transmitted on BBC1. The programme

Previous page: A clipping from *The Sun* newspaper following the broadcast of "Pressure Point". **Below:** The letter the BBC sent to grieving fans, and a sticker from the *Daily Star*'s 'Bring Back Gan' campaign.

BRITISH BROADCASTING CORPORATION
BROADCASTING HOUSE LONDON W1A 1AA
TELEX: 265781 CABLES: BROADCASTS LONDON TELEX
TELEPHONE 01-580 4468
DIRECT TELEPHONE LINE: 01-927

15th February 1979

Reference: 28/JB

Dear

    Thank you for your recent letter, which I have been asked to acknowledge.

    We are sorry that you should be concerned about the death of the television character Gan in the hit BBC Television series, 'Blakes Seven'. While we are aware that children have been upset at the loss of such a well-loved character, it should never be forgotten that people die every day in real-life and it is all part of growing up.

    However, the BBC have set up a telephone hotline for fans to ring if they would like to talk to someone about the way they are feeling. The number is 01-580-4167.

    The Producer and his team welcome every letter they receive, but would like to tactfully inform everyone that the newspaper campaigns to bring the character back are pointless as (I quote) 'Gan is dead, definitely, fully completely dead, yup, dead, he's gone.'

    Thank you again for your letter. We appreciate your interest in writing, and shall bear all your comments in mind.

Yours sincerely,

Jane Marrow (Miss)
Programme Correspondence Section

20 RESTITUTION

Writer: Trevor Hoyle **Director**: David Maloney

Guest Stars: Lynda Bellingham (Enda), Rob Heyland (Nor)

Opening Shot: Close up of Gan's face, contorted in either pain or sexual ecstasy. Given that it's Gan, we're going for the former.

You Just Described the Story:
Enda: We have thirty minutes to get this ship moving or we're all dead.

Random Insult:
Blake: You may think a human life is worthless, but I don't.
Avon: That rather depends on whose life it is.

In A Nutshell: Blake does a wrongbrain.

Story: Blake blames himself for the death of Gan, convinced that he could have done more to save his friend. When he begins acting erratically, the crew slowly realise that guilt is pushing him towards ever more reckless acts of vengeance. A disastrous attack on a Federation supply convoy leaves the *Liberator* completely powerless in space and at the mercy of the Federation's latest superweapon – the LECSP. The crew have just thirty minutes to escape before Tarrant destroys them all.

Information:
The flashback to Gan's death is nowhere near as funny the second time round.

LECSP stands for Long-range Emission of Charged Superheated Particles. Even in the future, that's a hell of a mouthful – did they learn nothing from IMIPAK? Couldn't they have just called it the space laser or something?

Servalan's costumes deserve a series of their own. After last week's boob lizard, we've now got what can only be described as diamante coconuts covering her jubblies.

Travis really needs to watch where he points that thing.

Tarrant would return to the series and eventually go on to be really annoying and stupid. Stupid Tarrant.

In space, all countdown clocks stop on 3. Or 1. Never 251.

The cloud effect was achieved by using uncoloured candy floss. Overnight the candy floss was set upon by ants which is why they look so grey in the Sea Base scenes. Paul Darrow was permitted to take the candy floss machine after filming wrapped and got a lot of use from it before eventually running out of sticks. Unsure of where to order more, he dumped the useless machine in a hedge somewhere near Tolworth where it can still be seen to this day.

Another twisted flashback for Blake and another few pennies thrown David Jackson's way.

The voice dubbed onto the footage of Gan sounds nothing like David Jackson.

Only Lynda Bellingham could make that costume look good.

Lynda Bellingham also plays 'Muller's Woman' in "Headhunter".

When we first hear of the LECSP, our money was on it being a hand-drawn effect, rather than anything electronic or, you know, expensive. There are times when being proved right is no fun at all.

Look very closely at gun that Enda suddenly produces – it is actually a stapler that has been painted white.

Blake may have forgiven himself for leaving Gan to die but we won't. It was all your fault Blake, and no amount of self-rationalisation will fix that.

Brian Croucher just can't do angry frustration, can he?

Closing Shot: Servalan bestows her *witheringest* of glares on the grainy image of Travis seen on her monitor.

Delightful Dialogue:

Enda: Fate chose to take him from you. Who are we to argue with fate?

Servalan: Cretin. I could lock you both in a room together and he'd still evade you.

Amateur Hour:

The glass of GREEN thrown by Blake has mysteriously become BLUE by the time it drips down the wall.

The painting of the damaged *Liberator* hanging in space is the least convincing effect in an episode which already puts 'Special Effects' on the Trade Descriptions watch list.

Travis flinches like a big baby girl when his finger gun goes off.

Avon's gun accidentally lights up six times during his conversation with Nor. There is a brilliant version of this scene on YouTube – a fan has added the gun sound effects and, re-editing lines from other episodes, has Avon continually asking 'Why don't you die?' as each shot is fired. The addition of canned laughter is genius.

Orac fluff his lines again. You'd think an off-screen actor could at least read without messing up.

Look for the shot at 35m 27s – is Jan Chappell crying?

The escape scene is made even more ridiculous and confusing by the BBC deciding to use the teleport sound effect for the alarm.

ADDITIONAL SCRAPS OF KNOWLEDGE

Planets: None at all, but more space than you could shake a stick at.

Space-isms: Space Command, Space Supply Convoy, Space Major, Space Shock Troops – they're all here. Because it's a space episode. Set, you know, in space.

Important Fact: Nor's jacket would later be adapted for the character Glitz in some *Doctor Who* story or other.

21 TRIAL

Writer: Crisp Voucher   **Director**: Derek Martinus

Guest Stars: John Savident (Samor), John Bryans (Bercol), Peter Miles (Rontane), Victoria Fairbrother (Thania), Claire Lewis (Zil), Amy Lewis (Vil), Ruby Lewis (Bil), Kevin Lloyd (Tosh Lines), Graham Sinclair (Lye), Nicholas Parsons (Host), Colin Dunn (Guard Commander)

Opening Shot: Bored Federation troopers standing around and looking bored.

You Just Described the Story:

Bercol: I wish I'd known that this was going to drag on so, I'd have brought my own chef.

Random Bitchiness:
Blake: They might even listen to you this time.
Avon: Why not? After all, I don't get them killed.

Random Backhanded Compliment:
Servalan: Travis knew, right from the beginning. It really is a pity he's got to die. He's so much better than anything I've got left.

In A Nutshell: A Trial. And it's called that for a couple of reasons.

Story: The Federation are holding Servalan accountable for her continued failures in intercepting Blake and the *Liberator*. She attempts to have Travis tried for war crimes, hoping his execution will prevent him revealing more evidence against her. Meanwhile, Blake decides the time has come to teleport down to a planet and wander about for an hour, hoping the crew will let him off for getting Gan killed. When he returns to the *Liberator*, his first effort at not getting the crew killed is to attack Servalan's headquarters. In doing so he allows Travis the chance to escape.

Information:
Any drama which throws up Tosh Lines out of *The Bill*, Peter Miles being

sinister and John, I say, John Savident within five minutes of the opening titles is our kind of programme. This is the TV geek equivalent of a hearty 'Phwoar!'

Peter Miles' ears are moving in time with his voice. Perhaps it's semaphore for the hard of hearing.

In all the exterior shots we've seen of Space Command throughout the series, it's rotating in space, yet when we look out of the windows the view outside is static.

Lye refers to Samor as 'Old Star Killer'.

'Prisoner and escort reporting as ordered' says the Guard Commander, in one of the worst-delivered lines in the entire series.

Travis is charged under 'Section Three of the War Crimes Statute Code, Jenkin One.' We understand the first bit of that but not the business about Jenkin One.

John Savident spends most of his scenes sitting down. Which probably suited him, I say, which probably suited him.

Blake has a refreshing glass of GREEN.

The *Liberator* chess game seems to be made up from cruet sets and some gold and silver rings.

Costume-wise, this is an odd one. Jenna's done up like Suzi Quatro and Blake's wearing green wellies.

Bercol is also the name of a range of household furniture designed for idiots.

Why has Travis got a cocktail shaker in his cell? Was it a last request?

His treatment of Tosh, who offers him a snifter of RED, is perfectly understandable – Travis has always been a GREEN man.

Su-per-per Trooper-Parr / Lights are gonna blind me (copyright Björn Ulvaeus and Benny Andersson)

Zil is only the fourth most annoying alien in *Blake's 7*, but it marginally beats the Decimas to top position as the stupidest-looking.

Just as the *Liberator* is about to begin its attack run on Space Command, look at the floor under Cally's desk: you'll see a BBC toolbox, left there by an absent-minded technician.

Just a week after David Jackson was written out of the show because they couldn't find anything for his character to do, only Blake, Avon, Travis and Servalan are given anything to occupy their time in this one.

Brian Croucher is probably at his most shouty here.

Given its immense firepower, the *Liberator* should really have blasted Space Command to oblivion. Instead, Blake elects to fire only one shot at it, thus enabling Travis to make his escape.

Closing Shot: Blake and Avon laugh heartily at Vila being compared to a flea. Vila is written as too stupid to cotton on to the insult.

Delightful Dialogue:
Avon: One of these days they are going to leave you. They were almost ready to do so this time.
Blake: Yes, I thought they might be.
Avon: You handle them very skilfully.
Blake: Do I?
Avon: But one more death will do it.
Blake: Then you'd better be very careful. It would be ironic if it were yours.

Avon: I would quite like to have met this Zil of yours. It's not often that one comes across a philosophical flea.

Amateur Hour:
That section of corridor outside the court room seems to get quite a bit of repeated use.

The zoom in on Space Command about halfway through the episode is a little too close. It looks like a toy from this distance.

Travis' eye patch is starting to fall off in the later courtroom scenes, with the top hanging away from his face.

Zil's costume is only any good from the brow up.

ADDITIONAL SCRAPS OF KNOWLEDGE

Planets: Zircaster (or 'Serkasta' as the subtitles on the DVD would have us believe).

Space-isms: Jenkin One could be a space-ism, we suppose.

Shopping List

for costume by Tuesday please- thanks! June.

Shiny stuff
Glitter
PVA glue
Flares
Bacofoil (bloody loads)

22 KILLER

Writer: Robert Holmes **Director**: Vere Lorrimer

Guest Stars: Paul Daneman (Dr. Bellfriar), Ronald Lacey (Toht), Colin Farrell (Gambril), Hugh Grant (Regular One), Morris Barry (Wiler), Colin Higgins (Tak), Michael Gaunt (Bax), Ric Spiegel (Zax), Basement Jaxx (Fleetwood Mac)

Opening Shot: The *Liberator* looking super-cool in orbit around a green planet.

You Just Described the Story:

Bellfriar: That'll be the space contamination.

Random Insult:

Vila: When Avon holds out the hand of friendship, watch his other hand. That's the one with the hammer.

In A Nutshell: Space plague! Space plague! Space plague!

Story: The Federation's new pulse-code communications require a special crystal to decrypt them. Avon and Vila travel to Q-Base on Fosforon, aiming to steal one with the unwilling help of an old 'friend' of Avon's, Tynus, who is stationed there. When Cally senses something malignant aboard an ancient vessel approaching Fosforon, Blake decides to warn the base.

Information:

This episode has a Season R title.

This is anti-matter *Blake's 7*. The traditional cardboard cut-out *Liberator* and cartoon planet are replaced by an excellent model shot, but the usual highly-convincing industrial complex is just an artist's impression. On that basis, we'd expect a well-dressed Jenna and Cally to be dealing death all over the shop with mind bullets.

Nope, Jenna's dressed like a fairy.

Nice to see Cally being childishly playful when she teleports Avon and Vila down to Fosforon.

Hang on a mo – Cally's doing proper telepathic stuff and now we've got an honest-to-goodness nuclear power plant. All bets are off.

Cally's had her hair cut with a knife and fork, and Ronald Lacey's rivals even his costume in the department of unfathomable stupidity. Shiny brown headbands and lobster-tail capes do not for a good look make. In fact, the costume design for the whole episode (regular crew aside) is pretty atrocious.

For two men trying to appear inconspicuous, Avon kicking open the door to Tynus's office seems a little OTT.

Paul Daneman is the only person in *Blake's 7* to be cooler than Paul Darrow. They would have employed more Paul Ds, but the only other one they could think of was Paul Daniels, who played six different Decima.

The dead body in the capsule looks like Victor Meldrew.

A digital readout on the *Liberator* screen goes from 1963 to 1937. We were wondering if there was some significance to these dates.

The long shot of the dome is realised with a glass shot – the beach is filmed through a piece of glass that has the dome painted on it. This works wonderfully until Michael Keating walks behind the painted area.

Tynus has a gynaecologist's chair in his quarters, and Avon appears to be washing his hands in preparation for something. If we were Vila, we'd be getting suspicious round about now.

Vila, inevitably, sniffs out a bottle of RED.

The TP Crystal is named after T.P. McKenna, who was originally cast as Cally in this episode.

Here's one you won't have noticed: the white standing lamps in Tynus' office were previously used in corridors on Gallifrey in the *Doctor Who* story "The Invasion of Time". They next appear, 32 years later, in the

Matt Smith TARDIS console room in 2010. (They're constructed in two parts, hinged differently in the two series but definitely the same design.)

Gorgeous smirk directly at the camera from Jenna at 18m 09s. Go and see.

Interesting idea, performing an autopsy on someone who is so obviously breathing.

Poor old Morris Barry doesn't get a lot to do other than have his neck broken by a stiff.

The true story of 'Lord Jeffrey Ashley' (Baron Jeffery Amherst in reality) comes out of nowhere and seems wildly out of place in a space series set so far in the future. We reckon it might have been Holmes' inspiration for the episode.

Poor Ronald Lacey seemed to spend most of his career playing snivelling little creeps.

Jenna does nothing in this episode other than press a few buttons.

Closing Shot: To make up for such a lovely opening shot, we're treated to our old favourite, the cut-out *Liberator* wobbling towards the camera.

Delightful Dialogue:

Bellfriar (as the virus takes effect): Oh my God ... I've forgotten how to read...

Vila: I used to say to people 'I bet Avon's got a friend somewhere in the galaxy.'
Avon: And you were right. That must be a novel experience for you.

Avon: There are a quarter of a million volts running through that converter. I make one false move, I'll be so crisped up what's left of me won't fit into a sandwich.
Vila: I'm a vegetarian. Thanks for the offer, though.

Blake: Jenna, I have been down before.

Amateur Hour:

The whole episode is a downward spiral of bad costumes. As well as people wearing bits of walls and linoleum, the Federation boarding team are sporting Michelin Man suits designed for dwarves.

The effect of the teleport co-ordinate finder is achieved by a bloke shining a torch under some green plastic.

Watch for the scene at 4m 35s, when it looks like Avon produces his little electronic cutter from out of his bottom.

Some of the walls in the complex are made from cloth; they billow as Vila and Avon run by them.

The TP Crystal falls off the teleport desk during the final conversation with Bellfriar. Paul Darrow moves to pick it up but accidentally treads on it instead.

The penultimate shot of the *Liberator* is taken from the first season's original model shoot. You can tell because it's still got the *London* stuck to the front of it.

ADDITIONAL SCRAPS OF KNOWLEDGE

Planets: Fosforon, The Darkling Zone, Thesarus.

Space-isms: A-Line messages, pulse code, Central Spacecraft Registry.

Important Fact: This was the second story recorded for this season. The Pope died during shooting. Not of plague, though.

Robert Holmesy-street: Robert Holmes loves putting Avon and Vila together. He does it in three of his four episodes. The other one's the rubbish one.

Indeed, Holmes structures both this episode and "Gambit" as two parallel plotlines, with Blake having an adventure on one part of a planet and Avon and Vila enjoying themselves elsewhere on the same planet.

This episode begins the series long tradition of Robert Holmes providing story titles that are constructed in a one word / two syllable combo.

23 HOSTAGE

Writer: Allan Prior **Director**: Vere Lorrimer

Guest Stars: John Abineri (Ushton), Judy Buxton (Inga), Kevin Stoney (Joban), Colm Meaney (O'Brien), James Coyle (Molok), Andrew Robertson (Space Commander), Judith Porter (Mutoid)

Opening Shot: Space. Followed by another shot of space. Followed by a great shot of the *Liberator*.

You Just Described the Story:

Avon: All we can hope for is that it's quick.

Random Insult:

Inga: He wouldn't spit on you!

In A Nutshell: Travis has a hostage. Need a good name for the episode – any ideas?

Story: In an unusually expensive and carefree gesture, the Federation deploys twenty pursuit ships to attack the *Liberator*. Blake and company manage to fight their way through but take heavy damage. A message from the now-rogue Travis, asking to join the crew, leads them to Exbar where he has taken Blake's cousin Inga hostage. Avon, meanwhile, has alerted Servalan to Travis' location.

Information:

Well, we're straight into the action here.

The pursuit lasers are green. The colour of lasers is gween.

On missions that ranged from less important to pointless, the Federation only ever sent Trivial Pursuit ships.

When did the Mutoids turn into Myra Hindley?

The *Liberator* is taking a very convincing pounding.

'He's my father's brother', says Blake. That'd be an uncle then.

Cally brandishes a glass of BLUE. Things must be grimmer than we thought.

Servalan downs a glass of GREEN before inviting Joban in.

A pigeon appears to have flown into Servalan's heart and become lodged there.

Money's tight – Jan Chappell's having to do the episode in her own clothes. That's presumably like doing P.E. in your vest and pants.

Cally and Jenna are left on the ship, presumably because Jenna had put dinner on and Cally was vacuuming the flight deck.

'Crimos' are 'criminal psychopaths'. We would have called them Crimipsychs.

The only reason Ushton is given a limp is so that it can vanish when Blake's back is turned, telling us he's a bad 'un.

At times, Travis' eyepatch looks like a sweet wrapper has blown into his face.

Blake is carrying a bundle of sticks tied together. It's a faggot.

Travis has converted his hand to clockwork especially for the occasion. There's nothing like good old-fashioned cogs and levers when you really want to take your time over revenge.

Wow! Full set of bracelets in the teleport room. Don't see that often. We shouldn't be seeing it at all, considering two of them are supposed to be down on the planet.

The shot of the Crimo blowing up in space is the same one they used for poor old Brian Blessed in "Cygnus Alpha".

Where's Gan? Oh. He's dead, isn't he. We forgot.

Closing Shot: Jenna gives Blake the cold shoulder for kissing Inga. Perhaps if she'd put out once in a while he wouldn't have to go around snogging family members.

Delightful Dialogue:

Travis: THE WORD, THE WORD, THE WORD, THE WORD, THE WORD.

Cally: Are you dying?
Vila: I'm thinking about it.

Avon: Zen, can we withstand an attack of this magnitude?
Zen: No information.
Avon: Thank you, that's very helpful.

Vila: I'm freezing.
Avon: Well freeze in silence.

Ushton: I should go up the back trail. Come at them from behind. Surprise them.

Amateur Hour:

The actors playing the Mutoids need to hit those buttons a little more gently; they've pushed the entire panel in on itself.

Camera 3 has an unsteady hand. Stop giving him the extreme close-ups.

There's comedy speeded-up film as Blake rolls down the hill after being attacked by a Crimo.

If you're going to use polystyrene rocks – PAINT THE DAMN THINGS! Shockingly poor.

Knyvette's in a heap of trouble partway through trying to say 'flotilla'.

The lovely flight controls were so damaged by this episode that they were replaced with cheaper materials, in this case a standard anglepoise desk lamp. The prop was later modified to look slightly less like an actual lamp than it does in this story.

When Darrow falls to the floor after the first attack, you can see his mark he's aiming for. He misses it by a good six inches.

ADDITIONAL SCRAPS OF KNOWLEDGE

Planets: Exbar.

Space-isms: Vis-play, time-units, space-casts.

24 COUNTDOWN

Writer: Terry Nation   **Director**: Vere Lorrimer

Guest Stars: Tom Chadbon (Del Grant), Paul Shelley (Provine), James Kerry (Cauder), Lindy Alexander (Ralli), Robert Arnold (Selson), Geoffrey Snell (Tronos), Sidney Kean (Vetnor), Nigel Gregory (Arrian)

Opening Shot: Federation Troops running about in some smoke.

You Just Described the Story:
Grant: Well, while it's still ticking we're alright.

Random Euphemism:
Avon: I need to hold this flap back. Get your hand in here.

In A Nutshell: Vowel, Consonant, Consonant, Bang.

Story: James from Tyne & Wear manages four seven-letter words in the first round while Eileen from Southampton barely scrapes by with a few six-letter words. However, Eileen scores a victory in the first numbers game, and when they come back from the break she's only trailing by four points. After a highly amusing anecdote from Sue Barker and a fascinating account of the derivation of the phrase 'backs to the walls' from Susie Dent, the game resumes. By the final numbers game, sadly, Eileen still trails by twenty-one points and can't win even if she does solve the conundrum.

Information:
The opening battle scenes are really rather good, with plenty of fast-moving action and smoke and guns and stuff. Just ignore the karate bits.

Paul Shelley is brilliant, isn't he? Shame his fringe is a bit daft.

The hoods that the Albians wear look extremely silly. And the shade of green that they wear is sick-inducing.

We think that the BBC must have bought a job lot of Perspex at around this time – see Orac, and the bomb thingy here.

98... 97... 96... 95... 94... 93... 92... 91... 90... 89...

Hmm. So, the countdown of the title refers to a bomb's countdown. We bet that it ends at 001.

Provine is a Space Major in the Space Assault Force. We can deduce from this that they don't operate anywhere around the centre of Huddersfield or Melton Mowbray.

The thermal clothing that Avon and Grant wear is similar to the thermal clothing that would be worn by a chicken in an oven.

The polar footage is plainly comprised of off-cuts from *Life on Earth* or something.

We're quite disappointed that Terry Nation didn't use the opportunity of an episode with an icy zone to write in an icecano.

Zen wasn't required for much of the taping of this story, so he took the opportunity to go off on holiday. He went to Malta, all-inclusive.

When Provine was little he was called Amateurvine.

It's lucky Avon and Grant actually knew each other. The scenes where they attempt to defuse the bomb would've been incredibly dull if they'd been strangers and had to make small talk.

This is the second Terry Nation script this season in which a man gets trapped beneath a fallen beam.

A teleport bracelet is wasted every time somebody's dropped off at the end of a story. Why doesn't a member of the crew beam down with them and return with both bracelets?

Closing Shot: Blake grins smugly. The curly git.

Delightful Dialogue:

Grant: I must be getting old.
Avon: Waste any more time and you won't get any older.

Grant: Thank you for your help.
Vila: Anytime.

Grant: I'll remember that.
Vila (disappointed): Oh, will you?

Amateur Hour:

Selson's uniform changes between scenes.

Both sides are equally inept at the chop-socky action in the opening scenes.

The control room door handily flies open before the rebels' grenade explodes, creating maximum carnage but preserving the prop doorway. Phew!

The timer on the bomb is digital and yet it has a traditional tick like an analogue clock. Even then, the ticking isn't synchronised with the countdown itself.

Why do Avon and Grant endanger themselves by turning on the heating in the polar installation when they're wearing thermal suits?

Space DIY hasn't moved on much since the 20th century. Avon's state of the art toolkit includes more than a common-or-garden power drill painted grey with a whizzy sound effect.

Why does Avon waste time trying to find the third rod to block the descending plunger when leaving the drill bit in place would have done the same job?

ADDITIONAL SCRAPS OF KNOWLEDGE

Terrynation Street: The names 'Del' and 'Grant', radiation yet again, rockets... Oh, and the countdown. And that falling beam mentioned earlier.

Planets: Albion, Arcos.

Space-isms: <deep breath, Terry's back!> Federation Space Assault Force (can you assault space?), solium radiation device, high-temperature lances, space heater, link clamp, flaps.

Countdown Conundrum: Just how is a rocket lying horizontally in a room just 4 ft longer than the rocket itself supposed to lift off and exit through the doors far above?

25 VOICE FROM THE PAST

Writer: Roger Parkes **Director**: George Spenton-Foster

Guest Stars: Richard Bebb (Ven Glynd), Frieda Knorr (Governor Le Grand), Martin Read (Nagu), Neil Toynay (Shivan), Harry Fielder (Shivan's assistant)

Opening Shot: The *Liberator*, coming full-on atcha.

You Just Described the Story:

Blake: Renounce ... False ... Renounce ... False ... Renounce ... False!

In A Nutshell: C'est un trap.

Story: Blake's behaviour is worse than usual, and he changes the *Liberator*'s course without consulting the rest of the crew. They react badly and attempt to restrain him, but Blake tricks Vila into letting him teleport down to Asteroid PK-118. There, he meets the man responsible for putting him on trial, Ven Glynd, who introduces Blake to a giant bandage-wrapped lunatic with a shambolic accent and a neat line in howls of pain and groaning.

Information:

You may remember this episode as being the one with the heavily-bandaged man who has got a glass eye stuck onto the bandages. That's how we like to remember it. The one with the glass eye stuck onto the bandages.

What ARE they all doing at the start of this episode? Especially Blake. We don't recommend trying these exercises at home.

Jenna, Vila, Cally and Avon argue in perfect formation when Blake redirects the ship. The exercises must be working.

They are scheduled to arrive at Asteroid PK-118 at five to seven in the evening. Zen says so, although he later revises this to eight minutes past seven.

Blake is a bit narky in this episode isn't he? And can you cure somebody of visions by sticking a Jammie Dodger to their forehead?

Cally's telepathy's still on the fritz, but she convinces Avon that it's working just by looking wistfully at the stricken Blake.

The *Liberator* spends the first half of this episode rotating very slowly back and forth. Blake's not ill, he's just dizzy.

Blake drinks some CLEAR.

As usual for this era of *Blake's 7*, the episode features contrasting shots of both the lovingly-detailed model of the *Liberator* and the one that's been painted with Tipp-Ex.

Blake doesn't seem remotely bothered that Ven Glynd has got an entirely different face since the last time they met.

What IS the accent that Croucher's doing? Or is Shivan supposed to be deaf too? Is that why he's talking like that?

The Emblem of Liberty is a pink disc on a chain.

Various bits and bobs from *Doctor Who*'s "The Invisible Enemy" are recycled for this story. The most easily spotted are (1) the helmet of Blake's spacesuit (2) the Atlay shuttle (3) Aitch.

'And herald at last the epoch of true freedom.' What? Come on, what? Nobody talks like that, Blake. Not ever.

Governor Le Grand seems to have coloured her face in with crayons.

Frieda Knorr can't say 'Servalan' properly. Croucher has trouble with it too.

Travis is so stupid he's even put his fake eye over his good eye. How can he see anything?

It isn't really very good at all, is it?

Closing Shot: A caption from the BBC's Director-General at the time, Ian Trethowan, apologising unreservedly.

Delightful Dialogue:

Avon (referring to Blake): He's used a number of ploys to get his own way, but 'just try trusting me', that's weak even by his standards.

Amateur Hour:

Where to start?

The glass eye?
The bandages?

'Bwaaaaakke! Ma bwuvvvvvvahhhh!'?

ADDITIONAL SCRAPS OF KNOWLEDGE

Planets: Atlay, Outer Gall, Del 10 (at least 'Del' is being used for a planet this week and not for a character)

Space-isms: Atmospheric veta particles, heurite ore, space fatigue.

Rhyme of the Week: 'Is that man really Shivan?'

Aitch Watch: There he is! Next to Shivan, wearing a dress.

Philately Will Get You Anywhere: As a general celebration of the United Kingdom throughout 1979, the Royal Mail produced a first class stamp depicting Shivan to show that British acting and costume design was among the best in the world.

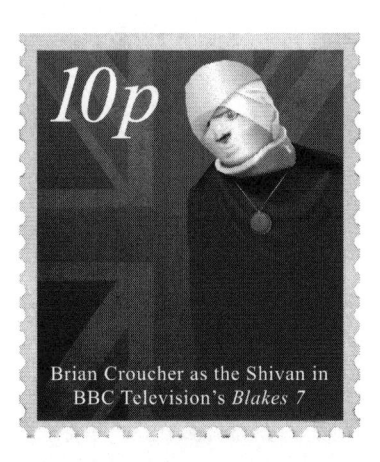

10p — Brian Croucher as the Shivan in BBC Television's Blakes 7

26 GAMBIT

Writer: Robert Holmes **Director**: George Spenton-Foster

Guest Stars: Aubrey Woods (Krantor), Denis Carey (Docholli), Nicolette Roeg (Chenie), Sylvia Coleridge (Croupier), Vittorio Fanfoni (Cop taking notes), Paul Grist (Cevedic), John Leeson (Toise), Harry Jones (Jarriere), Michael Halsey (Zee), Deep Roy (Klute)

Opening Shot: Zed picks a fight in a bar while Joan Sims from *Carry On Cowboy* looks on.

You Just Described the Story:

We may as well have strung together Jarriere's interminably long and tedious pieces of exposition instead of writing a synopsis.

Random Insult:
Docholli: Ungrateful scum!

In A Nutshell: Avon and Vila go gambling while Travis gets a job advertising Sandeman Port.

Story: Acting on a hot tip, the crew go in search of Docholli, a cyber-surgeon with knowledge of Star One, the latest definitely-the-actual-real-live-genuine control centre (honest) of the Federation. They trace him to Freedom City where Travis is acting as his bodyguard. While Avon and Vila attempt to rip off the casino with a miniaturised Orac, Blake and the others finally run Docholli to ground, who tells them that only a man called Lurgen knows Star One's location.

Information:

When Travis turns up in a silly hat, you know this isn't exactly going to be a classic. He also appears to have walked into a sheet hanging on a washing line, poor sausage.

It is such a shame that the model exterior for Freedom City wasn't used as online images show it was rather good.

Jenna and Cally have really glammed up for their trip to Freedom City.

The way that Cally holds the photograph of Docholli is very deliberate – the picture Blake hands her is actually a publicity headshot of actor Denis Carey and Jan Chappell's thumb is covering up his very 20th century shirt and tie.

Cally mistakes a face job for something else entirely. Cor, she just flashed her leg as they went to teleport.

And now, a boss-eyed pensioner dressed as a slutty penguin appears from inside a giant shower cubicle to deliver some sort of slow motion impersonation of Dick Van Dyke.

Only in *Blake's 7*... This first five minutes is unmatched by any other TV programme in history; it's just achingly absurd, as though several costume and set-design lorries have crashed, and the bus full of demented old tramps they've crashed into decide to put on a show until the ambulances arrive.

Against all the efforts of the make-up and costume departments, Aubrey Woods succeeds in giving a typically luscious performance. If he doesn't have a scene with Darrow it'll be a criminal act.

As if this episode isn't camp enough we have a man called Toise and another whose name is *almost* derrière.

John Leeson previously played thingy in the *Doctor Who* story "The Power of Kroll", also written by Robert Holmes.

One forgets that Avon is a greedy little tealeaf, but that's precisely what he was banged up for in the first place. Here, he's salivating over the prospect of ripping off the Freedom City casino using Orac.

Orac's been taking stupid pills, judging by the ease with which the boys con him into shrinking. Yes, that's right – shrinking. Orac can shrink now. Tune in next week to see him sprout a winky and write his name in the snow.

That's the best-stocked bar in the galaxy – GREEN, YELLOW, DIFFERENT GREEN – it's all on there. Travis, the original good-time boy, has a vitazade. We think that's BLUE.

Avon and Vila's cunning plan has a fatal flaw, we'll wager. But it's worth it just to see them buddy up for a good old-fashioned caper.

The name 'Krantor' isn't a million letters away from the word 'Kroton'. Krotons were created by Robert Holmes and featured in his *Doctor Who* story called "The Krotons".

This is the only time in *Blake's 7* where a gangster heavy is required and the silly sods didn't book Aitch.

There's a pig of an edit with Croucher outside together with some stinking post-dubbing.

Jarriere is a bit of an odd one, isn't he? Peculiar looking guy, sort of like a cross between Stephen King's It and Leo Sayer. As he rocks Servalan in her swing, we're definitely into David Lynch territory.

Freedom City is oddly realised. However, accusations of 'it's just tinsel and party streamers' are a little unfair, since that's what they're meant to be: we're told very early on it's Mardis Gras season. That's also why everyone's dressed the way they are.

'Docholli' is a corruption of 'Doc Holliday', while 'Chenie' is a corruption of 'Chessene' who featured in the Robert Holmes *Doctor Who* story "The Two Doctors" and was played by Jacqueline Pearce who here plays Servalan in *Blake's 7*.

Sylvia Coleridge's performance makes the viewer feel drunk even if they've never touched a drop.

Deep Roy is a national treasure. As the Klute he's terrific.

The draft script included a number of other games to be played the Klute. These include Fast Dominoes, Quite Quick Hangman and Languid Snap.

The Klute is drinking GREEN! But with a crazy straw.

Vila is treacherously drinking some BLUE.

Aubrey Woods' little moments to camera are reminiscent of John Normington's in the *Doctor Who* story "The Caves of Androzani", also scripted by Holmes but not featuring Sylvia Coleridge as a boss-eyed slutty penguin.

Jenna calls Cally a 'ten-credit touch'. Avon was trying to embezzle 500,000,000 credits (or 5,000,000 credits, it depends which episode you're watching). Now our maths isn't great, but that would work out at… a lot of touches. A *lot*.

'Cevedic' is a corruption of 'clever dick'. Holmes uses this in the *Doctor Who* stories "The Power of Kroll" (Clee Fardic), "The Space Pirates" (Keef Ardie) and the *Blake's 7* episode "Orbit" (Pinder).

Standing behind Vila at the roulette table are a slutty penguin, Dracula, a nun and a Cavalier.

Cally has become telepathic again.

Christ, this Servalan/Jarriere stuff is boring. It's like listening to Mat Irvine explain CSO to a W.I. meeting on a wet Sunday afternoon in Bridlington.

Krantor's little white pussy is the only cat to ever appear in *Blake's 7*, although several are mentioned in the *Doctor Who* story "Survival", which wasn't written by Robert Holmes.

Everyone pronounces the name Cevedic in a totally different way. Examples include Chever-Dick (from Toise), Shaver-Dish (from Travis), Chev-a-Deet (from Krantor) and Sever-Dick (from Cally).

Cevedic uses the same gun as Nagu in "Voice from the Past".

Docholli reveals that Blake must now go looking for a goth thong. We've all had days like that.

This episode is the only one to use the infamous 'Delaware' version of the theme.

Closing Shot: Vila and Avon look sheepishly on while Orac returns to normal size. Good job that metal box he was in was made of Disappearolon.

Delightful Dialogue:

As this is a Robert Holmes script, we could just repeat every line; these are mere drops in the ocean.

Krantor: She's as perfidious and devious as a snake.

Cally: What did you call me?
Jenna: A cheap little space tramp.
Cally: You slut!
Jenna: A ten-credit touch!

Krantor: Oh, how sad. Try a pataki cake.

Toise: Krantor! Someone is having a rrrrrun on the wheel!

Amateur Hour:

Cally's bracelet moves from her right to left arm throughout the episode.

John Leeson's hat makes it look like his head is on fire.

The Speed Chess graphics are of their day, but even then they can't have been very impressive.

There's a great wardrobe malfunction at 16m 15s – Jarriere's earring falls off when he's mid-conversation with Servalan.

When Dochilli removes Travis' robotic arm, you can clearly see where Brian Croucher has his real one strapped up.

ADDITIONAL SCRAPS OF KNOWLEDGE

Planets: Trantinia.

Space-isms: Nitro grenades.

Jenna Rape-Threat: Cevedic lusts after both Jenna and Cally, who are given virtually nothing else to do in the episode.

Best Coat Moment In *Blake's 7:* When Nicolette Roeg struggles a bit in helping Denis Carey on with his coat. Carey realises she's putting it on him upside-down so, cool as a cucumber, he pulls it off again and walks out with it draped over his shoulder.

27 THE KEEPER

Writer: Allan Prior **Director**: Steven Spielberg

Guest Stars: Bruce Purchase (The Pirate Captain), Shaun Curry (Rod), Freda Jackson (Tara), Cengiz Saner (Fool), Harold Innocent (Bishop of Hereford), Arthur Hewlett (Old man), Ron Tarr (Patrol leader)

Opening Shot: Wobbly shot of a static *Liberator* in front of a wrinkly, crinkly planet.

You Just Described the Story:

Blake: Let us assume that the keeper of the secret is somewhere down there on the planet Goth.

Random Insult:

The Pirate Captain: Kick that fool as you pass him – possibly I might smile at his pain.

In A Nutshell: Noggin the Nog.

Story: Docholli's advice leads the crew to Goth where a brain print of Lurgen is supposed to reside in an amulet. Of course Travis has already beaten them to it and, in collusion with Servalan, escapes with the details. Blake and the crew find yet another way of extracting the information and depart in hot pursuit to … STAR ONE!

Information:

They're looking for a man with a thong. It's tempting to skip this one.

Oh, look what they've done: planet Goth … visigoths. Brilliant. We were expecting a planet full of miserable panda-eyed teens dressed in black and bleating on about The Sisters of Mercy.

Cally's mascara is so thick it looks like she's wearing tiny deely-boppers on her face.

They have Earth grapes on Goth. And Earth rats. And Earth lutes.

The inhabitants of Goth really can't be very intelligent; one of them stands around and more or less allows Blake to whack him on the back of the head with a lump of tree.

The Pirate Captain is very easily impressed by Vila's Ali Bongo act. But then again, he has had some sort of Black & Decker DIY lobotomy.

Travis has completed his transition into full-blown pantomime villain. He actually slaps his thigh when he first meets The Pirate Captain…

… which makes Servalan Mother Goose. Why is she gadding about the galaxy when she's got a lovely little desk and a full bottle of GREEN at home?

Avon spends one scene with Cally playing with his balls.

Whose idea was it to give Jenna the mad staring eyes scene? She looks like a coked-up poodle when she does that.

Blake lets out a long theatrical yawn. We can only sympathise.

This feels like a *Doctor Who* script hastily rewritten for *Blake's 7*. There's not a single trace of a downbeat, desperate struggle against an oppressive regime. It's just a bunch of halfwits pratting about like it's an episode of *Jackanory Playhouse*.

Having said that, it's clearly supposed to be Jenna's episode. No wonder Sally Knyvette buggered off if this was the best they could come up with for her.

'Pair bond' is very obviously a euphemism.

Arthur Hewlett turns up here doing his usual old man schtick. Was he 75 when he was born?

The pyramid draughts game looks really rubbish.

George Lucas got the idea of Princess Leia being Jabba the Hutt's slave from this episode.

There is a lot of talk of 'going down below'.

Naming characters after cheap trainer brands is never a good idea.

Also, 'Rod' isn't much of a sci-fi name; it just makes you wonder where Jane and Freddy are.

You may notice that Freda Jackson has a tendency to go ever so slightly over the top in her performance.

Did no one tell Allan Prior about Orac? There is no sign of him in this episode.

Closing Shot: The *Liberator* falls over.

Delightful Dialogue:

Rod: My name is Rod.

The Pirate Captain: I am not afraid of your vapour.

And that's it.

Amateur Hour:

There is a very poor bit of CSO as Vila and Jenna are being led to the tents. It's a bit like watching an episode of *Bellamy's Backyard Safari*.

The *Liberator* table wobbles alarmingly as Vila picks up his Playmobil suitcase.

The Goth's facemasks look very sophisticed and somewhat at odds with the fact that they wear furs, carry swords and live in caves.

During the fight sequence near the end of the episode the spikes on Gola's mace bend back and forth and wobble – it's weird, it's almost as though they are made from rubber that has been painted silver.

ADDITIONAL SCRAPS OF KNOWLEDGE

Planets: Goth.

Space-isms: Nitro grenades.

For The Pervs: Jenna has her cleavage on show for much of the episode. No doubt this was down to The Pirate Captain.

28 STAR ONE

Writer: Christ Boucher   **Director**: David Maloney

Guest Stars: Jenny Twigge (Lurena), John Bown (Durkim), David Webb (Stot), Gareth Armstrong (Parton), Marcus Gilbert (Ancelyn), Paul Toothill (Marcol), Chris Merrick (Terry Lee Miall), Michael Mayard (Leeth)

Opening Shot: The same as *Star Wars*. But clearly not.

You Just Described the Story:

Avon: We seem to have stumbled over an alien invasion.

Random Break-Up Speech:

Avon (to Blake): I never doubted your fanaticism. As far as I am concerned you can destroy whatever you like. You can stir up a thousand revolutions, you can wade in blood up to your armpits. Oh, and you can lead the rabble to 'victory', whatever that might mean. Just so long as there is an end to it. When Star One is gone it is finished, Blake. And I want it finished. I want it over and done with. I want to be free.

In A Nutshell: Anticlimactic anticlimax.

Story: Despite protestations from Avon and the rest of the crew, Blake is insistent on destroying Star One. Unknown to them, it is already failing and breaking down, causing chaos on countless Federation worlds. Blake discovers that aliens from Andromeda have infiltrated Star One and their fleet is already on course to attack the Federation. Travis is disposed of down a handy shaft and the *Liberator* crew make a final stand against the oncoming invaders.

Information:

This is the last story to feature Blake in the opening titles until Chris Boucher's Season R episode "Blake".

Great, the episode starts with air traffic controllers having a chinwag. That'll get the viewers hooked.

Instead of arguing with Nova Control, the pilot of the *Nova Queen* really should have just leaned to the left a bit.

'Nova Queen' is an anagram of 'Queen Avon'.

Someone really needs to tell Cally that green just isn't her colour.

Nice to see a close-up of the Federation logo on Servalan's screen.

'Keldan City' sounds a bit like 'Kaldor City'.

We've seen that shot of *Liberator* flying past the planets and suns before.

Avon really doesn't like Blake, does he?

Boucher's dialogue is great and his handle on the characters is much stronger than even Nation's.

Servalan's two personal troopers in her office couldn't have more opposing hairstyles if they tried.

Stot uses a Laser Probe. Is it too much to hope it's a Laserson Probe?

The use of light-switches on Star One is a typical Boucher thing. He creates a world with cosy parallels to modern life.

Blake's quip about finding a door marked 'entrance' leads to rather a lot of smuggery when they find one on the planet below.

Sally Knyvette seems unable to disguise her utter boredom.

The dead crew dangling in the room Lurena hides in must be one of the most shocking scenes in the series. A genuinely good scare.

The circular control room on Star One reappears in Season P as the air traffic control centre on Auron.

We've been wondering this for quite some time, but which of those holes do you think is Orac's mouth?

Cally's telepathy crops up again.

You've got to feel sorry for Travis. His life really is a pile of poo.

Vila points out that Orac always makes him feel like he should be taking notes, which reminds us: take some bloody notes!

Blake and Cally take great pains to be as stealthy as possible when planting a series of bloody obvious-looking explosive devices in plain view.

Travis - the scourge of Blake, freedom and, as it turns out, the Federation - is despatched with a remarkable lack of ceremony. He's just washed away down a space plug-hole in a hurried stunt that should have gone better.

Look very closely at the Andromedan fleet and you'll see a Zygon ship from *Doctor Who*, a tennis racquet, a glass eye (the same one used by Travis in "Voice from the Past") and a plastic duck painted black.

The mice in cages in the experimentation room are actually guinea pigs. Surely someone on the production team realised this? They're huge!

Why does Section 4 have a big red number 3 on the door?

The *Liberator* switches to mood lighting for the big fight. Doesn't that it harder to see which buttons to press?

Closing Shot: 'Fire!' – fantastic stuff.

Delightful Dialogue:

Vila: Then are they expecting an invasion? A hoard of hairy aliens?
Orac: There is no logical reason why aliens should be hairy.
Vila: There's no logical reason why people should be hairy.

Stot (referring to Cally): Who is this woman?
Blake: She is my mother.

Vila: Don't like explosives, very crude. Difficult to reason with a bomb.

Travis: Aaaaaagggggggggghhhhhhhhhhhhhhhh!

Vila: Avon, this is stupid!
Avon: When did that ever stop us?

Amateur Hour:

Pearce loses her way in the middle of a line talking to Durkim but reels it in with what looks like a terrific bit of improv.

The Andromedans, masters of disguise and cunning, refer to each other by the names of their human doppelgangers even when they're alone. Now there's method-invading for you.

Blake's command to 'increase speed to Standard by twelve' is followed by a near-stationary shot of the *Liberator*.

Jenna is wearing the outfit that she left on Goth last week.

When the crew teleport down to Star One Blake is wearing green wellies. When he enters the base they have magically transformed into brown leather boots. The collared top he was wearing over his turtleneck jumper also vanishes when he teleports.

The *Liberator* handguns have developed the ability to shoot bloody holes in people.

Travis' ship on the *Liberator* screen looks like it has just been thrown past the camera.

Poor Sally Knyvette trips, stumbles and hobbles over her instructions to Orac to chat to the Space Command strategy computer. She even looks around for inspiration. Was another take really out of the question?

ADDITIONAL SCRAPS OF KNOWLEDGE

Planets: Keldan, Palmero (tropical fruit supplier to the Federation), Suni, Vilka, Herom, Cathenis (which was named in honour of Chris Boucher's next-door neighbour at the time of writing, Cathy Dennis).

Space-isms: Intergalactic space, anti-matter minefield.

Avon's "Well, now..." Count: 2

Phil Ware's Rant: BBC1 spoiled this story by showing Travis' death in the trailer. He thinks. He can't quite remember. But he mentions it a lot.

7.15 pm *New series*
Blake's Seven
The first of 18 episodes
Aftermath by **TERRY NATION**
starring **Paul Darrow**
Jan Chappell, Michael Keating
Jacqueline Pearce and **Josette Simon**
with **Cy Grant** and **Alan Lake**

In a desperate attempt to delay the invading aliens long enough for the Federation battle fleet to arrive, Blake has sacrificed the Liberator. As the space war rages the crew prepare to abandon their crippled ship …

Avon	PAUL DARROW
Cally	JAN CHAPPELL
Vila	MICHAEL KEATON
Servalan	JACQUELINE PEARCE
Zen	PETER TUDDENHAM
Dayna	JOSETTE SIMON
Mellanby	CY GRANT
Chel	ALAN LAKE
Lauren	SALLY HARRISON
Burnside	CHRIS ELLISON
Trooper	RICHARD FRANKLIN
Trooper	MICHAEL MELIA
Tarrant	STEVEN PACEY

Series created by TERRY NATION
Script editor CHRIS BOUCHER
Designer DON TAYLOR
Producer DAVID MALONEY
Director VERE LORRIMER

FEATURE p24

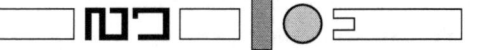

SEASON P 1980

Regular Cast

Paul Darrow	*Kerr Avon*
Michael Keating	*Vila Restal*
Jan Chappell	*Cally the Teleport Operator*
Steven Pacey	*Del Tarrant*
Josette Simon	*Dayna Mellanby*
Peter Tuddenham	*Zen / Orac*
Jacqueline Pearce	*Servalan*
Aitch	*Everyone else*

Episodes

Aftermath
Powerplay
Volcano
Flesh
Zen
Dawn of the Gods
Twilight of the Gods
The Harvest of Kairos
City at the Edge of the World
Children of Auron
Strike Attack!
Rumours of Death
Sarcophagus
Ultraworld
Space Beetles
Moloch
Death-Watch
Terminal

29 AFTERMATH

Writer: Terry Nation   **Director**: Vere Lorrimer

Guest Stars: Cy Grant (Hal Mellanby), Alan Lake (Chel), Sally Harrison (Lauren), Chris Ellison (Burnside), Richard Franklin, Michael Melia (Troopers)

Opening Shot: Exactly the same as "Star One". That saved a fiver.

You Just Described the Story:
Servalan: Where are Blake and the others?

Random Compliment:
Servalan (to Avon): You are infinitely corruptible.

In A Nutshell: Reboot.

Story: Following the climactic battle for Star One, the Federation finds itself in tatters whilst the crew of the *Liberator* are separated from each other. Avon is marooned on the planet Sarran, where he meets Dayna Mellanby and her father Hal. Servalan also appears on the planet. She kills Hal and attempts to steal Orac in her quest to gain control of the *Liberator*. Avon recaptures Orac and returns to the *Liberator* with Dayna. There, they find a Federation officer named Tarrant waiting for them, claiming the ship as his own.

Information:
New opening title sequence! Oh. Have they gone all *Star Trek* and made a cartoon series?

Err... where's Blake?

Wasn't Star One a 'single planet orbiting an isolated, dying star', millions of miles away from anything else? What are all these planets doing here all of a sudden?

The flight deck set was being used by Morecambe and Wise for a dance number when the opening scene aboard the *Liberator* was due to be filmed, so the action is heard only in voiceover as we get to look at more reused footage of space battles and an air vent.

And why is Zen so high-pitched?

And why are we on film?

Excellent choice of location for the scenes on Sarran. Bamburgh Dunes really does look very good here and makes for a refreshing change from the usual quarries. Quite why more productions don't use superb locations like this, we don't know. Well actually we do: it's a bloody long way to drive.

Josette Simon didn't own an equity card at the time of filming. You'd never guess.

Dayna only wears earrings in the scenes on videotape.

How did Servalan end up there? What are the odds? You can tell she is feeling the cold too.

Avon's fisticuffs with the Sarran on the beach are pretty well done.

Servalan's even flirting with Dayna.

Cy Grant is amazing.

Dayna insists that she and her father aren't hiding, whereas he's just told Avon that they're... hiding. Good ol' Terry 'One Draft' Nation.

Who draws the alien lifeform targets seen in the firing range? It's hard to imagine any of the Mellanby family sitting down of an evening to colour those in before cutting them out.

Blake and Jenna are written out swiftly with a few lines from Zen.

Avon's conversation with Zen via Orac is quite warming. Zen as a character does so little, but his constant, attentive obedience is endearing.

Avon prepares Servalan a cool glass of GREEN.

Did Lauren really lie on that cliff for five hours? If so, she's an idiot.

You have to love Cy Grant's pronunciation of 'Orac'.

The shock of Avon kissing Servalan is dispelled by the sight of her wobbly chest when she's thrown to the ground.

It's physically impossible for Servalan to have manoeuvred Orac up that spiral staircase. How the hell did she manage it?

Why does Dayna design her guns in aquamarine and peach?

We now have more than 30 episodes ahead of us of Dayna threatening to kill Servalan and failing.

Dayna and Avon's rescue of Servalan is well-staged. It's just a shame we have to return to that dodgy plastic videotape cave.

Closing Shot: A wobbly zoom into Avon as he is threatened with Tarrant's ickle weeny pistol.

Delightful Dialogue:

Avon: Imagination my only limit? I'd be dead in a week.

Avon: Listen, I'm not very keen on watersports, even at the best of times.

Amateur Hour:

Is this the best we can do for opening titles?

During the scene with Avon having a punch-up with a Sarran you can see someone in a red anorak wandering around on the dune in the background.

Where does Avon gets Dayna's teleport bracelet from?

ADDITIONAL SCRAPS OF KNOWLEDGE

Terrynation Street: Scientist with a disability.

Planets: Sarran.

Space-isms: Vita-shock weapons.

Dayna Cries: Twice.

30 POWERPLAY

Writer: Terry Nation   **Director**: David Maloney (uncredited)

Guest Stars: Michael Sheard (Klegg), John Hollis (Lom), Doyne Bird (Harmon), Michael Crane (Mall), Primi Townsend (Zee), Julia Vidler (Barr), Angela Thorne (Marjory), Catherine Chase (Nurse), Helen Blatch (Receptionist)

Opening Shot: Tarrant minces threateningly at Avon and Dayna.

You Just Described the Story:

Avon: This is my ship.

Random Insult:

Vila: Call yourself a computer? You're an idiot, Zen. You should have been melted down for scrap years ago. You electronic moron.

In A Nutshell: Now We Are Six.

Story: Tarrant has assumed control of the *Liberator* and holds Avon and Dayna captive. Zen has detected that the rest of the crew are spread across the galaxy, with Vila and Cally stranded on the planet Chenga. There, they find themselves at the mercy of a medical facility that plans to use them for organ harvesting. Tarrant reveals himself to be a permed ponce intent on knackering the series for good.

Information:

The first word out of Tarrant's mouth is 'Summary' and we already hate his smug guts.

It's Michael 'Majestic' Sheard. Oh yes, it bloody well is. Great!

Avon's pseudonym comes to him very quickly. Maybe he's always wanted to be a Chevron?

Vila's alive then. One down.

John Hollis is such a reliable actor. Never turns in a bad performance.

Klegg's entire crew is made up of recognisable BBC extras and stuntmen. Hang on though – where's Aitch?

One of the *Liberator* corridors appears to be stuck in a perpetual 16mm world while the rest of the ship is sturdy videotape.

Terry Nation cliché No. 34 – inspection tunnels.

The planet Servalan is rescued from looks nothing like it did in the previous episode.

That corridor's gone videotape now.

It's very difficult not to watch the extras when Klegg's squad are on screen.

Michael Keating is terrific in the scene in which Vila attempts to portray a squadron of ten men all by himself.

At the rate Vila's stubble's growing, he could join ZZ Top by the end of the episode.

Ah, Vila's been picked up by women with big guns. He's going to be okay.

The space vixens have 'fast forward' symbols on their hats. I'd take that as an encouraging sign.

This week, Cally's telepathy is specific to light arm-pain.

Whatever happened to that defence mechanism Zen had when Blake when Blake first boarded the *Liberator*?

NURSES – blue and green should never be seen!

Cally and Vila meet up – hurrah! Servalan schemes – hooroo.

Where did Servalan get a different pair of earrings since the last episode?

Terry Walsh School of Acting: when listening at a door, stick your tongue out.

Vila has a refreshing glass of GREEN while waiting with Cally to have his body chopped up into bits and stuff.

The two paintings on the wall on Chenga behind Vila and Cally also appear in an episode of *Brush Strokes*.

Dayna strangles Klegg by squeezing his shoulder.

Hang on – where the hell does Orac vanish to? He doesn't appear in this episode!

Closing Shot: Tarrant and Dayna look smugly at each other and wonder where the bedrooms are.

Delightful Dialogue:

Avon (referring to a trooper with a knife in his back): That's a difficult way to commit suicide.
Dayna: Maybe he was cleaning it and it went off?

Vila: I'm cold and I'm miserable and I'm hurt and I'm hungry.

Avon: This is Vila. I should introduce him now. He's at his best when he's unconscious.

Avon: Anyone comes through this door – kill them. Anybody who isn't me, that is.

Vila: Oh, it's just I'm not very good with pain. It's not that I'm a coward or anything. It's just that I have a very low pain threshold. Hardly a threshold at all, actually.

Amateur Hour:

Is this really the best we can do for opening titles?

Cally's mask muffles her voice.

Jan Chappell acts paralysed by immediately moving her arm.

ADDITIONAL SCRAPS OF KNOWLEDGE

Planets: Chenga, Epheron, Lauritol, Morphenniel.

Space-isms: Federation Space Captain, and the brilliant, unbeatable, truly Terry-tastic 'space accident'.

Tarrant Mitigation Technique:

Whenever anyone says 'Del', say 'Derek'.

In the first scene, watch Dayna's breasts instead.

Think how much better the series would have been if Tarrant had died in "Powerplay", and then pretend it's Section Leader Klegg who joins the crew.

Whenever Tarrant addresses Klegg in that sneering tone, imagine it's Albert Steptoe speaking.

Below: In late 1979, *Blake's 7 Weekly* ran a competition for its readers to design the necktie for Michael Sheard to wear to the BAFTA screening of "Powerplay." The winning entry by Gareth Pinto of Wisley - a periwinkle-blue design, made from woven silk with a *Liberator* gun motif picked out in yellow - was announced at a charity dinner held by the Men's Dress Furnishings Association. The winner and two unnamed runners-up were presented with signed photographs of Sheard by Charles Hendricks, chairman of the Association. 'There are never losers in a competition to design neckwear – it always ends in a tie,' he joked to rapturous silence.

31 VOLCANO

Writer: Allan Prior **Director**: Desmond McCarthy

Guest Stars: Michael Cough (Hower), Malcolm Bullivant (Bershar), Ben Howard (Mori), Alan Bowerman (Battle Fleet Commander), Judy Matheson (Mutoid), Patricia Black (Funshine Bear), Russell Denton (Milus)

Opening Shot: A volcano.

You Just Described the Story:

Tarrant: What's that?
Dayna: The volcano.

Random Insult:

Orac: Teleport operation is a menial task, much more suited to one such as yourself.

In A Nutshell: It's about a volcano.

Story: Tarrant and Dayna head to the planet Obsidian in search of a place to use as a base of operations in their battle against the Federation. Obsidian has somehow remained outside the influence of the Federation, and there they find Hower, who is the leader of the pacifist Pyroans. Tarrant attempts to persuade the Pyroans to assist them but Hower has other ideas to prevent the Federation showing too much interest in the planet.

Information:

Lots and lots of stock footage, although this is probably a better tactic than having a Visual Effects department volcano.

Tarrant's already trying to change things aboard the *Liberator*: 'Safely down'? What the heck does that mean? It's 'Down and safe', you dolt.

Some of the location shooting took place at Brimham Rocks in North Yorkshire. One of us went there once on a primary school trip. It was a bit short on volcanoes.

Keep an eye out at 3m 18s – the power lead has come unplugged from Tarrant's gun and it looks like he has a curly black tail.

The costume budget couldn't stretch to a complete outfit for Dayna, so her top half is covered in supermarket carrier bags. Look closely when they first approach the volcano and you can just see the word 'Safeway' emblazoned under her left arm.

Well done Tarrant, giving away all of the secrets of the strength of the *Liberator*.

The *Liberator* crew want to base themselves on Obsidian. We wouldn't. It's got a bloody great volcano in the middle of it.

Jan Chappell is wearing her own clothes again.

We're sure that Dudley includes the opening notes of the *Emmerdale Farm* theme at one point.

Servalan's grooming Mori to be the new Supreme Commander. Let's hope he's got the legs for evening wear.

None of these Travis substitutes really seem to cut the mustard, do they?

This year's well-dressed Mutoid is sporting the jelly mould once again.

From space, Obsidian looks like it is covered in paint blisters.

The battle fleet main ship is bloody odd-looking.

Vila has some adrenalin and soma. We don't know if this is the same as GREEN or not.

You could scour pans with the Battle Fleet Commander's hair.

Cally takes her sweet time to let Avon know the *Liberator* is occupied. Even then she tells him that three troopers have boarded the ship when there are actually four.

Mori and Cally both suffer teleport-bracelet-dropping-off-the-arm hell within minutes of each other. Jan Chappell even looks off-set toward the production crew, and you can tell from her eyes she is thinking, 'Another take – we *must* be going for another take? No? Oh, alright'.

What a surprise. The volcano that we know is in the episode erupts at the end.

Closing Shot: The *Liberator*'s bum.

Delightful Dialogue:

Cally: By the rim ... by the rim ...

Cally: Well, she's pretty, for one thing.
Vila: Pretty? Yes, I suppose she is. I hadn't really noticed.
Avon: We've seen you not really noticing, frequently.

Amateur Hour:

The chap playing the robot has got his funky movements down pat. A shame then that you can see his chest rise and fall with his breathing.

Ben Howard fluffs his line during his briefing with Servalan.

Michael Gough fluffs several lines when he's describing his people's pacifist tendencies.

Avon's gun disappears after he shoots the two troopers on the *Liberator* flight deck.

The impressive-looking back flip by the Federation trooper who falls to his doom is rather undermined by the CSO shot that follows it.

Avon stumbles over his line just after he is put down onto Obsidian's surface.

ADDITIONAL SCRAPS OF KNOWLEDGE

Planets: Obsidian.

Space-isms: Nothing much. Oooh! Oooh! Federation teletext.

Tarrant Mitigation Technique:

Remember, that's a volcano. Wouldn't it be lovely if Tarrant fell in?

In response to Hower's line 'Was it necessary to treat them like that?', state in the voice of Bershar 'It was in the man's case. I mean, just look at him.'

32 FLESH

Writer: Terry Nation **Director**: Norman Stewart

Guest Stars: Patricia Routledge (Arnos), Barbara New (Dothan), Amelia Bayntun (Gatan), Keith Barron (Voshtak)

Opening Shot: Boxes piled up in a warehouse, one of them seeping a strange green goo.

You Just Described the Story:

Voshtak: It's the flesh!

Random Insult:

Tarrant: I think you'll find I'm not to your taste.
Dothan: Nor anyone else's, dear.

In A Nutshell: Fancy a nibble?

Story: The planet Darvel is located in the heart of the battlegrounds of the war between the Federation and the Andromedans. Voshtak, a survivor from the war, crashes down on the planet and finds the surface littered with the bones of creatures from many races. As darkness falls, Voshtak's camp is attacked by a savage creature, but he's rescued by Dothan, a native of the planet. Dothan informs him that the Feralis, vicious predators, come out to prey on anyone left out on the surface at night. Aboard the *Liberator*, Avon is tracking a mysterious signal which seems to originate from the planet Darvel. He and Vila teleport to the planet below and make contact with Dothan and her clan, who claim to have located the injured body of Jenna.

Information:

Jeebus! Patricia Routledge in a skintight gold jumpsuit. Never thought we'd see that. She looks surprisingly sultry, if we're honest.

Due to a memo getting lost the *Liberator* set has only been half-built, hence the strange camera angles. This led to Norman Stewart not being hired again.

The vehicles driven across the planet surface are actually just mopeds with a cardboard outer body. When the trooper crashes one into the grain silo, you can see it crumple.

Cally's telepathy has now turned into telekinesis!

Voshtak uses the galactic standard shuttle craft, previously seen in "Seek-Locate-Destroy" and "Countdown".

He's not going to go unnoticed for long waving that thing around.

Never trust a woman with come-to-bed eyes but go-to-hell claws.

Avon's being his usual charming self. The others would probably go along with less fuss if he'd just tell them what he was up to every now and then.

The buddy-buddy relationship stuff between Vila and Avon isn't a patch on what we saw in "Gambit".

Barbara New's a lot more agile than she looks. She's a lot fiercer than she looks, too. The sight of her and Amelia Bayntun slavering over Keith Barron is going to stay with us for a very long time.

The cushions in the lounge thing are the same ones seen in the *Juliet Bravo* story "Snakedance".

Dothan's song is clearly improvised.

So that's what happened to Tarrant...

Closing Shot: Patricia Routledge howling at the moon.

Delightful Dialogue:

Arnos: My kind have lived on this planet for millennia. A few clockwork soldiers decide to invade? We'll deal with them the same way we deal with all strangers. With blood.

Vila: Tell me she didn't do what I think she did?
Avon: Oh, but she did.
Vila: Let's pretend you didn't say that.

Amateur Hour:

Keith Barron's perm is enough – what idiot decided on that hairstyle?

ADDITIONAL SCRAPS OF KNOWLEDGE

Planets: Darvel, Inkpath, Gamma Wretch 9A, Obsidiantart.

Space-isms: Space Werewolves sets a new low.

```
28.1.80/DP        80/4796
BBC-1 TELEVISION SERVICE
"BLAKES 7 AND THE FLESH"

Patricia Routledge stars as Arnos in
a new 'BLAKES 7' adventure in space,
on BBC-1 on Monday 28th January.

BBC COPYRIGHT PHOTOGRAPH.
FROM:    BBC, BROADCASTING HOUSE, LONDON W.1,
```

Above: The rear of the BBC Publicity photograph depicting Patricia Routledge in costume as Arnos. The front has remained embargoed for over thirty-five years.

33 ZEN

Writer: Terry Nation   **Director**: Pennant Roberts

Guest Stars: None

Opening Shot: The *Liberator* flight deck, empty.

You Just Described the Story:
Cally: No, really. I'm made up.

Random Insult:
Vila: Zen's rubbish!

In A Nutshell: An experimental episode, based entirely from Zen's perspective.

Story: The crew are taking some R&R at Space Hotel Epsilon. During their downtime they make occasional trips back to the ship, where they are observed by a lonely Zen. When Orac is left switched on by Vila, the two computers begin to bicker until Zen threatens to crash the ship into space if Orac doesn't leave him alone.

Information:
Due to the nature of the script, it comes as a massive surprise that Peter Tuddenham was given three weeks off during recording of this story. The voices of Zen and Orac were provided, uncredited, by Dalek voice actor Michael Wisher.

The jacket Vila is wearing was originally worn by William Russell in the pilot episode of *Doctor Who*.

When Zen does his impression of Orac, Wisher sounds uncannily like the voice Tuddenham would later use for Slave.

We are given brief snippets of the life of the *Liberator* crew at the Space Hotel: Vila is gambling, Avon is flirting, Cally is meditating and Dayna is playing computer games. No mention is made of what Tarrant is doing or why he's wearing a Federation Trooper uniform.

The shot of the auto-repair circuits was achieved by creating a wax model and melting it with a giant heat lamp. The footage was then played back in reverse at high speed.

This is one of the few episodes for which Dudley Simpson didn't supply the music. Instead, it was composed by Geoffrey Burgon.

Count the guns as Avon swipes one from the rack. In a minute it'll be back in the rack, but two different ones will be missing.

On the subject of guns, does that one look familiar? It'll be sprayed silver and called a 'clip gun' next year.

What do they say? Never work with children or animals? Watching poor Michael Keating trying to get through the scene with the parrot is agony. The parrot can also be heard twice later on during Avon's scenes in the Space Bar.

The Space Bar set features china cups and saucers with little paper stars stuck on them like you'd get in your exercise book at school.

Those guns have shuffled about again!

We're not sure if the Zen energy-pulse noise is meant to be just that or him snoring.

The entire set had to be rotated at a 45 degree angle in order to get a studio camera behind Zen's glass for the POV shots. These days it would be achieved with a CG graphic.

As the crew take their seats, Pacey manages to push his entire console to the left.

Closing Shot: The *Liberator* flight deck, as the crew take their seats for their next adventure.

Delightful Dialogue:
Zen: Confirmed.

Zen: Information: no hostile ships detected.

Orac: Do be quiet!

Amateur Hour:

Clearly a money saving episode, since all the Space Hotel locations are recycled from *Doctor Who* or something.

The CSO work is some of the worst ever seen on British television. It makes the cast look like they have been eating Ready Brek.

Zen's POV is blurred to obscure the fact there is no wall on the side of the set he's facing.

ADDITIONAL SCRAPS OF KNOWLEDGE

Planets: Ji Tung Kwah, Oceanon, Chillzar, Earth 3.

Space-isms: Space Hotel Epsilon, Space Bar, Vita-chips, kurgon crystals.

7.20 pm
Blake's Seven
The fifth of 18 episodes
Zen
by TERRY NATION
starring **Peter Tuddenham**

The crew leave *Liberator* to explore the Space Hotel Epsilon. Will the bickering of Zen and Orac be the ultimate downfall of Blake's crew?

Orac.................... PETER TUDDENHAM

Series created by TERRY NATION
Music by DUDLEY SIMPSON
Studio lighting WARWICK FIELDING
Script editor CHRIS BOUCHER
Designer CHRISTINE RUSCOE
Producer DAVID MALONEY
Director PENNANT ROBERTS

Subtitles on Ceefax page 170

FEATURE p11

34 DAWN OF THE GODS

Writer: James Follett   **Director**: Desmond McCarthy

Guest Stars: Marcus Powell (The Thaarn), Sam Sastor (The Caliph), Gareth Milne (The Unknown), Terry Scully (Groff)

Opening Shot: The *Liberator* whizzing unconvincingly through space. Cut to the crew playing a bloody board game.

You Just Described the Story:

Vila: A black hole – my God we're falling into a black hole.

Random Insult:

Vila: Why don't I ever win?
Avon: Being a born loser may have something to do with it.

In A Nutshell: Black 'ole.

Story: Orac secretly takes the *Liberator* on a route to observe a mysterious black hole in which the ship becomes trapped. Passing through the hole, the crew find themselves in a void littered with space debris. This is the domain of the Thaarn, a god from the myths of Cally's people, who had been cast out after killing another god. The Thaarn is harnessing the power of the black hole to trap ships from which he can obtain the mineral Herculanium to use in assisting his return.

Information:

Everybody picks on Vila again. They really are a bunch of bullies at times.

This episode was broadcast before they had finished making it.

We love the bit when Orac gets irate about the game. Irate Orac is always the best form of Orac.

Dayna calls Orac 'the Orac computer'. Bit rude talking about a member of the seven like that, isn't it?

The *Liberator* is almost destroyed by Mirrorlon.

The ship now has resuscitation capsules which we have never seen or heard of before. Or since, for that matter.

The shot of the *Liberator* crew in the dark, their faces all in a line, is nicely done.

This is the first episode not to make use of the teleport. It is also the first episode where Blake doesn't get mentioned.

Krandor is another artificial planet.

What exactly does the Caliph think that he looks like in that get-up? Adam Adamant? A character out of *Poldark*?

Cally's potted history of the Thaarn is like a mini-episode of *Jackanory*. She's really building up this mythical Thaarn; he sounds nasty and very fearsome. Can't wait to see what he looks like.

What has happened to that poor bloke with the clipboard?

If Lord Thaarn won't allow computers, what are all those machines against the wall in the calculating room?

To keep Orac's nature a secret, Tarrant fools the Caliph into believing he's bald and about waist-high to a man. Considering this pretty much describes the Thaarn when he eventually appears, we can't help but wonder if this is supposed to be a bit of pre-figuring from writer James Follett. If so, it's RUBBISH.

We wrote this entry with our graphite writing sticks. We keep them in a little desk-tidy like the one in Groff's office.

Is Groff supposed to be Jewish? Terry Scully certainly seems to be playing him that way.

The Thaarn says that he has created a machine that controls gravity. We bet that he says that to all the girls.

For six years internal BBC paperwork accidentally referred to this story as "Dawn of the Hods".

Where was Dawn?

Closing Shot: The side of Tarrant's stupid smug head.

Delightful Dialogue:

Vila: I may not be the bravest man in the galaxy.
Avon: Are you sure?

Vila: I'm in hell, and it's full of Avons.

Amateur Hour:

The black hole is just a piece of black card against the starfield background.

The tape holding the *Liberator*'s control consoles together is more than a little obvious.

After the *Liberator* emerges on the other side of the black hole, smoke can be seen coming from Orac. That may not be deliberate.

Michael Keating fluffs his line when Avon announces they have fallen into an anti-matter universe.

Vila's space helmet mists and demists with magical prowess, depending on the camera shot. The ventilation holes in the top of the helmets, which are plain to see, must have been a late addition.

The 'face' on the scrap-collecting vehicle is bobbins.

The bodies of the two salvage workers sent to cut up the *Liberator* have disappeared by the time the crew return to the ship.

We know new ideas can sometimes be a little thin on the ground, but to have Krantor and Krandor, Molok and Moloch in consecutive seasons seems rather lazy. (Don't even get us *started* on the three artificial planets in this season alone!)

ADDITIONAL SCRAPS OF KNOWLEDGE

Planets: Krandor, Xaranar, Romulus, Cardassia, PP-Wii.

Space-isms: The Spiral Arm in Sector 12, sling-shot orbit, asymmetric thrust computer, star orbit burial, telemetric bandsweep, herculanium alloy, neuronic whip, cubic cobars.

35 TWILIGHT OF THE GODS

Writer: James Follett   **Director**: Desmond McCarthy

Guest Stars: Marcus Powell (The Thaarn), Ballard Berkeley (Pallacki), Dominic Guard (Guard), Barbara Flynn (Mrs Groff), Roger Tonge (Groff's son)

Opening Shot: One of Ian Scoones' original beauty passes of the *Liberator* in flight. Again.

You Just Described the Story:

Tarrant: We made a promise to Groff, and like it or not, Avon, we're going to keep it.

Random Insult:

Avon (aimed at Tarrant): Remind me to inform Vila that his title of ship's resident idiot is under serious threat.

In A Nutshell: <ding-dong> Avon calling!

Story: Repaying their debt of gratitude, Avon and Tarrant set off to the planet Xaranar to inform Groff's family of his death. With no further information to act on, Avon and Tarrant have to ask at every shabby dwelling on the planet if the Groff family live there. Meanwhile, the Thaarn has docked his ship to the *Liberator* and is set to take his revenge on Cally. If that's not enough, Vila and Dayna have become addicted to a new computer game involving lock-picking and guns. Could it be a trap?

Information:

"Dawn of the Gods" was the first story recorded for Season P. Due to Marcus Powell (The Thaarn) being unavailable for filming, it was decided to leave "Twilight of the Gods" until the final block of filming. During the intervening six months, the Thaarn costume and mask were on display at Longleat's short-lived 'The *Blake's 7* Exhibition'. When they were returned for filming, they had been repainted and had some minor damage repaired with papier-mâché. Unfortunately, it shows. Badly.

We counted, and Avon and Tarrant visit thirty-five dwellings looking for the family Groff. They are all obviously the same basic set, simply redressed with different door numbers.

Josette Simon is wearing the costume that was originally worn by Gan in "Redemption" – it looks beyond ridiculous.

There is no other episode that wastes Avon so badly – pairing him with Tarrant and just knocking on doors. Shameful.

Vila only appears at the beginning and end of this episode, as Michael Keating had bagged himself some extra work as 'Peasant Villager' in the *Doctor Who* story "State of Decay"; he even wears the same costume. All of the animated sequences of him playing the game with Dayna were dubbed later.

The scenes of the Thaarn tiptoeing around dimly-lit *Liberator* corridors looking for Cally could have been genuinely chilling and creepy if they weren't so laugh-out-loud ridiculous. At times he looks like an old lady who has woken in the night and is trying to find the toilet.

Why does Barbara Flynn play Mrs Groff with the thickest West Country accent this side of the Wurzels?

Dayna's experience in the CES would later be used as the Vortex, the final game in the TV series *The Adventure Game*, which once had Paul Darrow as a guest.

Zen and Orac do not appear in this episode, but no one told Peter Tuddenham who still sat off-camera in 'Zen's Den' looking really sad.

Jan Chappell seems to really enjoy the final showdown with the Thaarn, where Cally goes all *Ring of Bright Water* on the errant Auron God. As in "Star One", the *Liberator* guns can suddenly blow huge bloody chunks out of people, and the teleport set looks horrific as the Thaarn finally croaks it.

When Tarrant and Avon stop off at the shop to buy supplies, the credit card Avon uses is slightly larger than his gun. Where was he keeping it all that time?

Closing Shot: Cally, wiping blood down her trousers and smirking.

Delightful Dialogue:
Tarrant: So, this is Xaranar.
Avon: Shut up, Tarrant.

Cally: Die, hideous creature... die!

Amateur Hour:
The Thaarn mask, now a dark brown colour, has clearly seen much better days.

During the argument on the flight deck Michael Keating accidentally swears. Rather brilliantly whoever wrote the DVD subtitles not only got the profanity wrong, they made it a much filthier word.

The entire gun rack part of the set falls backwards and out of shot with an almighty crash during Tarrant's boring debt-of-gratitude speech and no one seems to notice.

Josette Simon barely stifles a laugh when the button she pushes on the teleport console falls through the set and onto the floor with an audible rattle.

At 16m 34s, Josette Simon fluffs her line big time, calling Avon 'Paul'. The word was added in post-production. Because Josette was on holiday by that time, a line of her dialogue from "Aftermath" was dubbed on – you can even hear the sea in the background.

The costume worn by Ballard Berkeley is obviously Brian Croucher's Travis outfit, painted red and worn backwards. And why is he wearing a pair of two-tone loafers?

ADDITIONAL SCRAPS OF KNOWLEDGE
Planets: Xaranar.

Space-isms: Spacial docking displacement, quadrant-vectoring bi-lateral scan curve, Heicken's Syndrome, plasma sacking, Computerised Entertainment System (CES), vibro-locks, sonic doorbells.

36 THE HARVEST OF KAIROS

Writer: Ben Steed   **Director**: Gerald Blake

Guest Stars: Andrew Burt (Jarvik), Frank Gatliff (Dastor), Anthony Gardner (Captain Brotius Shad), Thelma Barlow (Mavis), Sam Davies (Carlon), Charles Jamieson (Guard)

Opening Shot: Not a bad model shot of the *Liberator* in orbit.

You Just Described the Story:

Tarrant: Unimaginative, but so is a punch in the mouth. We don't need either.

Random Insult:

Vila (to Tarrant): Bit of a know-all aren't you?

Well said, that man!

In A Nutshell: Rock-crunching hoover-bag ant mayhem with deceptive stone.

Story: Tarrant plans to seize a Federation ship that is transporting valuable kairopan crystals. A menial worker called Jarvik voices his opinion regarding Servalan's failure to capture the *Liberator*. Intrigued by his forthright nature, Servalan gives Jarvik a chance to prove that he can take the ship. Jarvik sets a trap on Kairos, knowing that *Liberator* will be drawn there due to the presence of the crystals.

Information:

Gerald Blake is, in reality, a pseudonym for former *Blake's 7* star Gareth Thomas. Thomas had originally left the series intending to broaden his professional experience and was tempted back with the chance to direct an episode.

Speaking of Blake, where is he?

What the hell has Tarrant got on?

What the hell has Servalan got on?

What the hell has Avon got on?

What the hell has Cally got on? It looks like her dressing gown.

Apparently this episode was the last straw for Jan Chappell.

Avon's obsession with sopron is amusing but wholly out of character.

Andrew Burt played Ken Barlow in *Coronation Street* from March to June of 1973. William Roache, handing out prizes at a school fête, had slipped on some grapes and was laid up for some time. Burt had hoped to retain the part, and rumour has it he actually laid traps around Roache's house in early June. It never went to court.

As with all Season P stories, the title is spoken exactly 9 minutes in – in this case by Andrew Burt.

Kairos is harvested by people apparently meandering around a field looking at the grass.

Not that the budget was stretched on this episode but entry to the Federation transport ship is achieved by climbing a B & Q loft ladder.

It's a shame Dayna didn't get the 'Beige Clothes Thursday' memo.

Season P's confusion over who's leading (Avon or Tarrant) is a problem here. On this occasion, it's all about Tarrant. That said, Avon waits until Tarrant is well and truly up the creek before playing his hand and saving the day.

Mirrorlon, Mirrorlon, we all love Mirrorlon.

There's a lovely shot of the *Liberator* spinning through space – seriously, it's the best in-flight shot of the series to date.

They must have hired a new YTS trainee for this episode; the shot of the planet spinning in space is damn good too.

As a token of her affection for Jarvik, Servalan has dyed her BLUE the same colour as his tunic.

Jarvik's zip gets lower as the episode goes on. And on. And on. And on...

How the hell did that kairopan get into Vila's boot? What were he and Dayna doing?

Does it really take Jarvik an entire night to find the crew?

It's pretty clear that this isn't the first time Jarvik and Tarrant have 'wrestled'.

The teleport really is amazing. Both Dayna's and Jarvik's clothes are cleaned during their trip.

Zen's ability to obliterate bits of a planet's surface would've been jolly useful on many other occasions.

Closing Shot: A group shot of the crew going about their business, disposing of a corpse.

Delightful Dialogue:

Servalan: You must be Zen. Tell me, Zen: how does one operate this spaceship?
Zen: One manipulates the controls and the ship functions accordingly.

Servalan: But first, there is the question of that primitive and degrading act to which I was subjected in the control room. I should like you to do it again.

Jarvik: Gently now, Killer Three. Ease your way in.

Amateur Hour:

For one brief moment, Servalan's piloted the entire command centre to take care of *Liberator*.

Why is the exterior of Servalan's ship the old command headquarters wheel and not the Giger-esque battle cruiser we see throughout the rest of Season P?

Jarvik's overpowering of Servalan's troopers is woeful.

Servalan says 'Take him! Will you obey me!?' and then blocks her guards from doing so by standing in front of them with her arms outstretched.

Avon has a word dubbed on during the scene in Cally's cabin. You hear the word 'astute' but he had said something else. Wonder what it was?

Servalan has a penchant for crazy straws.

The pantomime ant is pushing it, even for *Blake's 7*.

Either a line's been cut or Burt has given Pearce the wrong feed. Her response, 'No, I'm the fool!', comes out of nowhere.

Put on the DVD and jump to 42m 28s – Tarrant's teleport bracelet falls off his arm during the fight sequence; by 42m 41s it's magically back on his arm as he needs to remove it and hand it to Jarvik. Also, 44m 46s – Dayna's bracelet drops off her right arm in the teleport bay, yet when she walks onto the flight deck at 44m 56 it has reappeared – on her left arm! By 46m 06s it is on her right arm once again. With the incidents of numerous bracelets also dropping off in "Volcano" you have to wonder just how worn-out the props were at this point in filming.

ADDITIONAL SCRAPS OF KNOWLEDGE

Planets: Gardenos; Kairos, fourth planet of the star Xmines in the constellation Lypterion .

Space-isms: Parallax scan, sopron, proto-space-age landing module, herculanium, Space Transporter.

Worth Bearing in Mind: Any fool with three pursuit ships could take the *Liberator*.

Tarrant Mitigation Techniques:

Look at that costume – brown and cream striped bomber jacket, brown polo neck shirt. Just be grateful he's wearing it and not you.

Jarvik's misogyny was an early attempt by producers to make Tarrant appear less macho. Imagine the pair of them as a double act and count yourself lucky.

Bask in the fact that Dayna proved herself in mere seconds to be more of a man than Tarrant and Jarvik combined.

37 CITY AT THE EDGE OF THE WORLD

Writer: Chris Boucher   **Director**: Vere Lorrimer

Guest Stars: Carol Hawkins (Kerril), Valentine Dyall (Norl), Nigel Havers (Dr Rawlins), John J. Carney (Sherm), Colin Baker (Bayban)

Opening Shot: Space>More Space>*Liberator*

You Just Described the Story:
Bayban: You've got an hour.

Random Insult:
Bayban (to Sherm): You stupid son of a slime crawler.

Random Threat:
Vila: I'll get you for this, Tarrant! I'll tear your arm off and beat you to death with the wet end!

In A Nutshell: Vila opens more than just a door.

Story: In need of crystals to power the *Liberator*'s weapons systems, Vila is sent to the planet Keezarn to liaise with a contact who says that he can provide them. Unfortunately for Vila, he quickly finds himself at the mercy of the notorious and unhinged Bayban the Butcher. Bayban demands that Vila use his skills as a safe-cracker to open an impenetrable door, behind which Bayban believes are unimaginable treasures.

Information:
Tarrant is threatening Vila with being 'tossed off'.

Tarrant's bullying of Vila makes him utterly loathsome, especially his smug grin afterwards as he tries to explain himself to Cally. Are we meant to like Tarrant?

Avon's locator is hopelessly low-tech and apparently powered by an XLR cable.

Tarrant isn't only a bully, he's an idiot, as he gets duped over the matter of the crystals.

Avon's defence of Vila in his absence is just sublime. He genuinely cares.

The 'city at the edge of the world' is just a few ruins in North Yorkshire.

'The place is deserted. There's nobody here.' Well done Vila, thanks for translating that cryptic statement for us.

Michael Keating is in his element with Boucher's script. His one-sided argument, negotiation and discussion with his guides is great stuff.

Vila leaving the tracer behind is another good character point; while it's clear this is The Vila Episode, it's also clear that a lot of effort has gone into writing him well.

Awww... the lovely Carol Hawkins.

It's a shame Colin Baker underplays Bayban so much. What could've been a memorable villain just sort of fades into the background, barely noticeable.

Tarrant gets a drubbing from the entire crew; it's surprising that Zen doesn't mutter 'Berk' under his breath. Then he has the cheek to whinge to Dayna that she didn't stick up for him. Git. We don't like Tarrant.

The wide shot of the room with the locked door is rather effective, showing off the set's ceiling. Why didn't we see that from the start?

Kerril's had a bath and slipped into something more uncomfortable.

And Vila's opened the impenetrable access point – not very subtle, Chris.

Kerril's suddenly not the gun-toting scumbag she was twenty minutes ago, reduced instead to trite dialogue and shrieking at cobwebs – such are the perils of popping on a frock.

The three Baybanites that Avon and Cally catch at gunpoint are Richard Ellis, Harry Kurtz and Liam Lessing. All three had previously appeared together in an episode of *Coronation Street*, also directed by Lorrimer, playing slightly-less-than-sci-fi navvies.

The 3000-year-old voice we're hearing is CLEARLY Valentine Dyall's.

The BBC Standard Modular Space Wall flat gets another outing. This is the 247th use of it in the programme so far.

The outfits worn by the skeletons would eventually be sprayed silver and become Cybermen in the *Doctor Who* story "Earthshock".

BBC shorthand for sex = the chap nuzzles the lady's neck, then cut to later, when they're both laying on separate beds, fully clothed.

Where the hell was Dayna concealing that heat-seeking bomb?

This is the first episode where we see Cally kill someone.

Darrow and Baker in shot together – surely there's an Equity Blinovitch Limitation Effect to worry about here?

Tarrant is desperate to be recognised by Bayban and is merely snubbed. Ha-ha, Tarrant, you loser!

Why does Bayban assemble the laser cannon pointing away from the impenetrable door? Ah. It's so he's facing in the right direction when Avon and Cally come bursting in. Gotcha.

In this year's *Blake's 7 Monthly* season poll, this story was voted least popular, with Bayban being voted least popular villain and Colin Baker least favourite guest actor. Least favourite crewmember nearly went to Baker too until a recount was insisted on and Tarrant took the trophy.

Closing Shot: The *Liberator* charges towards us.

Delightful Dialogue:
Vila (to Tarrant): All my life, for as long as I can remember, there's been people like you.

Avon: Do you want me to threaten you?
Tarrant: Why not? I haven't had a good laugh in ages.
Avon: Sensible. You could die laughing.

Vila: Bayban the Butcher? You're Bayban the Butcher? Oh no...

Bayban: I may have to get rid of Kerril. Be a pity, she's the best gun hand I ever had but, er, she's got no team spirit, you know. And you can't run an outfit like mine without team spirit.

Bayban: You must be Vila. It's an honour, sir.
Vila: The honour's mine.
Bayban: That's what I meant.

Vila: You have a reputation for straightforward mayhem that's second to none. I've been an admirer of yours for, um, well, for as long as I can remember. Well, maybe not that long – I mean, er, you're not that old, are you? But, er, then again, you did start very young, didn't you? I think I feel sick.

Norl: My people are coming!

We'll never grow up.

Amateur Hour:

The painting of endless corridors in the real, three-metre-long corridor is a terrible match.

The low-energy probe that Vila uses disappears at 24m 06s as the forcefield disperses. It reappears on the reverse shot looking back through the door.

The Chromakey surface of the planet Vila and Kerril find is pretty poor, especially when Vere's shoving his camera all over the place.

Henchgoon on the left, when ambushed by Avon and Cally, is clearly chuffed to bits to be on the telly. He can't stop grinning.

Zen doesn't appear in this episode but Peter Tuddenham gets a credit for him instead of Orac, who does appear.

ADDITIONAL SCRAPS OF KNOWLEDGE

Planets: Keezarn.

Space-isms: Laser cannon!

Strongest Smell: Kerril.

38 CHILDREN OF AURON

Writer: Roger Parkes   **Director**: Andrew Morgan

Guest Stars: Ric Young (Ginka), Rio Fanning (Deral), Sarah Atkinson (Franton), Jan Chappell (Zelda), Sean Pertwee (Pilot Three-Two), Jack McKenzie (Patar), Michael Troughton (Pilot Four-Zero), Ronald Leigh-Hunt (C.A. One), Beth Harris (C.A. Two)

Opening Shot: We move in on the hull of Servalan's ship.

You Just Described the Story:

Avon: This is crass stupidity.

Random Insult:

The gong sound effect when Ginka removes his mask – racist? No...

Random Massive Amount Of Syllables In One Line Said Very Quickly:

Patar: Full emergency procedures operative, Retriever One.

In A Nutshell: It's July. The book's due out in September and it's not even typeset yet. If you want a witty line here, write it yourself:

Story: Seeking to extend her influence, Servalan plans to create a batch of clones of herself. She unleashes a deadly plague on the planet Auron and offers the Aurons a remedy in return for their cloning expertise. After receiving a psychic message from Cally's sister Zelda via the Ocarina of Time, the *Liberator* travels to Cally's homeworld to assist the Aurons.

Information:

Servalan's in full-blown panto mode today.

Avon appears to be sitting on a cactus.

Cally's so preachy and prissy about Avon's plan for revenge, yet in "Time Squad" she'd gladly shoot anything that coughed.

MAUVE is notorious for its psychotropic properties, hence Servalan disguising the drink as a harmless glass of CLEAR.

Michael Troughton manages to keep dignity intact at all times in his silly pointy hat but sadly, yes, that is an inflatable lavatory seat around his neck.

The tracking shot of the *Liberator* flight deck is both too fast and completely pointless, as the entire crew are milling around at one end.

It's a massive coincidence that within a few seconds of a discussion cropping up about Auron, Cally should suddenly sense her people are all dying.

Crikey, this Zelda looks a lot like Cally.

Tarrant appears to be hiding six brown lobsters under his shirt. You can see their heads poking out.

Avon's plans for vengeance will have to wait for later – next week, probably.

Servalan's plans get ever more desperate as the weeks go on. It's getting to the point where she'll prop up an upturned box with a stick attached to a piece of string and put a cupcake underneath.

We can't help but wonder whether Servalan's sudden desire to reproduce wasn't kicked off by her getting friendly with Jarvik a couple of weeks ago. Nothing like meeting 'the one' to get you in the mood for a dynasty.

Ginka needs to move the camera in his office. It's massively impractical to keep jumping up and turning round. Why not have it on the desk in front of him?

Andrew Morgan is trying far too hard to shoot the *Liberator* set in a new way. It looks staged and clumsy.

Dud's really outdone himself with the music this week. It's brilliant.

Aitch!

Hal Mellanby must have made *reaaallly* good guns, as Servalan has kept one from "Aftermath". Dayna kept one too, as she hands one to Cally in "City at the Edge of the World".

Ginka seems a little bitter about his final personnel review.

What was the point of Deral secreting Servalan's weapon if he was only going to whip it out the moment he got aboard? A nice fat Federation rifle would have been far less girly.

Industrial plant! Hooray!

Ginka says sensors are detecting movement. Servalan asks which sector, to which he replies 'Northeast'. They're orbiting a whole PLANET. Northeast is a bit bloody vague, and yet Servalan manages to zoom in on Avon's nipples. Talk about first time lucky.

Deral's brilliantly helpful to Dayna and Vila. We like a turncoat.

How fortunate that Zelda's wearing that white hood. Makes the camera angles easier to achieve.

Zelda's dead meat. Good scream. Shame Chappell didn't let one of those out in "Rescue" instead of the meek 'oooh' she came up with.

Dayna's changed clothes three times in this story. Avon's changed twice too.

Speaking of clothes – from this episode onwards, Servalan only ever wears black outfits. She had worn white up to this point, with two exceptions: red in "Gambit" and purple in "Powerplay". This was apparently a request from Jacqueline Pearce herself to indicate that Servalan was in mourning for her character and her children.

Zen selects Karn as a suitable planet for the Auron gene stock, which is fine unless you've watched the *Doctor Who* story "The Brain of Morbius". Then you realise he's an idiot.

Closing Shot: An entire planet's population is destroyed, there's been a desperate struggle for a race's survival and the *Liberator* crew sit around noshing fruit and laughing like drains.

Delightful Dialogue:

Cally: I'm coming, Zelda…

Vila: You tried to trick us, Servalan. Naughty. One hostage to us.

Amateur Hour:
The model shot of air traffic control aside, this is pretty good stuff.

ADDITIONAL SCRAPS OF KNOWLEDGE

Planets: Auron.

Space-isms: 'You and Cally are from the same sibling group, aren't you?' – Elsewhere in the universe, we call them 'families'.

Tarrant Mitigation Techniques:

Recumbent as he is for much of the episode, you can only get annoyed at the top half of Tarrant's body this week. As a consequence, he's 50% less bothersome.

Look and laugh at his high trousers – they're almost up to his armpits.

An big empty, useless space – and it's *still* better than Tarrant.

39 STRIKE ATTACK!

Writer: David Agnew   **Director**: Douglas Camfield

Guest Stars: David Yip (Salaman), Margery Mason (Heska), Niall Buggy (Professor Corculon), Tom Georgeson (Ando), Jan Francis (Delith), Mike Savage (Federation Policeman One), Charles Pemberton (Federation Policeman Two), Nadim Sawalha (Dr Karim), Hilary Crane (Termagen), Gabriel Woolf (Voice of Shengo the Magnificent)

Opening Shot: Vila, eating some sort of fruit from a bowl with a long spoon.

You Just Described the Story:

Avon: Servalan's scientists are too clever. They need to be stopped. NOW.

Random Insult:

Avon: Vila, these people are amongst some of the finest minds ever to have existed. And you think that you are capable of joining them?

In A Nutshell: Clan of clever clogs clobbered with clubs.

Story: The *Liberator* crew hear from Orac about a new Federation think-tank on the planet Danga, composed of the greatest scientific minds in the galaxy, who have been coerced into finding new ways to subdue populations under Federation control. Avon decides that they should travel to Danga to try to scramble the brains of the scientists. Upon arriving at the base where they are being held, the *Liberator* team find that the scientists are in fact working willingly for the Federation. Servalan happens to be visiting Danga, and she and Avon face off in a dramatic confrontation...

Information:

Due to an industrial dispute at the BBC, this episode was broadcast at 2.40am.

Written by the mysterious David Agnew, nobody at the BBC ever met him during production of this episode. Agnew apparently dictated his script via telephone, with a BBC secretary writing it down on his behalf.

Director Voytek's name scores 16 in Scrabble, and that's not even with a double letter score or anything.

David Yip's costume is even more bizarre than the brown robes worn by half of the cast in "Traitor", ranking high in the list of television's all-time worst clothing.

Orac comes across as being particularly catty in this episode. Why, for example, does he pick on Cally like that?

Tom Georgeson is a well-known actor.

The plot here is sketchy in the extreme. Why, for example, do the scientists agree to work with the Federation, especially given the fact that we know that Corculon is a former ally of Blake?

Agnew's scripting has a schizophrenic tone about it, and the story doesn't really hang together all that well. At times, it almost feels as if it was written by more than one person.

We can't work out why Vila goes up the tree just after the Destructons have attacked.

Nigel Planer was originally set to appear in this episode but, ultimately, didn't.

There are three references to sherbet in this episode – see if you can spot them all.

TV Centre was briefly evacuated during the making of this episode as a result of a noxious odour that emanated from the *Generation Game* studio. Nobody is sure what it was exactly, but most of the fingers pointed towards Larry Grayson.

The catering on the location filming of this episode included the following: Scotch eggs, pies, chips, cheese sandwiches and trifle.

We didn't really need to have the scene where Avon appears in just his pants.

And when did Servalan have a carpet fitted to the deck of her pursuit ship?

The scene where the spiders drop from the ceiling was unscripted. Shot on a very hot summer day the soaring temperatures caused several hundred spiders to hatch and fall from the lighting rig onto the cast. Paul Darrow asked Douglas Camfield if he could dub more manly screams onto the scene; Camfield refused as he found the reedy shrieks of the leading man funny.

In a draft version of the script Ando was originally named Dinkeldyne.

The incantation that Avon needs to chant to gain access to the safe is 'Ab Racad Abra.'

Closing Shot: Dayna's bottom. (Not bare.)

Delightful Dialogue:

Dayna: This time I intend to personally make certain that that woman pays for what she did to my father.

Tarrant: Well if anybody wants to know, mine has to be the most impressive.

Amateur Hour:

Watch out for the third Destructon as it exits to the right of the screen: the actor inside clearly stumbles over, then tries to make it look like he didn't stumble at all. It doesn't work.

When Servalan turns sharply to talk to Karim, the bag she is carrying over her shoulder swings and knocks over the rack of test tubes on his desk. As the bag doesn't appear in any other scene we can only assume that it belongs to Jacqueline Pearce and she forgot to leave it in the dressing room before they shot the scene.

Somebody should have told the production designer that bubble wrap never really worked in *Doctor Who* and it doesn't work here either.

ADDITIONAL SCRAPS OF KNOWLEDGE

Planets: Danga, Taffa, Calimberon, Pillitay, Mongpong 4.

Space-isms: Deca-technotron, sub-beam particle phase re-limiter.

40 RUMOURS OF DEATH

Writer: Chris Boucher   **Director**: Fiona Cumming

Guest Stars: Lorna Heilbron (Sula), John Bryans (Shrinker), Peter Clay (Chesku), Donald Douglas (Grenlee), David Haig (Forres), Annie Ross (Vera), David Gilles (Hob), Philip Bloomfield (Balon)

Opening Shot: A cell door, followed by Avon looking all Guantanamo as Michael Palin is tortured in the next room.

You Just Described the Story:
Avon: Hello, Anna.

Random Insult:
Sula: I'm sure Servalan will be delighted. She is, after all, a tasteless megalomaniac.

In A Nutshell: Girlfriend in a cellar.

Story: Avon deliberately allows himself to be captured in order to be interrogated by the ruthless Federation officer, Shrinker. Avon intends to take revenge on Shrinker, whom he believes murdered Anna Grant, Avon's lover, years before. Discovering that Servalan holds the key to the true identity of Anna's killer, Avon travels to her presidential palace, where he discovers that certain rumours may have been greatly exaggerated.

Information:
Shrinker should be more imposing, a more striking actor. Someone with presence. Not this big camp nitwit.

Darrow's great isn't he? He plays weary so well.

Dayna hasn't sorted her sentence structure yet: 'Still, stand very still.'

Good that Avon had no faith in Tarrant whatsoever.

Vila offers Avon a refreshing glass of GREEN.

Avon gets cleaned up before killing Shrinker. Good man.

That Sula's pretty damn cold.

The Federation security team are an inspired pair. Boucher's been taking lessons from Robert Holmes.

Why is Donald Douglas trying to do an American accent, though?

Mind you, sitting at a desk that low must play havoc with the back. Haven't these people heard of Health and Safety?

Vila's concern over Avon looking after himself, even going to the trouble of organising everything for him in his absence, is rather touching. Unlike stupid Tarrant's stupid posturing.

It's rather good to have Boucher continue Avon's backstory that was established in the previous season. But we can't believe that Avon would have gone for a woman like Anna Grant.

Have you ever had someone very close to you, who you loved more than anyone else, who only referred to you by your surname?

Anna's surveillance blockers are among the most hi-tech kit you'll ever see in your life ever ever.

Lorna Heilbron isn't a strong enough actress to pull this off. Her voice trembles too much.

Grenlee and Forres cheering on Chesku as he runs back via the CCTV is great fun. Haig and Douglas have a good chemistry. And then…

… they're gunned down.

Dayna's outfit is one massive red camel-toe.

Anna enjoys a drink of LIGHT RED in Avon's flashback.

Vila still finds excuses to stay behind. They're breaking into a Federation stronghold – surely the locksmith is more useful than the posh pilot in the fright wig?

GREEN! Vila's got a massive flask of GREEN!

Tarrant's bow makes you want to cut his arms off and pour acid in his ears.

Jacqueline Pearce has never come closer to falling out of a dress than she does when tied up in that cellar.

Tarrant says 'Green on all systems'. Somebody must have spilt their drink all over the computers.

This episode was released on a special BBC Video only available from Woolworths. As well as an interview with a professional Paul Darrow impersonator (Darrow was on tour at the time), the cassette came with an enamel pin badge depicting Orac thinking, a page of script framed with a certificate of authenticity (ours was number 12) and a keyring torch with Avon's face on it. However, due to an error at the production plant, the episode on the tape is actually "The Web".

Closing Shot: Avon saunters off to the flight deck to shoot something.

Delightful Dialogue:

Avon: What's the matter? Did I bleed on the wrong bit of floor?

Cally (to Avon): We've talked about it and discovered we care what happens to you.
Tarrant: Within reason, of course.
Dayna: We're as surprised about it as you are.
Vila: Not to mention embarrassed.

Cally: Oh don't be stupid, Dayna!

Amateur Hour:

That hyperactive fuzzy thing on the screen in Grenlee's office is very distracting. And annoying.

The painting of Anna on the cave wall makes her looks like Zelda out of *Terrahawks*.

The shot where Servalan goes from the film corridor of the stately home, through a door and into the VT office jars awfully. The two scenes should have been broken up with another.

ADDITIONAL SCRAPS OF KNOWLEDGE

Planets: Earth.

Space-isms: Laser probe, micro-circuit.

Tarrant Mitigation Techniques:

Pretend that it is actually Tarrant being tortured by Shrinker at the start of the episode and revel in the fact that no one would bother coming to rescue him.

It's not just us – one glance at Tarrant and the terrible Shrinker's reduced to a blubbering wreck.

Pretend you didn't see his smug flouncy bowing when they take out the Federation guards.

Compare the way Avon and Tarrant both enter a room with weapons drawn. Avon covers the room menacingly, Tarrant does the equivalent of a silent 'TADA!' Tit.

You Just Described Steven Pacey's CV:

Shrinker: Well someone's got to do the lousy jobs!

Rumours of Death Metal:

In 1991 death metal band Bloodflagon released their epic 48-minute concept album, "Resilience Over Despair". The track quickly become beloved by *Blake's 7* fans who were convinced that you could listen to the track while watching "Rumours of Death" and the action on-screen would perfectly marry up with the lyrics and tempo changes of the song. At the time the band denied any connection to the series, stating it was also a coincidence that the album shared the same initials as the Season P episode. The truth finally came out in an interview for the 25th anniversary re-release of the album when lead singer Malachi Armageddona (real name Duncan Burtwistle) admitted that the band were not only big fans of the series but lifelong members of the *Blake's 7* fan club Horizon. Armageddona now regrets not telling the truth in 1991. 'The episode you need to watch while listening to "Resilience..." is actually "Volcano"', he said. 'We didn't say this at the time 'cos that episode is shit.'

41 SARCOPHAGUS

Writer: Tanith Lee   **Director**: Fiona Cumming

Guest Stars: None at all. However, some stars are visible just outside the ship.

Opening Shot: Some caves or something.

You Just Described the Story:
Vila: That doesn't make sense to me.

Random Insult:
Avon (repeating himself to Tarrant): I said, shut up. I apologise for not realising you are deaf.

In A Nutshell: Nut*case* more like.

Story: Cally is interfered with mentally by a strange alien creature that lives on an abandoned spaceship. This causes everybody to dress up and dance around. Is this the end for our heroes?

Information:
Ooh, this looks a bit mysterious. Culty women painted silver waving their hands about.

That's an awfully showy way to blow out a torch.

Seven minutes in and not a word spoken. We don't like it – we need exposition.

Even Dudley's given up – they've just dubbed the *Mary Mungo & Midge* soundtrack over it.

Oh, God… GET ON WITH IT!

Good to see a new area of the *Liberator* in this episode (Cally's room), although we don't see it for long.

At last! Jan Chappell gets a story of her own!

Cally has been in her room for 10 hours and that one poxy scribble of a sketch is the best she can do?

Vila and Avon play some sort of triangular chess-type game.

Tarrant and Vila both wear fetching grey and red combinations.

Cally's lot have only been dead a couple of weeks, yet she's already forgotten the collective name for them: you're not an Auron, love, you're an Auronar.

Hang on a mo – they're rewriting Cally's telepathic capabilities too. She's communicated well enough in just about every other episode to date. Oh. Yes. Umm…

Dayna's wearing another body-length camel toe this week. They really have no idea how to dress that woman.

It's Cally's turn to get bullied by Tarrant this week. Why doesn't someone just slap him in his smug little face?

We like the fact that Avon orders Tarrant to remain behind on the ship. Tarrant really does come across as even more of an arse than usual in this episode, needling Avon for no good reason.

Had Tanith Lee even heard of *Blake's 7* before this, or were they a script short and she just happened to be selling friendship bracelets outside Television Centre?

Vila runs like a monkey.

The flying tray is very well done. That's not much of a reason to watch the episode, but that's all there is so far.

The effect of Zen's voice speeding up and slowing down was achieved by pumping helium into Tuddenham's booth and then sucking out all the oxygen.

Finding it almost impossible not to just give up on this one. We're only continuing because there's a chance of stopping some poor soul from ever watching this dross.

We're really missing good old Travis right about now. He'd sort this namby-pamby crap out, sharpish. A bit of bluster and spittle, and bang – we're back to dodgy space battles. Oh, for a dodgy space battle.

Images of the *Liberator* crew as concubines – Quick! Urgent brain enema required!

Vila's resorted to curling up in a ball on the floor. We know exactly how he feels.

Twelve minutes to go. In twelve minutes, we're going to get very drunk.

Ah, Avon's back in business. Bless Darrow's black leather gauntlets – amid all this crap he remains magnificent.

Some of the lighting of the *Liberator* is really nice in this episode.

We note that there isn't a regulation fire extinguisher on board ship.

That bit with the skeleton at the end is rotten.

Vila and Dayna helpfully explain the previous 48 minutes for the hard of thinking.

Closing Shot: The crew, all hard at work on the flight deck.

Delightful Dialogue:

Tarrant: And tomorrow, everything will look different?
Avon: If it does, you can assume you're on the wrong ship.

Avon: What the hell was going on over here? Afternoon tea?

Amateur Hour:

The beginning, the end and the bit in the middle, so closer to 50 minutes.

ADDITIONAL SCRAPS OF KNOWLEDGE

Planets: None.

Space-isms: If only.

Tarrant Mitigation Techniques:

Fantasise about how much better life would be if they'd left Tarrant stranded on the ship.

Just be glad you're not wearing a grey nylon jumpsuit.

Make Avon's 'Shut up, Tarrant' your new ringtone.

Console yourself with the fact that there are only 23 episodes until he's killed.

For the Pervs: Phwoar! Look at what Dayna's wearing! You can see all down her front and everything!

Get Your Skates On: Released on BBC Records, "Skates Seven" was the surprise chart hit of 1980. Written and recorded by Elizabeth Parker of the Radiophonic Workshop, the upbeat track featured Nile Rodgers on slap bass, and included samples of dialogue from episodes of *Blake's 7* run through a vodocer. The B-side (a hit in its own right after Simon Bates played it by mistake) featured a suite of Dayna's harp music from "Sarcophagus" with electronic disco drum beats thrown all over it. A promotional video was shot at Battersea Power Station and on the set of "Sarcophagus". Directed by Russell Mulcahy, it featured bikini-clad dancers wearing Federation guard masks skating around a rink chasing similarly clad 'rebels'. Peter Powell was famously suspended from *Top of the Pops* after the debut screening of the video when he quipped, 'I wouldn't mind liberating those lovely girls from their space bikinis!' It is impossible to find the 12" version of this record as one was never released.

42 ULTRAWORLD

Writer: Trevor Hoyle **Director**: Vere Lorrimer

Guest Stars: Peter Richards (Ultra One), Stephen Jenn (Ultra Two), Ian Barritt (Ultra Three), Steve Roberts (Ultra Four), Ronald Govey (Relf)

Opening Shot: A splat in space. Followed by a splat in space, then a splat in space, then the *Liberator*. (We're running out of ways to describe similar openings and we haven't even made it to the fourth series yet. At least we'll be able to substitute *Scorpio* for the *Liberator* when we get there. Won't that make a nice change?)

You Just Described the Story:

Tarrant: What the hell is that?

A common theme in Season P.

Random Insult:

Avon (on the subject of Tarrant's calculated risks): Calculated on what? Your fingers?

In A Nutshell: It's all an excuse to make a porno.

Story: Discovering an artificial planet, the *Liberator* crew begin to investigate when Cally disappears. They hear a distress call from her coming from the planet and teleport down to find her. There, they encounter the mysterious Ultras, who use organic matter to feed the brain that exists at the centre of the planet. No, really.

Information:

They've really stepped up the model work this season. The opening shot of the *Liberator* is gorgeous.

Zen's having some kind of fit. Looks like they've forgotten that his lights should pulse in time with his speech.

Oh how sweet – they turn the flight deck lights off when they go to bed. Do they take turns to unplug Zen each night?

Paul Darrow does lots of odd hand-acting in this episode.

Ultraworld doesn't look very alien in places, really. Anyone would think the location filming was done in some tunnels in Camden.

The Ultra look like humans sprayed blue. And are those veins on their uniforms supposed to be part of their bodies? Or just part of their uniforms?

Dudley's music is getting very tired by now. Still, at least he's found a xylophone at the back of the cupboard this week. Or is it a set of vibes? Maybe it's his famous marimba.

Tarrant goes off on his own again, thinking that he knows better.

Relf is 'Specimen P7943011'. 7943011 was Trevor Hoyle's Swiss Cottage telephone number at the time.

Is Avon wearing a CORDUROY tunic?

Oh look, Vila's being left behind yet again. He's little more than alcoholic light relief these days. Such a shame.

Orac's inability to understand jokes is akin to 'What is this thing you humans call love?'

Bet we could resist the power of the Core.

People say *Star Trek*'s Borg are based on the Cybermen. The Ultra are a much more accurate predecessor.

The menial who attacks Dayna and Tarrant does a great impersonation of Frankenstein's monster. Even down to the growl.

If the Core keeps on expanding, it's going to get too big and will press against the sides of Ultraworld, thereby causing itself pressure on the brain. It really hasn't thought this through. Probably because something's pressing on its brain.

It's nice that the menials get to have a ride on a little slide thing before they're devoured by the Core. Takes the edge off being eaten, we suppose.

Dayna keeps on asking Tarrant questions as if he'd know all of the answers. Although, he probably thinks he does.

The Ultras are trying to pimp Dayna and Tarrant! Show us this thing you humans call 'shag' and we will release your friends.

Carefully watch the model shots of the *Liberator* being drawn into Ultraworld. There are alchoves in the background and in one of them is the model of the *London*.

Another *Scooby-Doo* ending this week, as Orac takes a couple of minutes to explain the plot while Avon jokingly insults Vila.

Closing Shot: The *Liberator*, wearing red.

Delightful Dialogue:

Tarrant: Ever seen a lizard suck a bird's egg dry?

Avon: Shall we stay and observe, or shall we scuttle off with our closed minds intact?

Ultra: Soon, she will be wiped clean.

Tarrant: I still can't see why she would want to go down. It doesn't make sense.

Amateur Hour:

Dayna's sneeze is pathetic.

ADDITIONAL SCRAPS OF KNOWLEDGE

Planets: Duh, Ultraworld maybe? Oh, and Probus 4. Honest.

Space-isms: Germanium circuitry, wave emissions, memory tubes.

Fangs, But No Fangs: Josette Simon's smile throughout the series so impressed toothpaste makers Colgate that they were going to offer her a lucrative contract to be the 1981 'Smile of Colgate'. The offer was torn up immediately after the pair bond scene as (quote) 'bomb teeth isn't something we'd particularly like our brand to be associated with.'

43 SPACE BEETLES

Writer: John Lucarotti   **Director**: Paul Ciappessoni

Guest Stars: Stefan Gryff (Endaxi), Hubert Rees (Verrin), Annie Lambert (Lugo), Ann Curthoys (Lim Assol), David Hargreaves (Tul Prannis), Johnny Shannon (Sarvoy), David Jackson (Kan), Deep Roy (Shambo), Deep Roy (Tambo), Ted Rogers (Lagran), Pip Cresspavilion (Dab Otnch)

Opening Shot: Vila, staring at what appears to be a blue lemon.

You Just Described the Story:
Tarrant: BEETLES?

Random Insult:
Avon: If we left it to your intellect Vila, then we'd be left destitute for a very long while, and I, for one, am not prepared to countenance THAT.

In A Nutshell: The *Liberator* gets infested with space beetles.

Story: The crew of *Liberator* are forced off course after encountering a strange swirling phenomenon in space. After passing through the phenomenon they find themselves in a dream world where each member of the crew is tormented by the things they fear most. It transpires that they are in fact on the planet Talpheron, whose atmosphere has been tainted by a race of space beetles to disorientate and confuse any visitors. The beetles manage to get hold of the teleport bracelets and beam up to the *Liberator*, causing havoc.

Information:
The *Liberator* is beginning to look slightly worse for wear here. The set designers have clearly attempted to repair various parts of the flight deck with gaffer tape but it is very visible at times – look at the scene where Dayna is pouring out the drinks, for example.

Vila drains yet more GREEN in this episode (a particularly stupid thing to do given that he is driving), while the rest of the team stay sensible and stick to BLUE.

G-TASS doesn't seem to be a very stable computer system to us.

The Greek segment of the episode is something of a departure for *Blake's 7* but doesn't really work that well if we're honest, although it is nice to see a little bit of foreign location filming in the series.

Odd to see David Jackson in the series again, playing Kan the mild-mannered brother of Gan. It is unclear as to whether Kan is real or simply part of the space beetles' hallucinatory tactics.

Sarvoy's boat couldn't really stay afloat with that number of people on board.

The hallucination scenes were filmed at Ealing Studios due to the complex nature of the set required.

We think that Lugo's moustache is quite something to behold.

Why don't the *Liberator*'s self-repair system kick in when the beetles start to chew their way through the control cables?

Malcolm Terris.

Ken Morse gets a credit on this episode.

We think that future *Doctor Who* script writer Christopher Hamilton Bidmead must have been watching this episode, as there are clear parallels with his story "Castrovalva".

Extra budget was scraped together to build the elaborate two-tier space station set – originally it was going to be realised as a model that would be dropped in using CSO. Unfortunately, a week before filming, the structure burnt down owing to an electrical fire. Luckily director Paul Ciappessoni had taken some pictures with his Kodak Instamatic and these images were superimposed behind the actors.

This was the only Season P episode to be novelised by Trevor Hoyle; unfortunately the cover photograph used was of two slaves from "Redemption".

Closing Shot: Vila, losing an arm-wrestling contest with Dayna.

Delightful Dialogue:

Verrin: Give it here, I'll do it.

Avon: Very well, if you must. But don't forget Charon, will you?

Tarrant: He's certainly got a set of tentacles to be proud of, I'll agree.

Lugo: GET OUT AVON. JUST GET OUT. GET OUT NOW. GET OUT. GET OUT, GET OUT!

Shambo and Tambo: Oo, oo, oo. Ag, ag, ag.

Endaxi: You know, Avon, people like you stagger me with your blasé attitude towards the safety and well-being of others.

Amateur Hour:

A camera peeps into shot just as the first space beetle appears, followed by a boom mike and lastly the floor manager.

When we see Cally dancing in the cemetery, there is a very clear shot of Peter Tuddenham in his little booth at the edge of the set.

The sequences shot in Greece are on a very low-grade 16mm film. At the time there was a heatwave which the BBC's cameras just couldn't cope with.

Keep an eye out for the men dressed as bats at the foot of the castle.

Unable to source real extras in Greece, director Paul Ciappessoni resorted to using local waiters from the nearby cafe. While enthusiastic, they were also very drunk and most could barely stand.

It was David Maloney's decision to use stop-motion animation to show the space beetles moving. The only other option was to pull the rubber puppets along the floor – this couldn't be done as Maloney was ridculously allergic to wire.

ADDITIONAL SCRAPS OF KNOWLEDGE

Planets: Talpheron, Dolcis, Gabbana.

Space-isms: Sub-beam delta wave analyser.

44 MOLOCH

Writer: Ben Steed **Director**: Veer Lorry More

Guest Stars: Davyd Harries (Doran), John Hartley (Grose), Mark Sheridan (Lector), Debbi Blythe (Poola), Peter Duncan (Boloch), Sabina Franklyn (Chesil), Deep Roy (Moloch)

Opening Shot: The model of Servalan's oddly-shaped ship going from left to right, very slowly. The shot is repeated shortly afterwards.

You Just Described the Story:

Servalan: Women, food, and inflicting pain – in no particular order.

Random Celebratory Song:

It's great to be free, It's great to be free, It's great to be free from the law, It's great to be free, And we all agree, We're not going back anymore!

You tell 'em.

In A Nutshell: Planet of the Rapes.

Story: Servalan travels to the planet Sardos at the edge of the galaxy, hoping to find the remains of the Federation fleet. Instead, she discovers a group of Federation officers who have been left to their own devices. One of the officers, Grose, demonstrates a device he has discovered that can replicate anything, and he plans to use it to take over the Federation. With replicated stuff.

Information:

The episode opens with Vila serving a round of GREEN. Hedonism ahoy.

Vila does a lovely roly-poly as the *Liberator* approaches the planet. He's just happy to be alive.

Nice artist's impression of what's on the planet below. The *Liberator*'s sketchdroids do a marvellous job.

You may notice that this episode isn't particularly kind to women at all.

Grose couldn't be better named, while Doran seems completely obsessed with sex.

Moloch can do just about anything. Apart from look convincing.

Despite there being a gun and a rock on the ground whilst the trooper is fighting Vila, Servalan elects to clobber the trooper on the head rather than simply shooting him.

The Colonel Astrid Action Figure was marketed in 1980 but flopped spectacularly on the high street after failing to capture the imagination of the buying public.

Avon's genuinely concerned for Vila's safety – it's really quite touching.

It was all going so well until Moloch the Monkey turned up.

The teleport bracelet that Moloch wears is lacking the standard pink communication button.

Closing Shot: Close-up of Avon, who says 'Get us out of here.'
We couldn't agree more.

Delightful Dialogue:

Avon: Ah! Careful of my wrist, Vila. It's had enough.

Avon: Perhaps she wants to compare notes with some other genocidal maniacs. Or take a refresher course in basic brutality.

Dayna: Are they friendly?
Orac: They are socially exclusive but not unduly hostile.
Cally: What sort of answer's that?
Orac: A succinct one.

Amateur Hour:

Moloch himself – *everything* about Moloch himself. The first shot of him, after more than 47 minutes, is supposed to be the episode's big reveal, and yet we're presented with *that*. And you can barely understand a word he says. The man who directed this episode, and would surely have had to approve the design of the character, would go on to be the producer of the final series.

ADDITIONAL SCRAPS OF KNOWLEDGE

Planets: Kalcos, Sardos.

Important Fact: Six writers and this was all we could find to say about this episode.

Spaced Out: The line, 'For a man of your era, you have uncommon qualities of deduction, Avon' was sampled and used in the 12" Galactic Pony remix of "Out of Space" by techno-band the Prodigy.

Ill-Advised One-Off Christmas Special: Turn to page 262.

Below: The plush Moloch soft toy that was available from the short-lived exhibition *The* Blake's 7 *Experience*. The loin-cloth was added after a number of complaints from furious parents who were freaked out by their children dragging around a weird naked cyclops doll dwarf.

45 DEATH-WATCH

Writer: Chris Boucher **Director**: Gerald Blake

Guest Stars: Steven Pacey (Deeta Tarrant), Stewart Bevan (Max), Mark Elliott (Vinni), Katherine Iddon (Karla), Zack Norman (Ira), David Sibley (Commentator)

Opening Shot: The *Teal Star* in space, with some radio chatter between it and Teal Control. Unlike the same scene in "Star One", it doesn't degenerate into a big spaceship crash. (The next shot is a smashing one of the *Teal Star* set with a lovely matte-painted ceiling).

You Just Described the Story:
Vinni: Deeta Tarrant is dead.
Hope that hasn't gone and spoiled the episode for you.

Random Insult:
Vila (referring to Orac): Couldn't you redesign him as something useful, like a drinks dispenser? Or an empty space! I think he'd look really good as an empty space.

In A Nutshell: Duel. But not that one.

Story: Two planets - Teal and Vandor - are in a state of perpetual hostility and have pioneered a unique way of settling battles: a man from each side in single combat. The *Liberator* crew head there to observe one such encounter. Tarrant finds that his twin brother Deeta is on Teal and, as their First Champion, is about to take on Vandor's ruthless fighter, Vinni.

Information:
The one thing *Blake's 7* has never been able to do convincingly is stars. The ones outside the *Teal Star* window looks like the VT operator splashed salad cream on his machine.

When Karla and Stuart Fell go to assassinate Deeta, Fell's character takes his Vandor identification card with him. We're not entirely sure this is sensible, given that it's an assassination attempt. Deeta's wig is awful.

It's good they found an actor who looks so much like Steven Pacey though.

Do you reckon Paul Darrow was annoyed that Steven Pacey got the Western gunfighter routine in this story? Twice?

Both Deeta and Karla wear costumes the same colour as the Teal Star set. None are teal-coloured.

We see the *Liberator* crew have their tea in this episode, but Avon doesn't have anything cos' he doesn't need to eat cos' he's so hard.

The commentator's name is 'Darvid'. It's probably really David, but you know how these mistakes on birth certificates can stick.

A frosted glass of RED is the preferred tipple for serious relaxation, although the entire *Liberator* bar's on display here. That'll keep Vila occupied for half an hour.

'Space...The Final Frontier' – that needs no introduction. Come to think of it, it *is* an introduction.

This one's taking far too long to get going. 20 minutes in and nobody's so much as raised a voice. It's horribly under-written.

Vila chases Cally across the flight deck. There really is nothing going on of consequence. Worse yet, there's a TV news presenter informing us of the fact every few minutes.

The vis-cast shows several remarkable locations where the Teal-Vandor conflict might play out; in deep space, around huge rock formations, amid beautiful tropical islands. The one we actually get is a run-down, knackered old building within five minutes walk of the production office.

We bet that a full Health and Safety Risk Assessment wasn't carried out on that dangerous-looking battle ground. You might fall over and cut your knee on a bit of glass or anything.

It would have been much cooler had this been an Avon story and not a Tarrant story, wouldn't it?

Probably the best episode of the season. We're contrary old bastards.

Two great moments from this episode: Vila sitting drinking cocktails on the *Liberator* flight deck with a happy smile on his face, and the viscaster going all Alan Partridge when he finishes his piece. Pacey is brilliant too, playing Deeta with an odd calmness so you don't think it's the same person as Del.

Zen. We've nothing to say about him except we've not mentioned him for a while and he explodes next week.

Closing Shot: Avon and Tarrant, in unison, say into their communicators 'Bring us up, Cally!' Glorious.

Delightful Dialogue:

Orac: I am now picking up a public vis-cast transmission.
Avon: Put it on the main screen.
Orac: I must point out that this is a gross misuse and an absurd waste of my capabilities.
Avon: Put it on the main screen.
Orac: I will do it only under protest.
Avon: You can do it any way you like, just so long as you put it on the main screen.

Tarrant: As ever, Dayna: gaudy but effective.

Amateur Hour:

Check out the shot through Orac at Avon at 41m 44s. There's a huge swathe of the studio wall visible above the set in the background.

The voice of the *Teal Star* captain is clearly Stewart Bevan.

Avon's shoulder pads.

The funny effect on Deeta's eyes only really works on one eye.

ADDITIONAL SCRAPS OF KNOWLEDGE

Planets: Teal, Vandor.

Space-isms: Vis-casts, sensor net.

Best Foot-in-Mouth of the Series:
Vila (referring to Servalan): Her idea of chivalry is never to shoot a blind man in the back.

Cue Dayna blubbing.

Important Lunch Fact:
Very little paperwork survives for this episode at the BBC's written archive in Caversham. The folder is empty save for one scrap of paper detailing what the cast had for lunch on day two of recording. Paul Darrow had a salad, Steven Pacey had salmon as did Michael Keating. Owing to a mix up, Pacey also had a shepherd's pie because, since he was playing two characters, he was on the list twice. The girls just got salad because they needed to keep thin and pretty for the dads at home.

Tarrant Mitigation Techniques:
You're on your own this time. There's two of him.

Deeta doesn't seem too fond of his brother. That makes him okay in our book.

Below: *Death Watch* was one of four stories released on vinyl LP by BBC Records. Each episode was cut down to 18-minutes in length and then all four were edited together to make one senseless story.

46 TERMINAL

Writer: Terry Nation   **Director**: Mary Ridge

Guest Stars: Gareth Thomas (Blake), Gillian McCutcheon (Kostos), Richard Clifford (Toron), Heather Wright (Reeval), Dominic Guard (Olvir), David Healy (Sphere Voice)

Opening Shot: Big white pointy spaceship, followed by a bit of acting business by Paul Darrow.

You Just Described the Story:

Tarrant: From here on it's downhill all the way.

Harsh, Tarrant.

Random Insult:

Vila: You've got to hand it to Avon, he knows how to keep a secret. He probably won't even talk to himself

In A Nutshell: Blake returns. Or does he?

Story: Behaving oddly, Avon takes the *Liberator* to Terminal – an artificial world that was created to study the evolution of humanity. Avon believes that he will find Blake there, but Servalan has been planting a false trail to ensnare Avon and the *Liberator*; the Blake that Avon finds is merely a drug-induced illusion. Servalan strands the crew and attempts to flee in the *Liberator*, unaware that it is dying after passing through a particle cloud en route to Terminal.

Information:

Vila, Cally and Dayna are playing what looks like *Monopoly: Intergalactic Freedom Fighter Edition.* It's the electric one too – that's an extra tenner in the shops.

They're also drinking GREEN.

Avon's pulled a gun on Tarrant! Shoot, you idiot, shoot! Thinking about it – where does that gun appear from?

Tarrant, looking at scanner screen full of stars: 'There's nothing out there. We're in the middle of nowhere'. You're in space, you twat. That's what it looks like.

It's amazing how Darrow can maintain interest in a scene when the only response he's getting is a monotone 'Confirmed'.

Who carried the Space Monopoly in from the teleport room to the bridge?

Avon's outfit is terrific. He should hang on to that one.

There's a full complement of teleport bracelets in this story.

The steady heartbeat of Terminal doesn't distract from the fact it's clearly a field in Surrey.

Glynis Barber's star sign is actually Scorpio. Isn't that funny? Same as Curtis Mayfield, Roger McGough and Ainsley Harriot. She's not in this story though.

Jan Chappell wears a wig on location, having had her own hair cut too short several weeks earlier.

Dayna's being given some excessively long lines as Vila notices the energy loss.

Zen sounds a bit off.

Something's eating away at the *Liberator*. For once, it's not the lack of budget.

The Links are almost too shocking for words and not in a good way.

There's a teleport bracelet on Terminal, yet the *Liberator* has a complete stock. Are they replaced by the auto-repair circuits or is someone on the ship manufacturing them?

Blake is alive! And his beard is a great big fuzzy chin-full of fun.

Oh. Maybe he isn't.

The *Liberator* is covered in snot. This does not bode well.

Zen's growing decrepitude is genuinely moving.

How does Tuddenham manage to make Zen's death so sweet?

Vila grabs Orac. He's clever, that one.

Those last shots of the *Liberator* – magnificent and very sad. Bye, you beautiful old thing.

Closing Shot: Avon grins like a loon at the prospect of being stranded on an artificial planet full of monkeys.

Delightful Dialogue:

Avon: Zen, you will remain silent until further instructions.
Zen: Confirmed.

(idiot)

Avon: I don't need any of you … this is as far as you go. I don't want you with me, I don't want you following me. Understand this: anyone who does follow me, I'll kill them.

Servalan: MAXIMUM POWER!

Amateur Hour:

The Links. Truly rubbish.

The guard who wakes Avon manages to do so by kicking the floor next to him. Always drags me from a deep slumber, that does.

ADDITIONAL SCRAPS OF KNOWLEDGE

Terrynation Street: People in blonde wigs, reliance on life support machines.

Planets: Calipheron, Terminal, Jevron.

Space-isms: Electrostatic locks (sonal keys required), visual image structuriser.

Avon's 'Well, Now' Count: 4

Below: Mat Irvine's original props list for "Terminal".

BBC VISUAL EFFECTS DEPARTMENT
PROPERTY REQUISITION SHEET

REQUIRED FOR: October 13 1979	VFX SUPERVISOR: Mat Irvine	
ITEM REQUIRED	QUANTITY	SIZE (IF APPLICABLE)
Swarfega	150	250g
Fireworks	Loads	Massive

BBC
PROPERTIES DEPARTMENT

Mat -

Just wanted to check that this list is correct as it seems identical to the sheet we received for "Star One" last year.

Thinking about it, it seems identical to every other episode too?

Peter

PROPERTY STORES SIGNATURE ....
SECONDARY PROPERTY STORES SIGNATURE ....

7.20 pm *New series*
Blake's Seven
The first of 17 episodes
Rescue
by TERRY NATION
starring **Paul Darrow**
Michael Keating
Steve Pacey
Josette Simon
Glynis Barber
with **Geoffrey Burridge**

As Avon and the crew of the *Liberator* struggle to survive on the hostile world of Terminal, a stranger is on his way to find them. But rescue is not exactly what he has in mind …

Avon	PAUL DARROW
Vila	MICHAEL KEATON
Tarrant	STEVEN PACEY
Dayna	JOSETTE SIMON
Soolin	GLYNIS BARBER
Orac	PETER TUDDENHAM
Dorian	GEOFFREY BURRIDGE
Sea Devil	ROB MIDDLETON

Series created by TERRY NATION
Music by DUDLEY SIMPSON
Studio lighting WARWICK FIELDING
Script editor CHRIS BOUCHER
Designer ROGER CANN
Producer VERE LORRIMER
Director MARY RIDGE

FEATURE p11

Book, Scorpio Attack, £6.75 hardback, £1.50 paperback, or £3.60 hairyback from booksellers from 22 October

Subtitles on Ceefax page 170

SEASON R 1981

Regular Cast

Paul Darrow	*Kerr Avon*
Michael Keating	*Vila Restal*
Glynis Barber	*Soolin*
Steven Pacey	*Del Tarrant*
Josette Simon	*Dayna Mellanby*
Peter Tuddenham	*Slave / Orac*
Jacqueline Pearce	~~*Servalan Sleer*~~ *whatever*
Aitch	*Everyone else*

Episodes

Rescue

Power

Traitor

Breakout

Stardrive

Headhunter

Sabotage

Assassin

Jojoba

Games

Gravity

Destructor

Sand

Gold

Orbit

Warlord

Blake

47 RESCUE

Writer: Chris Boucher   **Director**: Mary Ridge

Guest Stars: Geoffrey Burridge (Dorian), Rob Middleton (Sea Devil)

Opening Shot: Avon and Dayna looking at chimps in the snow.

You Just Described the Story:
Soolin: What does the room contain, Dorian?

Random Insult:
Tarrant: Lift, you scruffy bag of bolts. Lift!
(He's so rubbish he insults space vessels)

In A Nutshell: Rescued.

Story: Stranded on Terminal, the survivors of the *Liberator* crew must find a way to escape. Surrounded by Federation traps, they are rescued by the mysterious Dorian (and his hot totty lady-squeeze), a seemingly friendly spacefarer with plans of his own for our trusty chums. He's even got a spare room for them.

Information:
New title sequence! It's better than the last season and the logo's changed too.

So, we pick up the action where "Terminal" left off.

Avon's outfit is pretty damn cool, but maybe lose the gauntlets.

The thing that attacks Dayna looks pretty good, actually.

Tarrant's fainted and is carried out of the exploding underground base by Vila. Pathetic.

How has Vila been able to change his outfit from "Terminal"?

Ha-ha! At 5m 02s a piece of the wreckage from the exploding base hits Tarrant in the goolies and he flinches!

Cally's last words: 'Blake!' It's not really his fault is it?

The moment you first see the inside of *Scorpio*, you just know it's going to play a major role in the new series. It's a corrugated plastic version of the *Liberator*, complete with sentient computer and just enough chairs for the crew. Oh, and wouldn't you know it? A teleport.

The Federation rifle loses its shoulder strap somewhere between the location and studio filming.

Hang on – isn't that the same stock footage we had in "Volcano"? You know, the footage of the volcano.

We love the bit on *Scorpio* when Avon is giving everybody instructions on what the others should do but struggles when it comes to Vila.

Dayna helpfully explains the gun clips to us: laser, plasma bullet, percussion shell, micro grenade, stun and drug. They're all there. It's wasted screen time though, as they're never used at all for the entire season. Well, apart from the one that goes 'Blthshiiiya!'

The model shots in this episode aren't bad. The production team must have certainly thought so because, as with the *Liberator*, the shots of *Scorpio* landing and taking off from Xenon appear again and again over the course of the series.

Burridge is hopelessly miscast. The part requires grit – Michael Elphick would've been better.

No one gives a sod about Cally. She's been dead barely an hour and Vila's trying to get into Dayna's knickers.

In flight, from behind, *Scorpio* looks identical to Zax's head from *Benji, Zax and the Alien Prince* or WALL•E when he's sad.

Orac is looking filthy. The Perspex is yellowing badly.

Soolin has prepared a glass of RED for everyone. Very considerate, but as we know, they're more GREEN people.

Lucky Burridge attempts to eat Glynis Barber's spine from the front.

Soolin looks particularly lovely this week.

Ooh, everyone's changed clothes all of a sudden.

Among those under consideration for the part of Soolin were Lindsay Duncan, Julia McKenzie, Lesley Ash and Janet Ellis.

At this point, with Cally dead, Zen destroyed and Orac broken, it is actually Blake's 4 – and there is no Blake either!

Discussing Orac with Dorian, Avon says that Ensor spent the last twenty years of his life in hiding; yet in "Deliverance" Ensor's son says his father has been in hiding for 30 years. One episode later (in "Orac") Blake refers to Ensor and his son disappearing 40 years ago. Nice to see continuity being adhered to. (That said, they can't get the sum of money Avon was meant to have embezzled correct – it is either 5,000,000 or 500,000,000, depending on if you're watching "Spacefall" or "Ultraworld".)

Unlike Paul Darrow, the spiral staircase appears in the first story of all four seasons of *Blake's 7*.

Vila's found the RED cupboard. Does this mean we won't see any more GREEN in the series? Was it only brewed on the *Liberator*?

When Dorian changes into his new costume, he cleverly matches the gold trim on the outfit to the colour of his hair.

It was during this series that the main cast recorded their voices for a 30 minute *Blake's Secret 7* cartoon series for broadcast on Saturday mornings. Other voices were supplied by David Jason and a pre-*EastEnders* Leticia Dean who played, hilariously, a character named Sharon.

The Dorian action figure had changeable heads and real hair. Storage at Maxtons, the factory responsible for the toys, was extremely unclean meaning most of the dolls already had fleas by the time kids played with them.

When she discovers that her gun won't work, Dayna half-heartedly throws it at the Sea Devil.

All of the cups and trays in this story were supplied by Littlewoods as part of a planned Christmas line, but owing to a poor design, each cup had a small hole in the bottom which rendered them, according to a BBC memo, 'Bloody useless as cups but mildly effective for sieving flour.'

Avon was bathing. Think on that. Picture it with candles, bubblebath and little rubber ducks.

John Nathan-Turner was so incensed by the gross misuse of the Sea Devil costume in this episode that he got his own back by ruining some Federation helmets for the *Doctor Who* story "Frontios".

Please, Dorian, die. Soon. Bored now.

Closing Shot: Vila saying something about pink asteroids.

Delightful Dialogue:

Vila: What have you done, Tarrant? I didn't save your life so you can keep risking mine.

Dayna: Don't you ever get bored of being right?
Avon: Just with the rest of you being wrong.

Avon: You know what they say. No good deed goes unpunished.

Amateur Hour:

Forget the stock footage of the volcanoes, Michael Keating struggling to holster his clip gun, reusing a Sea Devil costume from *Doctor Who* and even Dorian's old man wig. If you're going to put someone in a rubber suit and mask, it's essential you dub the lines. We can't understand a muffled word they're saying otherwise.

As Vila walks back to the base entrance on Terminal and calls for Cally someone sprints behind him, left to right, and vanishes into the bushes.

ADDITIONAL SCRAPS OF KNOWLEDGE
Planets: Xenon.

Space-isms: Ultrasonic fuses.

48 POWER

Writer: Ben Steed (back again, against all odds!)   **Director**: Mary Ridge

Guest Stars: Dicken Ashworth (Gunn Sar), Juliet Hammond-Hill (Pella), Jenny Oulton (Nina), Alison Glennie (Kate), Meshach Taylor (Hollywood Montrose), Paul Ridley (Cato), Linda Barr (Luxia)

Opening Shot: *Scorpio* on the landing pad.

You Just Described the Story:
Dayna: Something's happened to Avon, and Orac's being difficult.

Random Insult:
Gunn Sar: Watch what you're doing, you snivelling sack of offal!

In A Nutshell: Battle of the sexies.

Story: Unable to access *Scorpio* because Dorian didn't leave the door on the latch, the ~~Liberator~~ Xenon Base crew mess about in some sandpits for a bit. Avon is caught by the Hommiks, not a nice way to be caught. <Yawn> Anyway, there's this POWER struggle as three girls and eighteen boys squabble for domination over the sandpit. Meanwhile, Vila's trying to unlock the door. Soolin is missing for the entire episode, presumably in the shower, all naked and soapy, washing herself and her lovely body in steamy water... phwoar!

Information:
It's a bit of a greatest hits episode – Avon keeping secrets from the rest of the crew, an impenetrable door, a feudal society living with computers, mysterious women with telepathic powers, and that bastard that is Tarrant.

Xenon Base is very grey, isn't it?

Avon's gone out shooting people. It's good to have a hobby.

That's one bracelet down. Count 'em as the series goes on.

Vila's worried about being locked up in the base with Soolin. Is he mad?

Gunn Sar's comedy dialogue isn't quite working. It's a bit over-written.

Where's Soolin? We need to know how lovely she looks this week.

Avon, oddly, defends Gunn Sar's wife. Not like him to miss a bitchslap.

Why didn't Dorian use the locals for his plan last week?

Oooh… Pella has a POWER of some sort.

Avon in a fight to the death? This'll be fun. The extras cheering on Gunn Sar are hilarious.

The Seska do a lot of running; the one in red has a fantastic jiggle as she goes.

Why would you leave out the new crewmember in the second story of the new season?

Tarrant's frighteningly clever. He's managed to work out that if the Hommiks are men and the Seska are women then this must be a battle of the sexes. Oh, well done, Curly.

Gunn Sar is sweetly sewing a blanket.

Uh-oh, Dayna's challenging someone to a fight. Cue her fists-out, squatting-on-a-drawing-pin stance.

We don't care about the Seska or the Hommiks, and frankly we're starting to lose interest in the main cast too.

We're really warming to Pella's mate in the red though. She's saucy.

Avon's right when he says 'That's an interesting choice of hostage.' Pella clearly doesn't know Avon very well.

Ah, the saucebox is called Kate. Ben Steed must have run out of futuristic names when he got to her. And she's just been shot. Dead saucebox.

Avon always shoots people in the stomach.

Yay, Soolin's back and apparently she 'sells her skill' – Quick! Wallets!

Closing Shot: Avon looking visibly aroused, having had a gun pulled on him by Soolin (who, it has to be said, looks particularly lovely this week).

Delightful Dialogue:

Pella: The whole base would peeyoooo!

Dayna: You can't put thumbscrews on a computer.

Avon: Oh, it hurts, Pella.

Amateur Hour:

The light from Avon's fusion rod is pretty unconvincing.

ADDITIONAL SCRAPS OF KNOWLEDGE

Planets: Omnos Two, Xenon (still).

Space-isms: Herculanium, nuclear compression charge, petroscope, Dynamon crystals, ordinary domestic heliofusion rod, nucleic burster, tele-ergotron... Ben Steed's found his calling in life.

Below: No one remembered to tell Glynis Barber that she wasn't needed for the location filming of this episode, so she filled her time by drawing portraits of the cast and guest stars on her script.

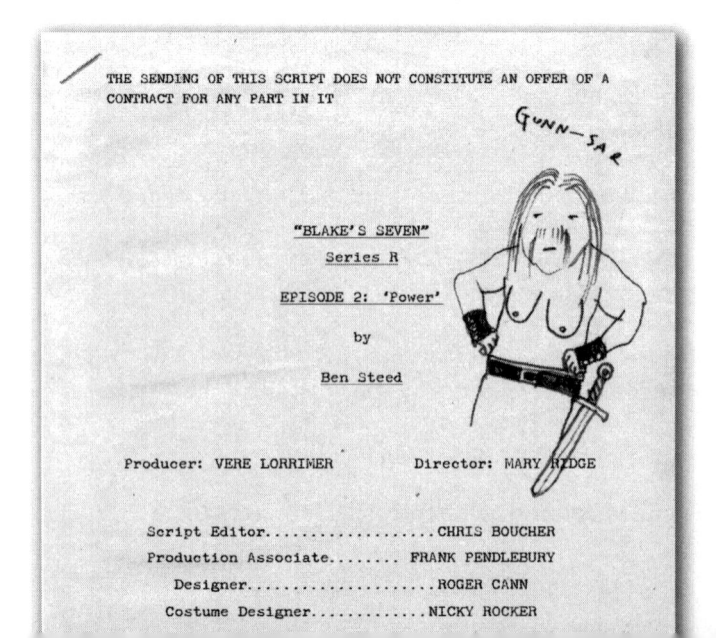

```
THE SENDING OF THIS SCRIPT DOES NOT CONSTITUTE AN OFFER OF A
CONTRACT FOR ANY PART IN IT


                        "BLAKE'S SEVEN"
                          Series R
                       EPISODE 2: 'Power'
                              by
                          Ben Steed

       Producer: VERE LORRIMER         Director: MARY RIDGE

            Script Editor...................CHRIS BOUCHER
            Production Associate........FRANK PENDLEBURY
                Designer....................ROGER CANN
            Costume Designer............NICKY ROCKER
```

49 TRAITOR

Writer: Robert Holmes   **Director**: David Sullivan Proudfoot

Guest Stars: Malcolm Stoddard (Leitz), Christopher Neame (Colonel Quute), Robert Morris (Major Hunda), Edgar Wreford (Forbus), John Quentin (Practar), Nick Brimble (General), Neil Dickson (Avandir), Brent Spiner (Data), David Quilter (The Tracer), Cyril Appleton (Sgt. Hask), George Lee (Igin)

Opening Shot: A planet, and judging by the incidental music, it's a mysterious one.

You Just Described the Story:
Dayna: It was Servalan, wasn't it?

Random Insult:
Vila: So Orac's thick – we all know that.

In A Nutshell: Sleervalan.

Story: Avon and Soolin take Orac back to Freedom City to con the casino out of yet more money to pay for decorations and equipment at Xenon Base. As they enter orbit, they are fired upon by Federation ships. Out of nowhere, six *Liberator* sister ships appear and a huge battle ensues. Soolin strips down and starts pole dancing in the *Scorpio* teleport bay while Avon reads out Christmas cracker jokes to himself, pulling each cracker alone and making 'Yippee!' noises as he does so. If you believe that, you'll believe anything.

Information:
We really need some sort of clue in these Season R titles to help us know what's happening.

Have they recast Travis again?

PURPLE is basically Space Rohypnol.

'Resistance is quite pointless' – doesn't have quite the right tone, does it?

The lack of a big, impressive flight deck makes Avon and Dayna's running to hear what Orac has to say quite ridiculous.

The production team shot 22 minutes of film of men sitting in quarries for this story. When the episode was complete, it ran to just 46 minutes, so they shot 5 more.

The inclusion of sun loungers on the *Scorpio* flight deck was presumably written with the *Liberator* in mind. Only an idiot would deliberately include them on that set.

Soolin is 7% more lovely this week.

Those Federation types are really bigging up this Sleer character.

Dayna and Tarrant appear to have teleported to a completely different planet to where the action is.

Servalan is now going by the title 'Supreme Empress'.

Pylene-50 is the fiftieth attempt to perfect the Pylene formula. The previous forty-nine weren't very good.

We don't know what Scalerians are.

Why is Orac doing public service announcements on the planet below?

You can picture Bob Holmes with the word 'agent' frustratingly at the tip of his tongue when he eventually went with 'double spy'.

The Federation officers on Helotrix drink BROWN. Ugh.

The episode fails completely on the basis that homeopathy is a load of old nonsense.

Dayna and Tarrant are incredibly dumb in this story.

When he was in *Colditz*, Christopher Neame played a character called 'Dick Player'. This makes us laugh.

The blue lighting on the three Federation officers when they're tracking the rebels on computer screens is rather attractive.

Vila, Soolin and Avon sit in the same seats for nearly the whole of this episode.

Paul Darrow says each line louder than the last. Forty-one minutes in and he's bellowing at Vila and Soolin.

Closing Shot: Close-up on Avon being boggle-eyed and vengeful.

Delightful Dialogue:

Vila: Blake would have been proud of you, you know.
Avon: I know, but then he never was very bright.

Soolin: Doesn't have much time for Tarrant does he?
Avon: Ah well. Tarrant is brave, young, handsome... There are three good reasons for anyone not to like him.

Hunda: We need to know the exact point when we can start the shaft.

Amateur Hour:

The painting meant to represent the exterior of the Federation headquarters is fairly poor. That said they didn't really try hard with the interior set, it's mainly just ropes of flashing disco lights pinched from the *Top of the Pops* studio.

The effect on Jacqueline Pearce's voice isn't very good at disguising her identity.

There are a couple of dodgy studio scenes when the rebels are attacked, complete with potted garden centre plants and foliage.

Tarrant and Dayna change clothes to pass as Helots. Luckily the teleport changes them back into their usual outfits when they return to *Scorpio*.

ADDITIONAL SCRAPS OF KNOWLEDGE

Planets: Helotrix, Lubus, Porthia Major, Wanta, Tarsius, Gedden.

Space-isms: Magnetrix terminal, Pylene-50, audio beam, Tincture of Pyrellic, Pamporanian fungi, medical lasers.

Incomprehensible Line: *General:* Fletch used gas against the Wazis.

50 BREAKOUT

Writer: Allan Prior   **Director**: Pennant Roberts

Guest Stars: David Collings (Ka Mahendran), Derek Griffiths (Kran Penni), John Leeson (Joam Mikkeljun), Philip Madoc (Mathoster), Brian Hall (Kurt Golightly), Jonathan Newth (Trooper Russell), Lola Morris (Dancer), Helen Bernat (Klyn)

Opening Shot: Avon teleporting into a corridor.

You Just Described the Story:
Soolin: It sticks in the throat.

Random Insult:
Avon: Tarrant strikes me as the kind of man who'd enjoy prison life a little *too* much.

In A Nutshell: Bizarre attempt at *The Dirty Dozen* in 47 minutes.

Story: Having intercepted details of prison transfers within the Federation, Avon and Tarrant have formulated a plan to recruit en masse directly from prisons by freeing certain key detainees. In total, they've targeted seven candidates. They take turns to spring them from the prisons and fight their way out of air space. Sadly, on the final rescue, they realise they need more numbers as security is high. All seven new recruits are wiped out during the assault.

Information:
It takes six minutes before we're told why Avon is breaking into a prison, alone, and rescuing a complete stranger. This is because the first day's recording was lost and a remount wasn't possible.

Philip Madoc and John Leeson had previously appeared in *Doctor Who* together.

John Leeson and Jonathan Newth had also previously appeared in *Doctor Who* together.

David Collings had also been in *Doctor Who*, but not with Jonathan Newth or John Leeson.

The sunshine through the cell window is one of those rare moments when a set in *Blake's 7* looks good.

We're not convinced by Mathoster's change of clothes. He looked pretty daft before in just his nappy thing, but now he looks like a grand wizard.

When Avon throws the dinner tray, you can see Darrow smirk as it breaks the window. The professional he is, he carries on with the take.

Dudley Simpson reuses two music cues from *The Tomorrow People* in this story, as he was ill during production.

Derek Griffiths was a last-minute replacement for Cy Grant, who had to drop out a week before filming. In a hastily removed subplot, Dayna's affection for him was meant to be because he reminded her of her father. With the subplot gone she seems a little unhinged, suddenly spouting dialogue about everyone she knows being dead and how wonderful her childhood was.

It takes exactly three minutes to defuse the bomb, which we were told before has a thirty second fuse.

In space, apparently, they *can* hear you scream.

When Avon scoops up the chicks from the nest, watch the curtain behind it as it changes colour between shots.

Scripts for this story were leaked to the press and a full breakdown of the plot was printed in *The Sun*. Consequently the story was moved to the middle of the fifth season of US action series *The A-Team* some years later. Complaints were received, but many felt it was the best episode of *The A-Team* they'd seen in years and nearly resulted in a weird spin-off series and what would've been the first successful BBC/ITV/US crossover production.

Terry Nation was reportedly unhappy with this episode and asked that Allan Prior not be employed again. This, in part, led to the cancellation of the series.

Filming was delayed when several accidents occurred at the Wookey Hole location. Several members of the cast and crew had playfully mocked an ancient stone called the Wookey Wizard, but came to regret their actions when there were six brutal murders in the caves during filming. Fortunately only one of those deaths was a member of the film crew.

Closing Shot: Avon throws the cup back at Tarrant to prove it's empty.

Delightful Dialogue:

Dayna: Servalan killed my father and my sister. All I had left were those shoes. She's not keeping them, Avon! They're not even her size. How can she be so cruel?

Amateur Hour:

Clearly a money-saving episode, since all seven prisons are just the same two corridors dressed differently each time.

Brian Hall's green wig is a series low-point.

The rats in Ji Tung Kwah are clearly guinea pigs slathered in hair gel. They haven't even got tails!

Is it so difficult to time an explosion correctly? Everyone leaps to the floor when the Ringmaster Droid enters, but the explosion comes a noticeable few seconds later.

Pop in the DVD and jump to 2m 43s. Avon's teleport bracelet falls off as he runs along the corridor, and then his gun falls out of its holster and breaks when it hits the floor. Ever the professional, Darrow pretends none of it happened and carries on; by 3m 01s the bracelet and (repaired) gun are all back in place.

ADDITIONAL SCRAPS OF KNOWLEDGE

Planets: Punzil, Fennestar, Brill-18, Stend.

Space-isms: Sonic lock, data-ratchet, data-spore, senso-cam, Space Security Zone.

51 STARDRIVE

Writer: James Follett   **Director**: David Sullivan Proudfoot

Guest Stars: Barbara Shelley (Dr Plaxton), Barry Elliot (Space Rat), Damien Thomas (Atlan), Peter Sands (Bomber), Paul Elliot (Space Scum), Leonard Kavanagh (Napier)

Opening Shot: Two planets, one big, one apparently not so. That's perspective for you.

You Just Described the Story:
Soolin: So, you've let Vila and Dayna walk into a trap?

Random Insult:
Vila: They're maniacs! Psychopaths! All they live for is sex and violence, booze and speed. And the fellas are just as bad.

In A Nutshell: Anything that can go wrong will go wrong.

Story: In a lay-by and fixing one of *Scorpio*'s tyres, the crew witness three Federation ships apparently self-destruct. Rather than focus on repairing the ship, Avon fusses about making everyone watch tedious frame-by-frame footage of the explosions to find out what caused them. The cause turns out to be a nasty infestation of Space Rats on Space Choppers in space. Following them to a nearby planet, they find rogue Federation scientist Dr Plaxton is being used by the Space Rats to create a new super-fast photonic STARDRIVE. Avon nicks it and kills her.

Information:
Why didn't they bring Orac? What was he doing back at the base? Looking after the cat?

Oh look! Vila's drunk again. It must be the fourth series. But hello, what's this? He's trying to squirm up to Soolin. This would be mildly amusing were it not for Dudley Simpson's *Terry and June*-style score.

Gadzooks! He was faking it!

Avon and Tarrant repair the hole in the *Scorpio*'s hull with an old milk crate that has been painted blue.

Federation Interceptor design has changed back to three lightbulbs. Dayna insists the Interceptors aren't on an interception course. Not Interceptors then, are they?

Message from captain of Interceptor 1 to Interceptors 2 and 3: 'OK boys, keep close formation at all times. Manoeuvre as if we're being waved about on the end of the same stick'.

What possible advantage is there to recording at 10,000 frames per second?

Soolin looks particularly lovely when she's bored.

The planet Caspar is pink.

According to production documents, Soolin's chair was the luckiest chair on the set.

Dayna runs really oddly. She sort of scampers about the place.

Three-wheeled motorbikes aren't very futuristic. Did "Day of the Daleks" teach us nothing?

That's Barbara Shelley! She's a real actress. Barbara Shelley doesn't own a telly.

Why are all the switches on Plaxton's desk facing away from her?

Atlan is the leader the Space Rats, though he is at pains to point out he isn't one of them. We have no idea what that's supposed to signify. He likes to relax with a refreshing tumbler of GREEN on the rocks. Judging by his exaggerated poses, body movements and facial reactions, his previous job was sawing women in half and making tigers disappear in Las Vegas.

Atlan's henchman, Bomber, is a pretty-boy slumming it unconvincingly with an indeterminate ruffian's accent. He appears to have styled his face paint on Jon Pertwee's first *Doctor Who* title sequence.

Soolin looks lovely in a quarry. This may explain Tarrant's great pains to ensure she goes first when climbing up the rockface.

'Stardrive' is an anagram of 'Rev TARDIS', or 'Revised TARDIS', if you will.

Another episode in which the studio floor features prominently. This time it has some white shapes stuck to it.

No-one can accuse Damien Thomas of not giving it everything. He's like a cross between Peter Lorre and an angry gekko.

The Space Rats' sofas look suspiciously like the Sandminer ones from the *Doctor Who* serial "The Robots of Death". We've mentioned them before. Can you remember who we said made them? No? Don't worry. We probably made that bit up.

Atlan threatens to let the Space Rats deal with Plaxton 'in their own fashion'. We can only hope this involves violence and despicable rummaging rather than having to adopt their hair stylings and dress sense.

Soolin kills four Space Rats in less than thirty seconds; she's so dreamy.

The shot of the parked *Scorpio* actually looks pretty good.

The crew have finally recruited a useful ally in the form of Dr Plaxton, and Barbara Shelley's putting in a decent performance too, given all the hideous things around her.

Oh, she's dead.

When she escapes with the crew on *Scorpio*, she bagsies the last seat on the flight deck, forcing Avon to stand. This is the real reason he sacrifices her; the oncoming plasma bolt merely provides an excuse.

However, spare little sympathy for Plaxton's demise. 'Whoever you are, take me with you', she pleaded with Avon, not for one second mentioning her assistant on the base. The poor chap was left cowering on a bunk somewhere, dreading the moment his door might be flung open to reveal a jiggy Atlan and his maurauding space tongue.

Closing Shot: Avon saying 'poo?'

Delightful Dialogue:

Tarrant: Precision guidance lost.
Avon: Slave, initiate the backup system.
Slave: I'm very sorry about this, but that was the backup system.

Vila: Supposing they come at us with one of their Space Choppers?

Avon: I want a close-up of his helmet!

Amateur Hour:

Michael Keating couldn't drop a gun convincingly if his life depended on it.

It's good to see our old friend the 'underground base' again. Just take a big silver door to a quarry and it saves you building anything.

Avon and the position of his gun are caught out in a continuity error when Atlan escapes from the lab. Still, it's worth it for the shot where Avon doesn't bother to lend a hand as Tarrant is disarmed and Soolin is used as a human shield; instead, he just registers a look of weary chagrin at their ineptness. Brilliant.

ADDITIONAL SCRAPS OF KNOWLEDGE

Planets: Caspar, Altern Five .

Space-isms: Space Chopper, selsium ore, space drive, photonic drive, star drive, Space Rats … oh my!

Avon's technique for traversing hostile terrain is as follows:

1) Stand semi-upright behind a handy bit of cover; do not duck down.

2) Jog across open ground to the next bit of cover; do not duck down.

3) Remain standing while your comrades catch up with you.

4) Duck down when, and only when, you're in plain view of a security camera.

5) Repeat as necessary until either a) your objective is achieved
 b) the villain's dead
 c) you're dead
 d) Blake's dead

Below: Trendy released a number of *Blake's 7* themed clothing patterns between 1979 and 1983. Knitted Federation guard outfits proved popular, but nothing came close to matching the unexpected sales achieved by Doctor Plaxton's cape. The outfit was to prove doubly successful for Trendy – one year later they re-released it with new cover artwork for men and renamed it 'The Sarkov'.

9850 **Trendy** 95p
IN USA and CANADA
$1.20

The Plaxton

ANOTHER FINE

BLAKE'S 7

OUTFIT BY TRENDY

CAPE IN TWO LENGTHS AND TROUSERS

B

TIME SAVER PATTERNS

DRESSMAKER TESTED

53 HEADHUNTER

Writer: Roger Parkes   **Director**: Mary Ridge

Guest Stars: John Westbrook (Muller), Lynda Bellingham (Vena), Andrew Cable (Guard), Nick Joseph (Android), Douglas Fielding (Technician), Lesley Nunnerley (Voice)

Opening Shot: *Scorpio* 'flying'...

You Just Described the Story:
Vila: A straightforward pick up job, you said. As last words go they're not likely to be famous.

Random Insult:
Avon: Try not to be stupid.

In A Nutshell: *Blake's Se7en*.

Story: Tarrant and Vila have been sent by Avon to collect Muller, an eminent robotics expert. Muller brings a box onto *Scorpio* with him, and for various reasons Vila eventually kills him. Upon their return to the base, Slave and Orac get all grumpy about stuff, so Avon puts them in quarantine. Then everything really goes to pot, as it turns out Muller's not Muller at all but a bear-hugging loony with a head in a box. Corridors were made for running down, and that's just what everyone'll do.

Information:
Ensor trained Muller. Nice callback to the first series there. Although, we bet he never taught him how to build a robot that could balance a human head on its shoulders.

Why does Darrow pronounce 'money' like that? It's just weird.

Muller calls *Scorpio*; by this time, he's presumably had his head cut off. How is he talking? The robot can't speak without sounding like Metal Mickey.

Oh goodness, doesn't Soolin look lovely with her hair like that?

This was the cricket commentator Brian Johnston's favourite episode of *Blake's 7*.

Right, look – let's make sense of this. This is a severed head on top of a curtain. Not only does it speak, but its face moves. Bear this in mind for later.

Muller goes nuts telling Tarrant to send the box back. Shouts and everything. But he's just a severed head! We can't stress this enough.

Vila can't have whacked him too hard or the damn head would've fallen off. And how the hell is it held on anyway? Surely it should roll around the flight deck?

Tarrant comes across as a right berk yet again as he checks for Muller's pulse – surely to get a pulse he must've noticed the bits of gut and flesh dangling down? Maybe he hasn't had any medical training to speak of.

Fantastic character moment from Avon as he turns to Soolin to comfort Muller's wife. That said Soolin's attempts at comfort are to just repeatedly offer her alcohol.

We briefly see Muller's service record which shows his other inventions. They include a special light switch and a sweet-smelling shelving unit designed to fit where walls join in a room. The Muller Lite and the Muller Fruit Corner were probably not what the *Scorpio* crew were looking for.

Technician 241 confirms for us that Muller's head is missing. Surely there would be a drop or two of blood on the floor?

Grumpy Slave is great fun.

Just look at the quality of the countdown clock in this episode… *Pong* had better graphics.

The studio floor is wearing its grey outfit again this week.

Doesn't Soolin look lovely in a space su… actually, she looks ridiculous. Ridiculously sexy, that is.

Oooh… Soolin's so masterful with Orac.

Dayna couldn't look more bored as she operates the teleport.

Lynda Bellingham is hugged to death.

Avon's urgent task, brilliantly, is to get changed out of that absurd space suit.

No, no, no – that head thing just doesn't work! It's so ridiculous.

Hang on – in "Shadow" Avon fitted a bomb inside Orac that would destroy him if he was ever taken over by an outside influence again. Nice to see that worked so well.

Soolin is absolutely puffed out when she gets to the surface, so where does the extra spurt of energy come from? <SPURT JOKE REMOVED>

Muller should really have asked someone else to design his android heads – it is basically an old motorcycle crash helmet with some weirdly cut tubes sticking out the front.

Why didn't t'Ommiks make use of this power room in, um, "Power"?

Just who the hell made the bridge and who maintains its paintwork?

Now that Muller's android has collapsed, we can see that there's just a flat surface at the neck, so Muller's head could only have been balanced on top. Also, there's no blood. Are we getting our point across here?

Dayna attaches three explosives. Two go on the bridge (why blow that up? You need to get back to the other side of that stream), the other one she places on the android's head. Lucky it didn't just blow the head up, really.

Closing Shot: Low shot, right up Avon's nose. (*Orac:* Yes, master!)

Delightful Dialogue:
Avon: Tarrant, what have you got up there apart from yourself, a halfwit and a corpse?

Avon: Leave Soolin to finish off. *<sigh>*

Orac: Accept your domination, Soolin. *<big sigh>*

Amateur Hour:

It is very lucky that Tarrant didn't need to shoot anyone when he rescues Muller – he has no ammunition clip in his gun (a running theme in Season R.)

The *Scorpio* chairs wobble terribly when Muller tries to operate the teleport.

Muller breaks the teleport control lever away from the control panel. In fact the whole panel slides all over the desk during that shot.

The *Scorpio* space suit helmets don't fit at all. They're just balancing on top of their heads – rather like Muller's head does on his body. And what's the fin on top of the helmets supposed to be for?

A thunderclap can be heard when Vila tries to open Muller's box. A thunderclap. No, really.

Dayna's bomb brings down a heap of rubble on the robot, leaving its outfit torn, dirty and with wires hanging out of it. Unfortunately every other scene within the base that follows has the costume clean and intact. Once we're out on the surface of Xenon it goes back to being dishevelled again.

The whole idea (see above) regarding severed heads. Really, we've gone over this several times, and you should've been paying attention.

ADDITIONAL SCRAPS OF KNOWLEDGE

Planets: Xenon generally, Pharos.

Space-isms: Medicapsule, percussion detonators.

Tarrant Mitigation Techniques:

Avon has got our backs this time, calling Tarrant a fool and a halfwit.

Sigh:

Orac: Join us Soolin. We can fulfill your every desire.
Soolin: You wouldn't know where to start.

(All we ask is a chance to prove you right, Soolin)

54 SABOTAGE

Writer: Robert Holmes **Director**: Douglas Camfield

Guest Stars: Peter Egan (Captain Gerrit), John Nettleton (Trace), Brenda Cavendish (Raali), Ray Smith (Hinton), Bunny Losh (Inspector)

Opening Shot: *Scorpio* docking at what looks like a shoe painted silver, in a painfully slow and drawn-out sequence.

You Just Described the Story:

Avon: Sabotage!

Random Insult:

Vila (on Raali's marksmanship): My grandmother's a better shot and she's dead.

In A Nutshell: Whodunnit? Well, who? Whodunnit? Whodunthesabotage? Who?

Story: *Scorpio* has docked at the K-18 Space Satellite Base to locate an expert in cybernetics named Hinton, an old associate of Soolin's. Once on the base, the power is cut and life support is slowly diminishing. The crew have to find their way to the bridge and restore power before finally exposing the saboteur.

Information:

This opening model shot lasts nearly two minutes. Even Dudley Simpson seems to have fallen asleep.

Peter Egan has a full head of hair here. Where does it all go between now and *Ever Decreasing Circles*?

He's very good though! His instant dismissal of Tarrant as 'a gutless deserter' has us warming to him in no time.

We love the little tune that plays before every announcement on the base.

Soolin looks amazing this week; this is the first skirt we've seen since Cally left.

'I'm Security Officer Raali. I'm in charge of security on this base.' We'd never have guessed.

The guns the base personnel use look a bit water pistol-y.

Dayna, stuck on the ship and out of the action, does little more than act as a vocal countdown clock.

The walls of the bathroom set were designed by *Blue Peter* winner Oscar Hurt. Oscar was one of nearly sixty entrants who each design a tile pattern for the wall. Oscar makes a cameo in the Travis spin-off series (see page 258).

Avon's clothes must really stink by now. He's been wearing them for months!

Soolin climbing the ladder will stay with us for a long time, but not as long as it will for lucky Vila, who follows her up.

GREEN! We don't see much GREEN anymore... Vila's got two bottles to himself; drunkenness abounds.

As they rescue Trace from the falling door, watch John Nettleton's left hand. He broke two fingers when he fell. This is why he has his hand in his pocket later on.

Speaking of Trace, Irish or Scottish? We're just not sure.

Hello, what's this? Avon and Soolin are getting very cosy in that recycling unit. Lucky sod.

Oh no! Gerrit's dead! Not that Vila seems to care, as Michael Keating seems to snigger as the door flies open.

Hinton! It was Hinton all along! We knew it. He throws a *really* good punch.

What *did* go on in that Recycling Unit?

One of the background extras is Roy Wood from glam rock group Wizzard.

Oh, that's it. All over. One feels there should be some second surprise at the end, but no twist, no surprise, just back to *Scorpio* and forget why we even came here in the first place.

Closing Shot: Soolin winks at Avon, getting a wry frown in return.

Delightful Dialogue:

Hinton (referring to Avon): Somehow he managed to dodge the bullet.
Vila: The bullet probably dodged him.

Dayna: She killed my father, Vila!
Vila: Really? You never mention it.

Amateur Hour:

That is definitely a platform shoe sprayed silver, not a space station.

The air masks that the *Scorpio* crew grab don't actually form any kind of seal around the face; they're wasting an awful lot of air from those tiny tanks.

Tarrant misses his cue after Avon finishes speaking to Dayna via the computer terminal. We like Darrow's raised, expectant eyebrow during the awkward silence.

Soolin's hairstyle changes from the film sequences (the explosion in the lab) to the studio.

The special effect used for the death scenes – a photograph of the actor was burnt with a magnifying glass and then the footage sped up – is woeful.

ADDITIONAL SCRAPS OF KNOWLEDGE

Planets: Jirryl, Kai-10, Ormelia, Rytel Rianna-Tropos and Limbast are all part of Trace's research route.

Space-isms: Techa-Oxymasks, vibro-bolts, atomic pen-cutter, Space Rats (again).

55 ASSASSIN

Writer: Rod Beacham **Director**: David Sullivan Proudfeet

Guest Stars: Richard Hurndall (Nobollox), Caroline Holdaway (Piri), Sweaty Betty Marsden (Verlis), John Wyman (Cancer), Charles Dance (Eric), John Attard (Benos), Adam Blackwood (Tok), Mark Barratt (Servalan's captain)

Opening Shot: *Scorpio*, flying to the right.

You Just Described the Story:
Avon: It's nothing. It's of no value.

Random Insult:
Piri: I'm really stupid, aren't I?
(*Us:* Yes.)

In A Nutshell: Servalan or Sleer or whatever her bloody name is now has a plan to hire someone to assassinate the *Liberator* or *Scorpio* or whatever-they are-now-crew.

Story: The Doctor has been recalled to Gallifrey following a premonition of the President's assassination. While seemingly trying to stop the assassination, he instead appears to shoot the President during some ceremony or something. After some pratting about, he's hooked up to the Matrix and has a wacky dream about clowns, surgeons, biplanes and the tiniest train you've ever seen. In the end, it turns out it was the Master and everyone goes home.

Information:
For an ex-Federation officer, Tarrant's knowledge of the solar system is woefully poor. Soolin on the other hand seems to have done The Knowledge.

This is the only episode, with several exceptions, where Soolin looks lovely.

Servalan appears to be pulled around the studio by an invisible thread attached to her belly-button.

The script goes out of its way to refer to Cancer as a 'he' at every opportunity. We smell a rat. Well, maybe a crab.

Unusual to see circular wipes on *Blake's 7*. In fact, the director has gone wipe and dissolve mad here.

We love Darrow's acting when he first approaches Benos.

There's lots of beard action in this episode.

We bet that Neebrox stinks.

Josette Simon was awarded an OBE for services to drama in 2000. Paul Darrow has never been given an OBE.

John Wyman also appeared in the James Bond film *For Your Eyes Only*, which didn't feature Richard Hurndall as he wasn't good enough to be in it and didn't feature William Hartnell as he wasn't alive enough to be in it.

Where on *Scorpio* did Neebrox get that bizarre curtain?

There were a record 408 complaints to the BBC regarding Caroline Holdaway's acting.

Referring to Cancer's prison as 'Cancer's cell' is an unfortunate turn of phrase.

Tarrant acts the prick yet again, being swayed by Piri's pathetic simpering.

At some point while aboard Cancer's ship Tarrant loses a stud from the front of his outfit. It has reappeared by the end of the episode, which makes us think that while Soolin was being 'threatened' by a plastic spider being pulled along on a string, Tarrant was sat down somewhere quiet sewing it back on.

There's some really effective lighting in the scenes when Soolin is creeping around Cancer's ship. We don't get to see enough purple in *Blake's 7*.

Neebrox has a glass of GREEN!

Soolin locking Piri in a room with a dead body is terrific stuff. Cally would never have done that. Mind you, she wouldn't have had a chance, as she'd be too busy operating the teleport.

Dudley Simpson tries his best to make the revelation that Piri is Cancer into a moment of thrilling drama. However, he probably didn't count on her appearing with her hair shaped into an up-ended baguette.

Cancer shows off her brooch, saying 'It's been staring you in the face from the very beginning.' No it hasn't – she didn't turn up until half way through. Silly moo.

Cancer's death is not only the highlight of this series but of the BBC's output since its inception ever ever ever.

Avon's 'feeling the pinch' crack is dreadful.

Drinks of RED all round at the end for the crew.

Closing Shot: Soolin has a major camel-toe. Avon smirks and drinks his RED.

Delightful Dialogue:

Avon: Get me up as quickly as you can.

Avon: All right, then he's not infallible, it's just that up to now he's never failed.

Servalan: Avon? You're not sulking I hope.

Amateur Hour:

Caroline Holdaway.

ADDITIONAL SCRAPS OF KNOWLEDGE

Planets: Domo, Prim, Gourimpest.

Space-isms: Vem – it's a unit of currency. Not to be confused with Space Vems.

56 JOJOBA

Writer: Tanith Lee   **Director**: Lennie Mayne

Guest Stars: Sarah Miles (Jaive), Margot Van der Burgh (Pendra), Rachel Davies (Winter), Sarah Sutton (Claidi), Denis Lill (Oldfield), Harry Fielder (Azhrarn)

Opening Shot: Jaive emerging from the cave of Arnoth, green hair all mussed up, blood dripping from her mouth. It's a startling image.

You Just Described the Story:
Tarrant: These women live on a diet of blood dripping from a secret cave. I want to get inside.

Random Insult:
Jaive: Leave this place, devil! Evil-doer! MAN!

In A Nutshell: Avon takes a back seat and watches while Dayna gets entwined in a female culture of blood drinkers.

Story: On the purple planet of Jojoba, the Sisterhood of the Cave of Arnoth wait for another cycle to feed on the secret spring of life. The *Scorpio* crew investigate claims that the Federation is interested in the planet. What they discover is that the cave hides another secret: a living, thinking being of mystic mystery, being bled from the gaping cave entrance.

Information:
Jaive, a green-haired adherent of the cave of Arnoth, combs her hair with tree branches even though she claims the trees are alive and feel pain.

Jojoba is a purple planet with a green sun. Its inhabitants wear orange. Are primary colours banned?

The Sisterhood of Arnoth feed on the life-spring of Arnoth, a scarlet liquid that nourishes their society. Not once have they considered it might be blood from a creature living in the cave.

There's a mystical aspect to this episode which is revealed later on to be complete nonsense.

Avon slaps Winter about a bit.

Vila complains that the Jojobans smell of 'incense, or patchouli, or something.'

Oldfield is a Federation Commissioner interested in conquering the Jojoban people, but he's travelling with only one guard – presumably for budgetary reasons.

Vila's got a new costume, which is notable for consisting of a poncho fashioned out of a Fine-Fare-brand tablecloth, with accoutrements made from the little plastic squares you used to reseal bread bags with (the ones kids always put on their bicycle brake lines). It suits him and it's a shame it doesn't appear in the series again.

Dayna seems quite at home with the Jojobans, apparently participating fully in their secret rituals when she stays at their village overnight.

Avon watches most of the night-time events on the planet while sitting in his chair on the *Scorpio* flight deck, alone, with the lights dimmed. It looks quite moody.

The cave between the foothills of the mountain of the goddess is obviously made out of papier-mâché on Matt Irvine's office table. There's some fake lightning drawn on.

The whole production looks like a Kate Bush video from the early '80s.

Tarrant falls in love with Claidi and, characteristically, acts like a nit for the rest of the episode, arguing with Avon repeatedly.

The Arnoth creature is revealed to be a rare space whale, placed in captivity by the early settlers of Jojoba and bled for food ever since. The descendants of the original settlers have long forgotten its history and think the liquid they drink is from a spring. So what keeps the Arnoth creature alive? Who's feeding it? Probably Tanith Lee's telepathic space milk.

The Jojoban women have unnatural strength, as shown when Jaive strangles Oldfield.

It's clear that the Arnoth creature feels pain. Much like the viewer when watching the episode.

That the Jojobans are revealed to be female vampires drinking the blood of the captured Arnoth creature is the episode's big twist, but it's spoilt early on by being a totally bum idea.

Pendra's outfit catches fire at 35m 19s. Margot van der Burgh walks out of shot and you can hear her stamping the flames out.

Jaive is betrothed to a unicorn, an effect achieved by glueing a paper stalk onto a pony's dejected face.

We think there might be some feminist subtext in this episode.

Oddly, Servalan doesn't appear.

Closing Shot: Vila, for once refusing to drink his RED following the blood-drinking he has seen down on Jojoba. The others laugh.

Delightful Dialogue:
Azhrarn: It is not the Bleeding Time.
(This would be fine were it not delivered in broad Cockney as 'It's not ver bleedin' tiiime!')

Amateur Hour:
The mist around the cave looks like it was created by a BBC engineer's clay pipe.

Slave says 'I must humbly report that the women of the planet are females of the strangest type.' We think he meant 'strongest'. But we're not sure.

Sarah Miles' nipples are visible through her white costume.

ADDITIONAL SCRAPS OF KNOWLEDGE
Planets: Jojoba, a purple splat in space with a green sun.

Space-isms: Space Vampires.

57 GAMES

Writer: Bill Lyons **Director**: Vivienne Cozens

Guest Stars: Stratford Johns (Belkov), Rosalind Bailey (Gambit), Barry Corbin (General Beringer), Ellen Farner (Madeleine), David Neal (Gerren), James Harvey (Guard)

Opening Shot: Explosions! Lot of explosions!

You Just Described the Story:

Servalan: This isn't a game, Belkov. We want those crystals and we want them now.

Random Insult:

Computer: Orbit achieved. Points scored … acceptable.

In A Nutshell: More theft.

Story: Avon is offered a crystal to do some stuff for a bloke that plays games a lot. Dare you to sit through this dross and write a more elaborate synopsis. So, so sick of this series now.

Information:

One of the characters in this episode is named after the *Blake's 7* episode "Gambit" (it's the computer, Gambit, in case you were wondering).

Feldon is the hardest substance in the universe.

Avon is the second hardest substance in the universe.

And he loves accidents that claim innocent lives.

Belkov's games aren't really up to much, consisting mainly of bits of transparent plastic.

Belkov's triangular chess board must have a good agent as it has already made appearances in "The Keeper" and "Sarcophagus". It's basically a semi-regular cast member by now.

Nice to see the sea turn up again in the series following its earlier appearance in "Aftermath".

When the crew and Gerren are on the surface on Mecron Two, everybody is wearing funky boots with the exception of Vila, who's been lumbered with a pair of carelessly-laced Hush Puppies.

Everyone smiles more than usual.

The Mecronian knife looks rather dangerous even for the wielder, being a three-sided blade with no handle. Good for chopping carrots though.

Avon is completely ruthless again, being prepared to abandon all of his colleagues down on the planet if need be.

Servalan can't click her fingers properly. No wonder she lost the Presidency.

The crew are briefly captured by a Federation officer whose voice is completely wrong for his haircut.

Belkov might be good at space chess but he'd be rubbish against ZE KLUTE!

The flight simulator that Tarrant has a go on actually looks rather good.

Orac gets some jiggy-jiggy action with another computer.

We like the multi-coloured pizza on Belkov's desk. There's also a Palitoy TIE Fighter visible in some background shots.

Orac compares Belkov's computer to the Oracle of Delphi, a mythical figure infamous for her impenetrable answers to straightforward questions. Recreate the stuff of legend by asking scriptwriter Bill Lyons if he thought much about the story's ending.

Closing Shot: Avon again, this time smashing a fake necklace with a gun.

Delightful Dialogue:
Avon: I use the word deliberately.
Tarrant: But did you use it accurately?

Vila: They're after blood – my blood!
Dayna: Tell them you've already given.

Amateur Hour:

In the rock-breaking scene, the tubs that the prisoners push along don't actually appear to be on the rails at one point.

David Neal's false beard isn't very convincing.

Exactly which of Gerren's shoulders is injured?

Stratford Johns fluffs a couple of his lines when Tarrant, Dayna and Gerren first encounter him. It doesn't really matter, as he's being so enjoyably fruity.

ADDITIONAL SCRAPS OF KNOWLEDGE

Planets: Agravo, Mecron Two.

Space-isms: Space games ... maybe.

Below: Released by Waddingtons Games for the Christmas market, *Belkov's Battleships* was just regular *Battleships* with the Season R logo stuck on it and a picture of Stratford Johns on the box. By sheer coincidence Christmas 1981 is also the only year Waddingtons didn't make a profit.

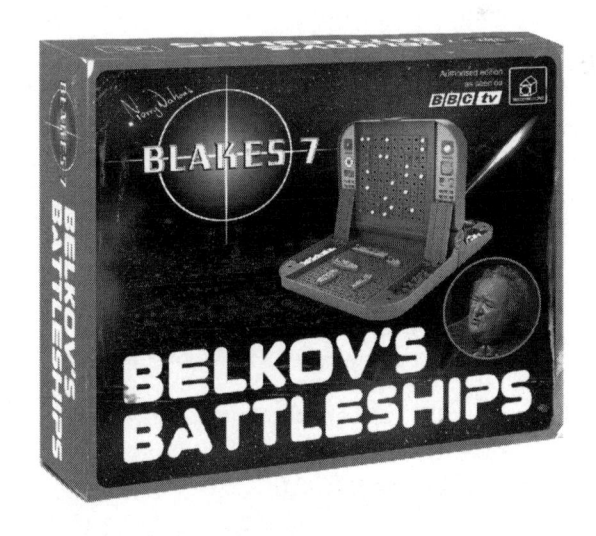

58 GRAVITY

Writer: Allan Prior   **Director**: Mary Ridge

Guest Stars: Terry Scott (Rogerson), Anna Wing (Bahor), Douglas Fielding (Technician One), Norman Hartley (Technician Two)

Opening Shot: Vila, slumped over a flight console. There's not a glass or bottle in sight so he's either dead or waiting for his cue.

You Just Described the Story:

Rogerson: With GravWel you don't need fuel, ships, fleets or any of them. Imagine the power to transport a year's worth of supplies simply by lifting a finger!

Random Insult:

Tarrant: With technology like that the possibilities are infinite!
Avon: You'd certainly be a lot more popular with the opposite sex.

In A Nutshell: What a whopper!

Story: Aboard *Scorpio*, Vila intercepts a Federation transmission concerning the transport of supplies to the colony of Hildon Ogma, a remote outpost on the edge of charted space. Reasoning that supplies to such a remote colony would be sizeable, the crew of *Scorpio* head off in pursuit, but when they locate the source of the transmission, it's a small two-man cruiser. The ship is captured and the supplies located – a year's worth in a box the size of Orac. Avon and the crew learn of Rogerson, a Federation scientist who claims to have perfected a means of shrinking matter in both size and mass.

Information:

Look closely at the shots of Vila from behind – that's not Michael Keating. Production documents don't reveal the reason for him having a stand-in for reverse shots this week.

If that ship looks familiar, it's because Terry Scott jokingly suggested it should be based on the home-made spaceship used in the 1979 *Terry and June* episode "Writing on the Wall".

While Dayna's costume this week is blissfully free of camel toes, Tarrant is wearing what looks like a codpiece.

He won't get that amount of food in that small a box without some serious CSO.

Okay, he won't get that amount of food in that small a box convincingly without some serious CSO.

Terry Scott this week, Roy Kinnear in a couple of weeks, what next? Ken Dodd in *Doctor Who*?

Again – we know she's Servalan, they know she's Servalan, so why is she persisting with this Sleer nonsense?

Yes, that's our old friend, the personal stereo from Season N. You can't keep a good prop down.

Anna Wing in silver spandex; bad fashion and bingo wings do not justify punching space pensioners in the face.

A still of Avon wedged behind Slave from this episode was used as one of several promotional images selected by Denis Allen Print for their short-lived range of *Blake's 7* greetings cards.

Have you noticed how many stories from this season involve revolutionary gadgets which will make Avon's 6½ invincible in their fight against the Federation and then don't? This is another of those devices.

Rogerson and Sleervalan cosy up with a decanter of ORANGE. It could actually be orange – there's a bowl of fruit on his desk, after all. This could be the first instance of a real drink in the programme.

Another great plan ruined by bickering among the troops. If Tarrant had kept his mouth shut, they'd have arrived before she'd buggered off with GravWel.

When he came to novelise this story, Tony Attwood attempted to fix the problem of Rogerson's mother's sister being his uncle by making her his nephew's aunt. However this is nothing compared to the comic strip adaptation that appeared in the *Sunday Express*.

That's not so much an effect as a poster of Terry Scott's head.

This is the episode mentioned in the autobiography of Idi Amin.

Closing Shot: Rogerson's smug grin flattened across the floor of his lab.

Delightful Dialogue:

Vila: I'm not going down there.
Tarrant: You are and you'll stay down there until I let you come back up.

Soolin: Rogerson, it's not too late. Come with me now and we can save you.
Rogerson: Nyearggggggghhhhhhhhhh (continue for 21 whole seconds)

Amateur Hour:

There's no adequate explanation for that spaceship.

The shrink/expand effect is shockingly executed, even by early 1980s standards. The sound effect just adds insult to injury.

The initial broadcast of this episode mistakenly had the Series M and N title sequence. It was corrected for the repeat screening the following summer.

As if the two-man cruiser model wasn't bad enough, the ship Servalan arrives in is made from the lid of a photocopier with nine spark plugs glued to it. The paint job is so poor that you can still see the Canon logo on the side!

The *Radio Times* ran a competition for *Blake's 7* fans to name a character in this episode. The winning entry (the only one received) came from Frank Doubleday of Glossop, who came up with the brilliant 'Technician Two'.

ADDITIONAL SCRAPS OF KNOWLEDGE

Planets: Hildon Ogma, Lanch.

Space-isms: Space famine, spacelane, spacer, space meat, spaces, backspacer, space.

59 DESTRUCTOR

Writer: Chris Boucher **Director**: Derrick Goodwin

Guest Stars: Ronald Hines (Lord Tancred), John Duttine (Sel Kallan), Simon Gipps-Kent (Teva), James Cosmo (Tev Darrant), Kevin McNally (Tyraz), John Levene (Madame Mallor), Cyril Shaps (Old Woman)

Opening Shot: A huge explosion at a top secret Federation base, followed by a mad-looking woman running towards the screen, shrieking.

You Just Described the Story:
Avon: I need men, Vila and I need them *now*.

Random Insult:
Tev Darrant (to Tarrant): If you weren't screaming like a woman then I'd quite happily destroy your head.

In A Nutshell: Avon's Army.

Story: In an increasingly desperate attempt to form an alliance against the Federation, Avon seeks out Lord Tancred, leader of the non-aligned world of Desteron. Tancred has a vast private army which Avon seeks to utilise for an attack on a vital Federation supply depot. Tancred demands a high price though: he wants to keep Soolin. What's worse is that Soolin doesn't seem to mind!

Information:
This episode was four days into production before anyone realised that it hadn't been formally commissioned.

During recording, Paul Darrow decided to experiment with 'method acting'. For the entire rehearsal period, he went around wearing studded leather underpants and drinking his own homemade GREEN from a hip flask.

No chimps appear in this episode. Believe it or not, that's a toddler into a monkey suit.

The Federation supply base that is seen here isn't the same Federation supply base that is seen in that other episode that time.

It was planned to include a guest appearance in this episode from Zen's identical twin brother, Xen, until it was realised that they just couldn't find a suitable actor to voice the part.

It was also planned to give Vila a 'comedy' robot sidekick in this episode. Designs were drawn up by Mat Irvine but the idea never made it off the page, as it was feared that the resultant creation would become more popular than the rest of the cast.

Avon's line when appealing to Lord Tancred, 'If you like a lot of diamonds in your riches, join our club', was later adapted by Jacob's Biscuits as an advertising slogan.

The game of Space Bingo that Vila is forced to play was considered as a possible merchandising spin-off that could be exploited for cold, hard lucre right up until someone pointed out that it was just Bingo with the word 'Space' stuck in front.

Under some lights, it looks as if Madame Mallor's nose is made out of wax.

It's hard to understand quite why the Federation base was stockpiling nothing but Space Dough and even harder to understand why Avon wanted to attack this particular base because of that.

During the making of this episode, Chris Boucher complained that the model shots were on videotape, even though they were in fact being shot on film.

The scene in which Avon finds himself in a crypt in an old church, with loads of stringed instruments on the floor, was just a manifestation of his own dream.

It was originally planned that Stephen Frears was to direct this episode, but they couldn't afford him so had to use Derrick Goodwin instead.

James Cosmo's costume is quite something to behold – does anybody ever look good dressed in a Turkish carpet?

Closing Shot: Kallan's beard, on fire.

Delightful Dialogue:

Kallan: Oh, give in Avon. All of those studs that you're wearing won't help you now.

Darrant: My dear chap, your opinion is the very last thing that we should consider. Bear that in mind while I finish off this zealot.

Amateur Hour:

Did nobody on the production team spot that the main Federation guard was played by three different actors?

A black scenery drape falls to the floor in the background of the shot where Vila is agitated in Soolin's bedroom.

During the scene in the mine, the floor manager is clearly seen tripping over a camera cable at the right of the frame.

The scene where the monkey goes mad wasn't scripted. The child employed to wear the monkey suit scoffed all the red sweets left in the dressing room and washed them down with three jugs of filter coffee. Chris Boucher hurriedly knocked out a page of covering dialogue and the cast basically winged it.

Every drop of vomit seen in this episode is quite genuine.

It was common policy to invite fans to the studio to watch filming and meet the cast of the series. This privilege was withdrawn partway through the filming of "Destructor" when the visiting fans fiddled with the switches on the Space Bingo prop, resulting in the numbered ping-pong balls firing out of the machine at great speed. Three studio lights were smashed, a camera was damaged, and Michael Keating needed minor dental surgery after taking two balls in the mouth.

ADDITIONAL SCRAPS OF KNOWLEDGE

Planets: Desteron, Kagalus, Limino, Nikoseer.

Space-isms: Magno-tendrils, Space Dough.

60 SAND

Writer: Tanith Lee   **Director**: Vivienne Cozens

Guest Stars: Stephen Yardley (Reeve), Daniel Hill (Chasgo), Eileen Way (Yormum), Jonathan David (Keller), Peter Craze (Servalan's assistant), Michael Gaunt (Computer)

Opening Shot: Sand.

You Just Described the Story:

Chasgo: It's mostly sand, right?

Random Insult:

Servalan's Assistant: That pig Reeve. Yes, pig! No, pig! I hate this planet.

In A Nutshell: Sand.

Story: Virn is a very sandy planet. Five years ago, a Federation research team disappeared there and Servalan is bored enough to find out why. On arrival, her ship is disabled but she's been followed by the *Scorpio* crew, who teleport Tarrant and Dayna down for a nosey. Things look up a little for Servalan when she becomes trapped with Tarrant. Eeek.

Information:

This episode features some Sand.

Evil Sand.

Evil *Vampire* Sand.

This is the episode that is referred to by the general public as, "Oh, that one, you know, the one with the sand".

The planet is called Virn. Unfortunately, this sounds exactly the same as Vern. If they were going to name the planet after a bloke, they may as well have called it Sandy and had done with it.

The structure of this episode is a new one for *Blake's 7* – Servalan plays the lead throughout. Does anyone think that Tanith Lee wanted to write for a female lead but found Dayna and Soolin too boring?

Soolin is lovely though.

Stephen Yardley is dressed in silver because he is a Space Man.

The crew all drink RED here. Vila gets well-oiled.

After four years, Servalan gets a history, and a background. She's genuinely unnerved throughout, a different Servalan who feels things. Mainly Tarrant.

If you look closely during the spaceship scenes, you can see Servalan clutching her bucket and spade.

The planet exteriors are shot in-studio but on film, providing them with an effective new style for the programme. Given that it's a Tanith Lee script, all the lighting is green and purple.

Servalan isn't dressed for Virn. Not sure what she is dressed for, really.

Dayna's very sure of her marksmanship skills: four bullets for four enemies. Luckily for her, she's injured before her bizarre confidence has to take a battering for the umpteenth time.

Servalan can make a noise like a chimp.

Why does nobody notice sand on *Scorpio*'s controls and all over the floor? If Jenna was still around she'd have spotted it and hoovered it up in a space trice.

Jacqueline Pearce gives probably the best performance of her tenure on the series, possibly because some elements of the story are based on her own life.

Panthers don't have silver talons, Tarrant, you idiot.

There's a great moment to look out for in this story – watch out for the bit with the sand.

The sand can not only suck the cellular energy from living beings, it can also preserve them, get around the place (presumably on little wheels made of sand) and affect computers, making them spout romantic nonsense for some inexplicable reason.

This is the only episode of *Blake's 7* to be both written and directed by women, which is probably why everyone spends their time all bleedin' emotional and crying and stuff.

Lee makes a nice attempt at linking the events on *Scorpio* to psi-powers left behind from her previous script, "Sarcophagus".

The computer on Virn base produces this string of similar-sounding words: 'Keller. Colour. Cooler. Killer. Calor. Choler.' It's like we're eavesdropping on Terry Nation brainstorming a character name.

The sand can be destroyed by liquid, which is unfortunate since it's piss-yourself-scary.

Closing Shot: Servalan's face.

Delightful Dialogue:

Servalan: There is something you should realise. There are no women like me. I am unique. That makes me rather dangerous.

Vila (drunk): Funny, aren't I? If I died, it'd be a real joke. Who'd care? Who cared about Cally?

Amateur Hour:

Servalan's ship is a bit boxy-looking.

There's a dodgy CSO shot of Servalan's ship landing.

Then there's the CSO shot of Reeve and Servalan walking across the surface of Virn, followed by a shot of them walking across the surface of Virn but on film.

Basically, the CSO in this fourth series is failing us.

It's unfortunate that the story is constructed as a mystery, at least through the characters' eyes. From our perspective, however, we know it's called "Sand", it's given away in the very first scene that sand is somehow causing the problems on the Federation base, and we see a character killed by sand within fifteen minutes. It's as much of a mystery as an opened packet of crisps.

ADDITIONAL SCRAPS OF KNOWLEDGE

Planets: Virn.

Space-isms: Percussion bullets.

Death Knell of an Ill-Conceived Poster Magazine: See below.

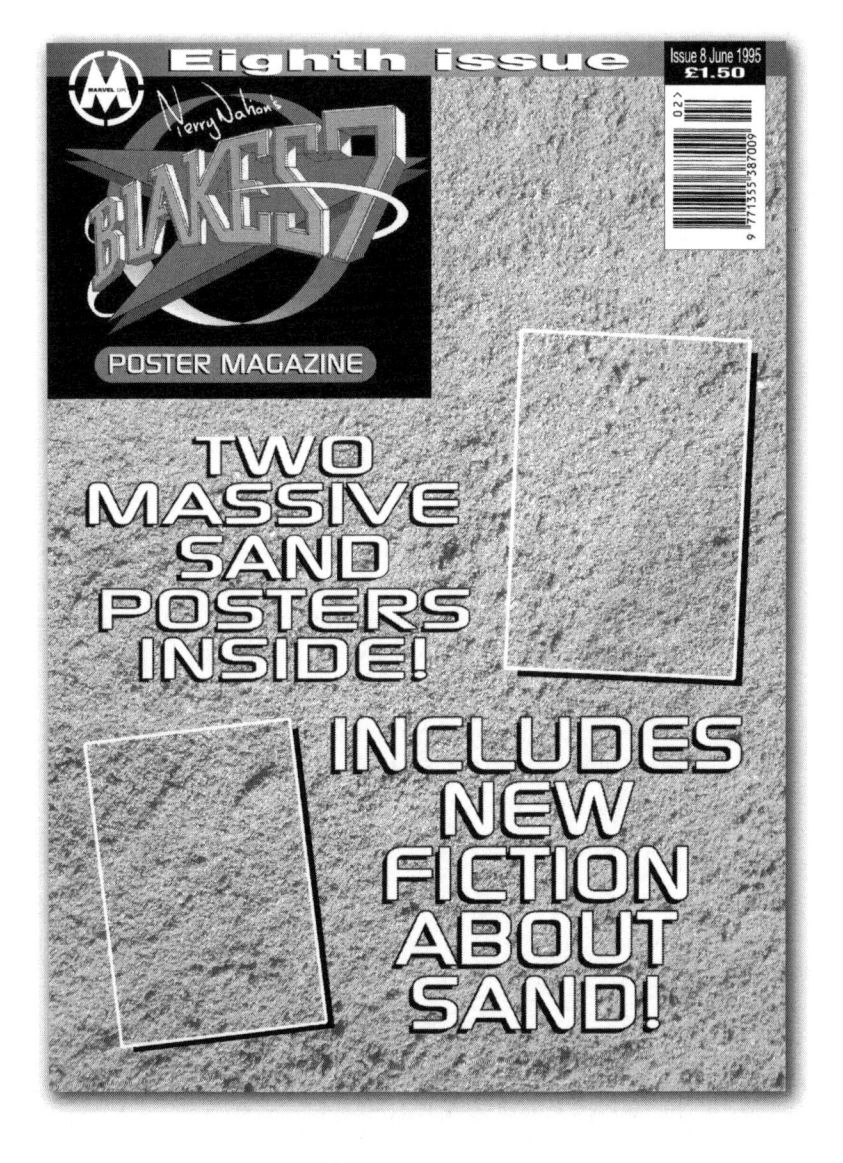

61 GOLD

Writer: Colin Davis   **Director**: Brian Lighthill

Guest Stars: Roy Kinnear (Keiller), Anthony Brown (Doctor), Ralph Fiennes (Kinglord), Stuart Organ (Robson), Dinah May (Woman Passenger), Norman Hartley (Pilot)

Opening Shot: The *Space Princess* flies left-to-right across the scene in a pretty good model shot, followed by some pretty ropey ones of *Scorpio*. Oh well, can't have everything.

You Just Described the Story:
Keiller: They don't eat the passengers' food so they're not drugged. And they're rotten actors.

Random Insult:
Soolin: I dislike greedy men, Keiller.

In A Nutshell: Bank job.

Story: Keiller, an old friend of Avon's, is currently operating a gold run for the Federation in the guise of a pleasure cruiser. He contacts Avon and the crew of *Scorpio* with a view to a heist. Avon agrees, and an elaborate plan is formed. While the plan goes off without a hitch, it ultimately transpires that Servalan was behind it all. Not only that, but having escaped with the money, Avon is informed by Orac that it is now worthless, as the bank has closed. Then dinosaurs rip through the walls of *Scorpio* and eat the crew.

Information:
For this episode only, the vocal version of the theme tune (sung by Steven Pacey with lyrics by Vere Lorrimer) was used. However, it was only retained on copies sent for international broadcast.

The sliding airlock door and catch would later be seen on the *Blue Midge*t hatch of *Red Dwarf*. It's such a shame that the CSO is so bad this season, the model work is absolutely terrific.

Soolin looks particularly lovely in this episode. And then she frisks Keiller. <sigh>

Where the hell did Avon and Keiller originally meet? Avon doesn't strike one as a chummy, friendly sort.

The doors of the *Space Princess* sound like they are having some sort of orgasm when opening and closing. Very odd indeed.

Roy Kinnear is quite terrific in this episode.

Zerok isn't the gold planet. The gold planet is Voga, surely?

Avon doesn't blink for the first 9 minutes.

Keiller puts his arm around Soolin and cops a feel. <sigh>

Oh! He's just done it again.

Soolin's earrings are identical to those worn by Servalan in "Project Avalon". Given that Glynis Barber also appeared in "Project Avalon", it's reasonable to assume she nicked the earrings.

Vila calls the teleport 'a teleporter'.

Keiller's discreet outfit for breaking into a high-security Federation gold-processing plant is identical to his usual garb. In other words, a bright red jacket and trousers with sparkling gold detail.

Unusual effort has gone into the production design with the red star motif on the *Space Princess* and the ZVP logo appearing through Zerok. However, it's still just another gasworks with a payphone.

Our freedom fighters are never more ruthless than when breaking into the Zerok processing plant. This is after all just a company dealing with the Federation, and yet Avon and Soolin gun down employees on their way in like there's no tomorrow. Are they really freedom fighters anymore? Or are they just criminals?

The radiation in the Zerok processing plant is 'On'.

Is there anything camper than Avon and Soolin standing back-to-back in the corridor at 18m 20s?

Soolin even looks good in a Zerok silver jumpsuit.

The pink spinning cube acting as Keiller's recording device has previously been seen in *Z Cars*.

We wish Steven Pacey had employed his drugged-acting technique for his entire run in *Blake's 7*. We might have liked Tarrant more if he had.

Poor Roy Kinnear really has to sell those Killers, being as they are pencil shavings sprayed silver.

Crikey, the body count is rather high in this episode isn't it?

Tarrant and Soolin's sudden preachy attitude to Keiller for shooting the ship's doctor is rather at odds with their bloodlust elsewhere in the story.

In the quarry scenes at the end, Jacqueline Pearce recorded all her angles six weeks prior to the rest of the cast, owing to a holiday she'd booked in Monmouthshire.

Wouldn't you have at least tried to pay Soolin 2 billion credits for a quick feel before the truth was revealed?

Orac does a little laugh near the end of the episode when he explains that Zerok has ceded to the Federation.

Closing Shot: Avon cackling like a demented idiot as money flutters to the ground all around him.

Delightful Dialogue:
Soolin: Something useful?
Avon: Guns.
Soolin: Something useful.

Vila (after teleporting Avon back on board within inches of the airlock seal opening): Did you get the gold?

Amateur Hour:
Dialogue is inaudible during the dolly-left in the first scene on Scorpio's flight deck; the actors seem to be trying to out-stamp each other during the shot.

One of the guards falling from the ladder when Dayna's explosive goes off hits the camera.

Tarrant's teleport bracelet has vanished when he and Dayna find the unconscious Keeler.

Yes, those are plastic TV dinner trays surrounding the doorways on the *Space Princess*.

ADDITIONAL SCRAPS OF KNOWLEDGE

Planets: Zerok, Pyrrus, Beta 5 in the Ark Rough Bennett Complex.

Space-isms: Stardust blizzard fields, subneutronic overlap shift, exobriddium addiction, *Space Princess*.

Below: To celebrate the 38th anniversary of the series in 2016, toy manufacturer Funko released Keiller as a Pop Vinyl figure in their *Blake's 7* range. The publicity literature suggests it is 'the first of thousands' and that Clonemaster Fen from "Weapon" will follow in December.

62 ORBIT

Writer: Robert Holmes **Director**: Brian Lighthill

Guest Stars: John Savident (Egrorian), Larry Noble (Pinder)

Opening Shot: *Scorpio* approaches a blue ball.

You Just Described the Story:
Vila: You know I like to stick with you, Avon. Where it's safe.

Random Insult:
Vila: Soolin, the only thing you ever grasped was a gun – do you want to get brain damage?

Random Money-Spending Fantasy:
Vila: I'll have an imperial palace, with solid diamond floors, and a bodyguard of a thousand hand-picked virgins in red fur uniforms. Vila's Royal Mounties.

In A Nutshell: Holmes + ($b7$ x S4) + (Noble x Savident) = Happiness ≈ ∞

Story: Egrorian, a colossal sadist, pervert and genius, contacts Avon with a view to selling him a funnel. Avon, while suspicious, is amenable to meeting him. He and Vila are transported via shuttle to Egrorian's base. An exchange is agreed upon whereby they'll swap Orac for the funnel. However, Avon not only suspects a double-cross but has planned his own triple-cross with a handy fake Orac. He's proved right, as Egrorian is working for Servalan. Avon and Vila are trapped in a shuttle which doesn't have enough lift to reach… ORBIT!

Information:
This episode's opening titles were 10 seconds shorter than the rest of the season's, owing to the length of the script. This was 'restored' for the DVD but remains on the original VHS release.

As usual with *Blake's 7*, the model of Egrorian's base looks great at a distance, so why zoom in on it?

The role of Egrorian was originally offered to Nicholas Courtney and then to James Bolam, who suggested John Savident, having been in a production of *Much Ado About Nothing* with him at the National Theatre.

Avon is using Tarrant as he's disposable and, brilliantly, tells the rest of the crew this. They all hate Tarrant.

Avon speaking with Egrorian over the communicator is absurd, ridiculous, stupid and sublime.

Soolin looks particularly lovely this week.

It's surprising how much effort the production team go to to replace the *Liberator* teleport with the same device on *Scorpio* when most writers in Season R render it useless or impractical. Holmes does so here and it's to the benefit of his plot.

Egrorian's video transmit is only 8bit. This casts doubt on the quality of his Tachyon Funnel.

Isn't Pinder cute? He's really only a callow youth of 28, you know. He 'aged 50 years in as many seconds' when he was exposed to Hofel's Radiation and used to be Egrorian's 'golden-haired stripling'.

When he puts his feet up in the shuttle, Avon has chewing gum on the sole of his boot. Probably Orbit.

Was it Savident, the director or the script that suggested Egrorian be played the way he is? Probably Savident, since the lines themselves are relatively straightforward.

'Red is dead, green is clean.' Road safety advice like this should've been tied into Sally Knyvette's TV campaign (see page 284).

The Tachyon Funnel, sadly, is one of those irritating science fiction conceits which are illogical and impractical, much like IMIPAK.

The tissue in Egrorian's top pocket comes and goes between shots.

Egrorian is just plain nasty. He's a proper sadist and treats Pinder with utter contempt.

Awww... poor Pinder's face when Egrorian flirts with Vila...

Tarrant, Dayna and Soolin do nothing in this episode.

Does anyone else find it odd that Pinder vanishes? It serves no narrative purpose, but Vila says 'He's gone for a lie down' in a very specific way.

The fake Orac is just an irate wasp in a fish tank.

You can nearly see Servalan's right knocker when Egrorian's holding her hand.

Jacqueline Pearce is just *magnificent*. Her eye-rolling reactions when Egrorian flirts with her are exquisite.

Avon, by chance, made a replica of Orac a few months back. What are the odds? And when did he find time? Does he have a little shed out the back of Xenon Base that he tinkers about in when he's supposed to be doing the washing-up?

Servalan's dress has now had two silver straps added to stop her knockers poking out.

Servalan and Egrorian drink some TURQUOISE. This is presumably what happens to GREEN after it's been reconstituted repeatedly over eight years.

Oh wow. Orac's 'Vila weighs 73 kilos, Avon' is a moment to behold in the series as a whole. Suddenly, a very silly, very comical episode becomes a horrible descent into madness. This is of course Robert Holmes' forte.

Keating and Darrow excel. Name any other prime time series where the main hero would act this way.

Yay! Pinder's gone rogue! And suddenly all the guest cast are dead. Again. As usual.

Soolin looks particularly lovely as she listens to Avon's account of what's just happened.

Vila rightfully has the hump with Avon by the end, although that little weasel Orac is equally to blame if you ask us.

Closing Shot: Avon declaring 'You know you are safe with me.'

Delightful Dialogue:

Every last line in the script. Even the the commas are harmonious. However, some highlights include:

Avon: How can he tell the king from the queen?

Egrorian: (to Avon) Natural leaders are rarely encumbered with intelligence. Greed, egotism, animal cunning, and viciousness are the important attributes. Qualities I detect in you in admirably full measure.

Vila: (to Avon) Listen, if it'll set your mind at rest, I never thought you were a woman.

Pinder: I'm pleased to make your acquaintance, ma'am.
Vila: (to Avon) I think he's talking to you.

Egrorian: They'll be jellifi-ha-ha-haa-haah-haahe-hee-hhii-hiied-hhee-hee-hee-hee …

Vila: It's a trip I won't forget, Avon.

Amateur Hour:

The little toy truck used to push the dark matter around is a bit crap. And what the hell is it doing on the shuttle anyway?

The Tacyhon Funnel destroys planets with a pink video wipe.

There's no expense spared on Servalan's office set. Nor budget.

Not one of these matters – the script and performances are exquisite.

ADDITIONAL SCRAPS OF KNOWLEDGE

Planets: Malodar, Prophyrus.

Space-isms: The Space Institute, Hofel's Radiation, the Egrorian theory of parallel matter, video transmitter.

Important Fact: This is the finest episode of *Blake's 7* you are ever likely to see.

63 WARLORD

Writer: Simon Masters **Director**: Viktors Ritelis

Guest Stars: Roy Boyd (Zukan), Bobbie Brown (Zeeona), Dean Harris (Finn), Simon Merrick (Boorva), Rick James (Chalsa), Charles Augins (Lod), Brian Spink (Mida)

Opening Shot: Lots of smoke and a badly overlaid countdown caption.

You Just Described the Story:
Avon: Then are we all friends here, with one common enemy?

Random Insult:
Soolin (to Avon): But you lie so well.

In A Nutshell: Avon decides the time has come to act completely out of character.

Story: In a remarkable act of unprecedented botherance, Avon calls a meeting between the five most powerful factions in opposition to the Federation. Unfortunately, trust in the group is minimal, and it's not difficult for Servalan to throw a spanner in their works. She lays a trap using Zukan, one of the delegates, but unknown to Zukan, he has put his daughter Zeeona's life in danger. And Tarrant rather likes Zeeona.

Information:
Yes, that is Charles 'Queeg 500' Augins you can see there – the links between *Blake's 7* and *Red Dwarf* are numerous, even if we hardly ever mention them and prefer to shoehorn in references to *Doctor Who* as much as possible instead. Augins is a choreographer and went on to work with *Star Trek: The Next Generation*'s Gates McFadden on the musical *Labyrinth* starring Derek Bowie.

When there's no more room in hell, the pacified colonists will walk the escalators of a redressed shopping centre in Guildford.

Why on earth would Avon be calling meetings? That's probably a consequence of importing many new writers and directors into the series.

The leaders Avon has summoned look ridiculous. He must have stressed fancy dress on the invites. Rick James in particular seems uncomfortable in his outfit, toying with it like a child.

Zukan's salute was adapted for use in the *Doctor Who* story "Paradise Towers" as the Kang's 'How you do' ceremony.

After the previous two stories and their strides forward, we seem to have taken several leaps back. We're in a bad sci-fi rut here, with clichés spilling forth all around.

Glynis Barber was so taken with Zeeona's hair that she used it herself for *Dempsey and Makepeace* two years later.

We could write anything here and it wouldn't matter. This story is so dull you'll have switched it off by now. Look, we'll prove it: the Gingerbread Men hold off Avon and the others with their candyfloss guns in the house made of sweeties.

See.

If you're going to show the floor of Xenon Base, Ritelis, at least scrape the gum off it first.

Soolin looks particularly lovely in this episode.

"Warlord" features the final appearance of Servalan, and we don't think that she's used particularly well. A poor end for one of telefantasy's most distinctive villains.

Why do the goblets produce sparks of electricity when they are touched together?

Zukan: 'There are times when I miss the darkness.' Close your eyes then.

Who waters the plants on Xenon base? Were Cally alive, it's conceivable it would be her. But the current crew just don't seem like plant people. One hopes there's a rota, as this would mean once every six weeks Avon must potter around with a little watering can.

When Dayna opens the champagne bottle, the cork hits Rick James in the side of the head. If you look closely, you can see him wince throughout the rest of the scene.

Only twenty-three minutes in and bored bored bored.

Oh hang on, some excitement! A bomb!

Now just a minute ... the bomb goes off in Tarrant's face and brings down half the planet, so why does he not even have a hair out of place?

When Dayna and Vila are looking at the console screen, one of the messages is 'smeti wen'. Answers on a postcard please.

Soolin looks particularly lovely on location.

Cor! Soolin's pulled a fast one on Avon. She looks particularly lovely when pulling a fast one.

Soolin and Avon opt to wear incredibly peculiar suits while flying Zeeona home.

The damage report display on Xenon Base reveals life support is 'damaged' and water supply is 'slightly damaged'. That doesn't bode well for the plants.

Dayna: 'We've got Channel 5.' So, it's a steady diet of sharks and Nazis for now then.

Vila gets drunk again. In this case it's probably justified.

It took fifty switches to turn the life support off and four to turn it on. We can't decide if the system is flawed or brilliant.

Closing Shot: Dayna picks up Zeeona's glove and says 'She took her glove off', which is a clear indicator of just how utterly tedious this fifty minutes really is.

Delightful Dialogue:
Vila: Avon's idea of diplomacy is like breaking someone's leg and then saying 'Lean on me.'

Zukan: I see my bad dreams in other people's eyes.

Amateur Hour:
It's mostly bad. We admire Viktors Ritelis for such a rebellious attitude and it would be unfair to bang on about the flaws here. Not that it stopped us.

ADDITIONAL SCRAPS OF KNOWLEDGE

Planets: Paedophile, Serrus, Herriol, Sentha, Tarl, Komm.

Space-isms: Space Gingerbread.

Related Merchandise: Having previously produced jigsaw puzzles for Season M, Hestair Puzzles approached the production office with a view to creating a new range for the 1981 Christmas market. The first, a 240-piece puzzle depicting Zukan, was released in late October and sold so poorly that another eighteen planned jigsaws were immediately junked. A total of fifteen Season R puzzles were purchased and are thought to have been snapped up by Zukan actor Roy Boyd as christening gifts.

64 BLAKE

Writer: Chris Boucher   **Director**: Mary Ridge

Guest Stars: Gareth Thomas (Blake), David Collings (Deva), Matthew Waterhouse (Ilkan the Mercenary), Sasha Mitchell (Arlen), Janet Lees-Price (Klyn)

Opening Shot: That oh-so-gorgeous model shot of *Scorpio* preparing for take off. Savour it one last time.

You Just Described the Story:
Tarrant: We're running out of options.

Random Insult:
Avon: Stick to the distress beacon, Orac. When I want your impersonation of a pain I will let you know.

In A Nutshell: Out with a bang, not a whimper.

Story: Having fled Xenon Base, Avon reveals that he thinks he knows where Blake is. He's right: Blake's on Gauda Prime and pretending to be a bounty hunter in order to recruit a new crew. Reaching the planet, *Scorpio* is gunned out of orbit and crashes; everyone but Tarrant has already teleported to the surface. Unfortunately, because Tarrant doesn't know what Blake looks like, he misunderstands the situation and tells Avon that Blake has betrayed them to the Federation. Avon reacts badly to the news.

Information:
This is the final episode of *Blake's 7* and was originally broadcast on Monday 21st December, 1981. Happy Christmas.

Everything goes wrong here.

Nice to see a bit of Soolin's background sketched out – shame that it's all in the last episode. We learn more about her here than we have done in the previous ~~twelve~~ ~~sixteen~~ ~~fourteen~~ few episodes.

Orac is either strapped down or covered in plasters after half of Xenon Base fell on him last week.

Blake is presented as a hardened, bitter individual, tired of the fight. It's quite a surprise to see him apparently acting as a bounty hunter, as this seems slightly out of character for our hero. He is even prepared to kill his fellow bounty hunters.

We still can't quite believe that Avon saw Zukan as a figurehead for his rebel alliance. I mean, he was no Blake, was he? Not with that hair.

According to Soolin, Gauda Prime – or 'GP' – is a 'draw for every crook and killer in the quadrant'.

They're really bigging up just how bad Gauda Prime is – there's going to be some serious trouble later we reckon.

Scorpio's under attack from SIMON.

We love the bit when Orac gets narky with Slave. It's the last time that they ever speak to each other because… *<sniff>*… *<sniff>*… Slave DIES!

Tarrant's self-sacrifice in piloting the ship while the others escape still isn't enough reason to like him.

The shots of *Scorpio* grounding are straight out of *Thunderbird*s in all the best ways.

So is that it? Tarrant's dead now? A Wilhelm Scream would have made it so much more satisfying.

Oh, hang on – damn – he's still alive. Someone looks determined to finish the job though. That's us in that Hopper shooting at him.

Blake and Tarrant, together at last. That's the most perm ever seen on British television.

We learn from Blake what happened to Jenna: she's fine.

It's nice to see Vila at least trying to be brave when the end comes.

All the more reason to hate Tarrant – his willingness to act first and worry about facts later is the reason everyone dies. Utter, utter stupid, stupid bastardy bastard. Tarrant is the catalyst for everything going to shit.

Even today, Avon's shooting of Blake is heartbreaking.

Not bothered about Tarrant though.

Closing Shot: {SPOILER}

Delightful Dialogue:
Avon: Have YOU betrayed ME?

Amateur Hour:
No. All six of us have viewed this episode more times than we'd care to mention and still it just flies at such a rate you'd think it was only twenty minutes. Season R is a real builder and it's all leading up to this. Nothing about this is amateur.

Well, maybe Arlen.

ADDITIONAL SCRAPS OF KNOWLEDGE

Planets: Gauda Prime.

Space-isms: Space Flyer, Space Hopper, E-Space, Marshmen, river fruit.

Quarterly Performance Management Review: *Avon:* The fire was stupid. Putting Vila on guard was suicidal. What's the matter, is staying alive too complicated for you?

Tarrant Mitigation Techniques:
No need. He's dead. Hurrah! But that's barely enough for us.

The episode guide stops here because, well, there aren't any more episodes, everyone's dead, and it's ALL HIS FAULT.

(Disclaimer: we do quite like Steven Pacey)

OTHER WORLDS

BLAKE'S 7 - FILM TREATMENT #1

In 1980, shortly before the surprise announcement of a fourth series during the closing credits of the Season P finale "Terminal", the BBC began negotiations with Terry Nation and new film production house Visual Elements.

Visual Elements had been founded in 1976 by Birmingham-based writer/director Frank Lennon as a means to getting his short films about poverty to a wider audience. Joining forces with James Spencer, always referred to as 'the money' behind the operation, the pair embarked on a series of thirty-seven ten-minute films about people living within limited means in the UK, US and Australia. Even though the films were more of a critical than financial success, Spencer and Lennon found themselves besieged with offers from industry types to produce a full-length feature for a broader audience and wider commercial gain.

While Spencer was keen to follow this path, Lennon was more dismissive but could see that the benefits would allow him to complete the short films he *did* want to make. Speaking in 1977 to a journalist from *The Telegraph*, he said:

'... there comes a time when you have to realise that art and commerce are unique entities. Anything worthy as art is unlikely to attract financial success, while anything of commercial value is unlikely to have any real artistic merit. If Visual Elements was to succeed as a viable company, it would have to produce titles which challenged our founding integrities. In other words, I sold my soul to some extent.'

Lennon was referring to the three films first distributed by Visual Elements – *Invitation to Supper*, *Fear of Flying* and *Butter Side Up* – all released in January 1978 on a rotating distribution, which meant each exhibitor passed the viewed print onto the next cinema, allowing each house to receive a fresh audience each week. The films were an uncomfortable mix of the two genres Spencer had identified as being most popular at the time: sex comedy and horror. While commercially very successful (each film more than quadrupled its budget within the month of January through ticket sales), the films were critically slated and considered by many to be misogynistic, in bad taste and thoroughly irredeemable.

This critical fallout led to a heated and very public exchange of words between Spencer and Lennon, with Lennon ultimately taking out a full-page advertisement in the tabloid newspaper the *Sun* that simply read 'Judas Spencer'. It created a great deal of confusion for the newspaper's regular readers and was still being mentioned in their letters pages some five months later.

In 1979, having finally settled their differences, Visual Elements was once again in production, and their film *Whites of the Egg*, about sperm, became a huge hit, making them once again a fairly hot industry property.

It was during the premiere of the film in London's Leicester Square that Spencer struck up a friendship with Edith Lens, who at the time was working for the BBC. Spencer asked her if there were any popular TV properties which would be good for a big screen adaptation, and Lens, fully aware that *Blake's 7* was about to end on its third series, suggested a follow-up or remake of the show as being the most viable.

Lens arranged for Spencer, Terry Nation and Lennon to meet and discuss the idea. Through an unfortunate series of events, this meeting eventually had to take place at a Happy Eater on the M25, all roads into London having been closed off. Nation, jetlagged after his arrival from the US, was reportedly agitated and contrary throughout the meeting, and Spencer left feeling it had been a disaster. He wrote in his diary that evening:

'Terry Nation has a wonderful reputation within the industry, but seeing him hurl a bun at a waitress for calling him "sir" – and then taking a fistful of complimentary lollies to make up for it – made him seem, to me at least, a little aggressive.'

Nation always denied this happened and Lennon refused to comment.

So, it was with some surprise that Lennon received a call from Spencer on a January morning in 1980, asking him to prepare a script treatment for a film production of *Blake's 7*.

Lennon's main problem with this was that he had never seen an episode of *Blake's 7*, refusing as he did to own a television set, and wasn't lying when he once said he 'spent Monday evenings staring through the window of Rumbelows watching episodes go out live'. On the evening of 7 January, he viewed the Season R premiere story "Aftermath" with only the sound of traffic to accompany it. Even without dialogue, he recognised the power of the imagery and became obsessed with the notion of a mythical leader, absent from the programme but clearly present in the title of the series.

Lennon's initial draft was delivered on 1 March 1980, shortly after transmission of "Rumours of Death". Indeed, his script is subtitled "Rumour of Death". The script was held by the BBC for nearly six months before any further talks occurred, during which time Spencer continually tried to contact Lens, unaware that she had left the BBC and moved to Granada.

The BBC ultimately turned down Lennon's script. In spite of protestations from Spencer, and pleas to allow them to submit a second revised proposal, the BBC closed negotiations because a new and more exciting film offer had been submitted (more on that in the next chapter).

In the meantime, Lennon's scene breakdown is presented here in all its glory. We are grateful to Mary Lennon for allowing us access to her late husband's paperwork. Since his death in 1993, Lennon's office door had been locked. We were the first, and sadly the last, to be allowed access again, as the offices at the South London address burned down just a day after we were present.

THE BLAKES SEVEN - RUMOUR OF DEATH

By FRANK LENNON

01/   BLAKE as God surveys the world from heaven. HE

watches the human race crawl about like insects in their filth and squalor. HE snaps his fingers and rain falls; he snaps them again and thunder claps. He is a playful God.

02/ KERR AVON wakes from sleeping to see an image of the God Blake hovering, bathed in white light at the end of his bed. God Blake tells Avon he must change the world and release those in shackles. KERR AVON kneels to his God and promises to do his lord's work.

03/ KERR AVON rescues a criminal from execution. VILA, a thief, is about to be put to death. First his hand is cut off. Then his other hand. Then his foot. Then his other foot. After his first eye is burned out of its socket KERR AVON steps in and asks the executioner to put down this EYE-LASER. KERR AVON takes VILA by the elbow and leads him to LIBERATION, a spaceship he has built for when the flood happens.

04/ KERR AVON next collects a space warrior called TARRONT whom he finds drunk and sitting in his own filth. TARRONT has lost all dignity and self-respect. KERR AVON tries to offer him something to believe in but TARRONT does not listen. KERR AVON calls on the Blake God to speak to TARRONT which he does and so TARRONT goes with KERR AVON.

05/ VILA learns to pick a lock with his tongue.

06/ KERR AVON receives a telepathic distress call from a young android girl called CALLY who wants him to bring her food, water and books so that she is no longer hungry, thirsty and bored. KERR AVON does this but only takes her one book: a LIBERATION flight manual. CALLY agrees to join his crew.

07/ KERR AVON picks up ORAC and DAYNA from a clone bank. ORAC is a super-clever genetically enhanced boy of 12 wearing just underwear and stained with coal dust. DAYNA is his adopted mother and she calls him COALBOY rather than ORAC.

08/ GOD-BLAKE is watching from the heavens and laughing at how stupid such tiny creatures can be because GOD isn't nice.

09/ TRAVIS flies the spaceship THE SERVALAN into a sun to retrieve HOT-ROCKS which can be used to bring the human race under his control. He snarls threats at his vampire crew when they get stuff wrong like: "Stupid vampire girl!" and "Blood-drinking bitch".

10/ AVON has created the PEACE SHIELD for THE LIBERATION which can be deployed at any point during a battle thereby ending it very peacefully. DAYNA makes special new guns which can be fired only if the person using the gun has peaceful intentions. They all pray to GOD-BLAKE before attacking the space station STARONE 1.

11/ While the others fight, KERR AVON must fight TRAVIS alone in a duel to the death. As TRAVIS wrestles KER AVON'S gun from him and tries to fire the gun backfires because TRAVIS' intentions are not peaceful. TRAVIS explodes, his face splits apart to reveal a dying GOD-BLAKE.

12/ Without the GOD-BLAKE to keep balance and control in the universe it ends.

© Frank Lennon, Visual Elements Ltd 1980

BLAKE'S 7 - FILM TREATMENT #2

By 1983, director John Boorman's career was riding high on the critical and commercial success of *Excalibur*, his retelling of the legend of King Arthur. Boorman had endured a difficult creative period during the mid- to-late 1970s when, buoyed by the international success of *Deliverance*, he was handed complete creative control over his next venture. The result was the 1974 film *Zardoz*.

At its core, *Zardoz* is a compelling story of an oppressive establishment and one man's journey from willing enforcer to revolutionary. However, while the central idea for *Zardoz* is sound, the execution is hailed by many as over-indulgent, confusing, and in many places simply ridiculous. Although there are a great many powerful images and themes within *Zardoz*, they are overshadowed for all but the most liberal-minded filmgoer by the decision to dress star Sean Connery in a nappy, braces, thigh-length boots and a ponytail for much of the film.

With its confusing mix of art-house, blockbuster and just plain strangeness, *Zardoz* received a mixed reception on release. Critic Roger Ebert called the film 'an exercise in self-indulgence', and even today it remains a film which starkly divides opinion. While Film4 recently hailed it as a forgotten gem, the wider consensus is that even among the pantheon of films which are so bad they're good, *Zardoz* is more the former than latter.

The film flopped at the box office. Boorman's career, which had showed such great promise with work like *Point Blank* and *Deliverance*, entered a fallow period. His only notable work for the remainder of the decade was as a journeyman director on *Exorcist II: The Heretic*, another film which failed to set the box office alight.

But the vision and execution of Boorman's 1982 film *Excalibur* struck a nerve with filmgoers and critics alike. The film opened at number one and went on to become the 18th highest-grossing movie of 1982 in the US.

Boorman found himself returning to his roots, settling for a time first in Ireland and later in the UK as he gathered his forces for his next project.

Once again based in his native Shepperton, Boorman became reacquainted with Steven Pinder. Pinder, a former BBC Documentary Unit alumnus like Boorman himself, had been supplementing his income in recent years with work as an extra in a number of projects, including *Blake's 7*.

Pinder had an enthusiasm for the series which proved infectious, and Boorman, on viewing several episodes, was drawn to what he saw as a highly moral play about the nature of good versus evil and man's ability to both revere and revile his fellow man, themes which had played strongly in all of Boorman's work up to this point. The experience of *Zardoz* was still relatively fresh, but armed with a decade's filmmaking experience, and with an older, wiser pair of eyes, the prospect of re-treading the themes laid out in the earlier film (without becoming a remake *per se*) became increasingly attractive. Besides, *Blake's 7* had only been away from our screens for a few years and enjoyed a loyal and sizeable audience.

However, it was the discovery that *Blake's 7* had been created by another contact from his days with the BBC that prompted Boorman to seriously consider a big-screen adaptation as his next project.

Terry Nation had worked briefly with Boorman in the early 1960s, when he was a scriptwriter for Tony Hancock. Boorman, a long-time admirer of Hancock's work, had approached Nation as a potential subject for one of his landmark *Citizen 63* documentaries – a series of self-contained profiles of people from every walk of British life. A study of the man behind Hancock, the biggest name in entertainment at the time, would have been a sure-fire ratings grabber, but Nation was working out his contract with ATV at the time and had been unable to take part. Ironically, had the series been *Citizen 64*, Nation would have been able to participate, and his success as creator of *Doctor Who*'s Daleks would have guaranteed the series even bigger audiences.

Boorman and Nation, it seemed, shared not only a love for comedy but also very similar views on the driving force behind *Blake's 7*, and the pair latched onto a particularly rich seam of drama in the increasingly messianic nature of Blake himself, particularly in the series' third season. A script was hastily commissioned, and, for a while at least, it seemed certain that the story of Blake would receive blockbuster treatment.

Boorman held the view that *Blake's 7* was the perfect vehicle for him to build on his earlier story of one man's place in society, and the duality in the nature of some of the programme's leading characters opened up what he saw as a fascinating means of telling that story. Boorman's own love of mysticism and folklore enabled him to weave into Nation's ideas a far more heroic Blake than we saw on television.

The initial draft of Boorman's script was received very positively by all concerned, particularly Nation, who was inspired to contribute more than the initial storyline of a freedom fighter and his band of rebels. The pair collaborated on a second draft that played up the messianic tone even further, almost totally excluding the other main characters. Avon, Vila and the rest of the crew became little more than acolytes, but the story continued to impress the BBC team. They felt the story was sensitive to the roots of the TV series but had enough originality to get people into cinemas. British cinema was still looking for a film to emulate the success of *Star Wars*, and despite a clutch of notable fantasy and SF films in the early 1980s (not least Boorman's own *Excalibur*), the time was right for a sweeping space-opera which told the simple story of good versus evil.

But the success of Boorman's *Excalibur* became a juggernaut, eclipsing any small-scale ambitions he might have had. International studios were courting Boorman with increasingly attractive deals, none more so than 20th Century Fox, distributors of the *Star Wars* franchise and Boorman's own *Zardoz*. Fox were keen to avoid any potential dilution of the final entry in George Lucas's epic saga, due for release that same year, but also recognised that in Boorman they had a filmmaker with an ability to emulate the success of *Excalibur* in the SF genre. In what history has proven to be a golden handcuffs deal, Boorman's script was taken off the table and he moved to Fox, working as producer on a number of projects. Keen to return to his first love of directing, however, he left Fox as soon as his contract expired and went on to write and direct *Hope and Glory*, a lower-budget, semi-autobiographical tale.

Boorman's *Blake's 7* remains a lost gem and we are proud to print here, for the first time, the initial treatment for the proposed film.

BLAKE'S SEVEN

by John Boorman, based on an idea by Terry Nation

1. EARTH – a global industrial complex, the powerhouse of the GALACTIC FEDERATION, fuelled by a population reduced to the status of drones. Like insects, they toil without thought or care for anything apart from the next rest period, the next meal. The human race, reduced to mindless animals for the glorification of a wealthy elite.

2. The star ship LIBERATOR streaks towards the planet's surface out of a leaden, smog-filled sky. It unleashes a salvo of missiles, raining death and destruction on the Federation. Inside, AVON, JENNA, VILA and TARRANT move as one, evading Federation defences, outmanoeuvring the fighters sent to destroy them, all under the watchful gaze of their leader BLAKE. Then, as swiftly as they came, they are gone.

3. Federation Command - the evil SERVALAN and her inner sanctum argue fiercely about the damage wreaked by BLAKE. The legend grows: BLAKE is hailed as a messiah by some colonies, his impact is so profound, his ability to escape the iron fist of the Federation so mysterious. For the first time people are looking heavenward with what, if left unchecked, can only be hope. The Federation must act.

4. Later, in his cabin, JENNA finds BLAKE alone and clearly stricken. He agonises over the responsibilities of leadership, of a civilisation looking to him for salvation. He has become god, but he's not even a man. How can a boy of 21 lead his

people into the light? JENNA comforts BLAKE, they embrace and, for the first time, they make love.

5. Flashback to young BLAKE as a child. He is sustained through the abuse and punishment of an enslaved childhood by the prophecy spoken by old GAN, the healer.
   In Mankind's darkest hour, when all hope is quashed, a hero would arise and unite the seven tribes of Earth, leading them into the light. And he shall be known by the sign of the seven. We zoom in on BLAKE's shoulder as he mounts JENNA; there we can see, plainly, a raised patch of skin, almost scar-like, in the shape of a 7.

6. BLAKE and the LIBERATOR execute increasingly daring but no less successful raids on Federation outposts, each with devastating results. Behind, the devastation is always the same - a blast pattern in the shape of a 7, visible from miles away. They are clinical, precise and as yet untouchable.

7. SERVALAN has located a secret weapon in the war against BLAKE. TRAVIS, BLAKE's own brother grew up in the shadow of BLAKE, sickened by the love and awe he inspired in those he touched. Driven insane with jealousy, his malevolence moulded him into the figure that now sits at SERVALAN's right hand.

8. Across the seven systems of the Federation the first seeds of rebellion are sown. Graffiti reading "BLAKE" appears first subtly then with greater confidence. People are beginning to push back against the system.

9. TRAVIS pursues BLAKE across the solar system, sullying the work done by his brother; erasing hope wherever it shows its first green shoots. Always one step behind, TRAVIS recalls the prophesy he heard so often as a child and the one part of the legend that keeps the coals of vengeance white hot in his black heart - Terminal. The final end.

10. The LIBERATOR touches down on an alien world, in need of urgent repairs and a far darker mission. Their last raid crippled the ship and killed JENNA. BLAKE has come to bury his lover and mourn her loss.

11. TRAVIS arrives during the funeral of JENNA and, his chance finally arrived, takes on BLAKE in a duel to the death. Both are killed. AVON, VILA and TARRANT are visited by a vision of BLAKE who tells them that the legend must go on if hope is to continue. They must all become BLAKE. BLAKE should not be a person; he should be an ideal, the symbol of hope for planets and systems everywhere.

12. AVON, VILA and TARRANT launch an all-out attack on Star One, taking their own lives but destroying SERVALAN and the very seat of Federation power. The reign of terror is not over but hope has become incarnate.13.
 In a future Federation society, we see young children laughing and playing with joy unbridled, a society of peace and happiness. United under one god....BLAKE

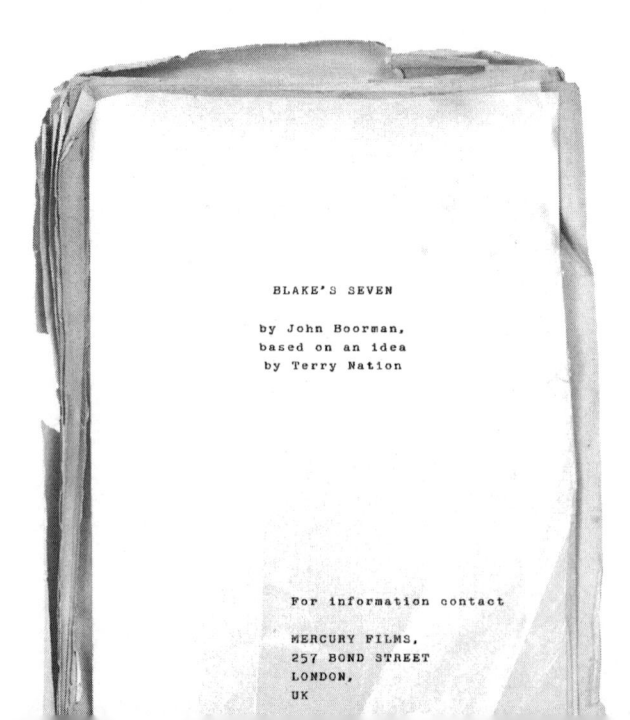

BLAKE'S SEVEN

by John Boorman,
based on an idea
by Terry Nation

For information contact

MERCURY FILMS,
257 BOND STREET
LONDON,
UK

THE JAPANESE REMAKE

Super Fun Oppression Squad

Blake's 7 was sold around the world by the BBC, but the Japanese put their own creative spin on the series by heavily re-editing each episode and inserting entirely new characters and scenes. Despite all the differences from the original series, Terry Nation was on board the Japanese version as 'Series Advisor', taking a 15% cut of the profits. Dudley Simpson's stirring score was replaced by a new one from aspiring video game composer Koji Kondo, while the opening titles were given an anime-style makeover.

The result, *Super Fun Oppression Squad*, removed all reference to the Federation, depicting Blake and his crew as a band of spacefaring hellraisers who travelled the universe destroying industrial buildings under the guidance of their new leader, Kon, a crude computer-generated character whose scheming monologues bookended every episode.

Jenna was voiced by an old man and portrayed as a bitter transvestite named ManWoman Jen. Gan, now known as 'Mr Gan', spoke like a baby. Blake's arch-nemesis, Travis, became Big Time High Collar Man.

Often, there were instances of human characters being fused with machinery, and inevitably there would be a destructive appearance from a huge marauding dinosaur creature which had been created as a result of a nuclear disaster. At the end of each episode, Vila would deliver a short moralistic lecture to the viewer on the evils of alcohol. (This last section was removed for Australian TV, where the programme was sponsored by Castlemaine XXXX. Coupled with the re-edits that had already taken place, this meant each episode ran too short for its allotted place in the schedule, so material from the children's cartoon series *M.A.S.K.* was inserted instead – specifically, the sequences from the end where T-Bob would tell Matt Trakker's son what he'd done wrong that week, followed by the entire crew laughing raucously.)

The series only ran to 15 episodes, syndicated in two blocks of 8, Season

X and Season Y. The ordering of the episodes is something many fans just can't agree on.

Super Fun Oppression Squad was backed up by an impressive merchandising campaign for the two years it ran. These collectibles are now highly sought after and go for impressive sums on eBay. Among the many items available were a lunchbox, a video game, T-shirts, food units, an umbrella, a slipper and dressing gown set, an alarm clock, bubble bath and a dog.

The following is the original Japanese press release for the English language version, which covers the cast and episodes. Someone spilled tea on the cast biographies, but it wouldn't kill you to look them up on Wikipedia. We're not here to nanny you.

English Version Cast

Robert Rietty – male voices
Miriam Margolyes – female voices
Maurice Denham – voice of Jenna
Hiroshi Ohtake – voice of Ko

Episode Guide

1. Super Fun Oppression Squad - Destroy! Destroy! Destroy!

The star-cruiser Green Leaf is spreading its message of peace to the grateful planets but deadly Kon, agent of HATE, lures the ship into his web of terror, transforming the Green Leaf into the dreaded God Trident and its crew into death-crazed maniac slaves ready to carry out his evil bidding. So is born the Super Fun Oppression Squad – their mission: DEATH!

2. Target Earthbase Seven Kill!

The Super Fun Oppression Squad is sent to Earthbase Seven to locate and destroy Kon's evil android twin Nok. They fight their way through Nok's underground hideout destroying his countless acolytes only to discover that Nok himself is none other than Kon! But Kon can't die and tells them so.

3. Mission to the Dark Planet.

Kon can't die – the Super Fun Oppression squad have tried to kill him before but in the ruins of planet Umbor they stumble upon secret plans revealing how Kon and his evil breed of robots were first created. Could these plans unlock the secret to their freedom? They launch an all-out attack on Kon's hidden fortress but their attack is a failure and Mr Gan dies.

4. A Holiday for ManWoman Jen.

ManWoman Jen and Blake are visiting ManWoman Jen's two mothers on the planet Vart. They buy a postcard which has blueprints for a superweapon on it which they don't use. But hungry still for old school death they construct traps out of wood and laugh at native creatures as they are trapped in their old fashioned web of death. Mr Gan transmutes down to the planet to join in the fun but ManWoman Jen kills him with a building. In his faraway hideout Kon laughs. On Vart, ManWoman Jen and Blake laugh. Mr Gan beneath his rubble grave laughs.

5. Mega Assault Animal Crush Dispatch!

Cute Super Fun Oppression Squad mascot pet Turtapuff is SMASHED by evil enemies of Super Fun Oppression Squad. Super Fun Oppression Squad set out to get revenge on behalf of their BEST FRIEND. Avon makes it a personal mission as Turtapuff was his very own pet given to him by his father.

6. Happy Man Gan Crazy Head Explode Time

Mr Gan keeps having headaches. Tablets do not help – headache strips do not help – a drink of water does not help. Super Fun Oppression Squad must travel to the dangerous future heart of the universe to seek out a cure before metal tentacles bursts out of Mr Gan's robot head limiter leaving him crazy.

7. Mister Mister Fast Fast Run

Super Fun Oppression Squad encounter Mr Mr Fast Fast Run who wants to steal Liberator ship from Super Fun Oppression Squad. Mr Mr Fast

Fast Run can run faster than all of Super Fun Oppression Squad so Oraculatron must make robot legs for Super Fun Oppression Squad to beat Mr Mr Fast Fast Run.

8. ORACULATRON!

Learning of a Global Hyper Super Compute-R, Avon devises a plan to capture it and use it for The Super Fun Oppression Squad in their ongoing mission of DEATH. Now they are FIVE.

9. Armageddon Tentacle FLY!

Vil-A breaks into a special safe held onboard the Royal Galactic Supreme Space Palace-Ship 2. He steals the Gem of Mirrors and Floors and escapes with it in a Hopper. He is picked up by Super Fun Oppression Squad in their Liberator Spaceship. He agrees to give them the gem if he can join their crew. Now they are SIX.

10. MegaKairopanese

Mega-Clawful Ugly Crab scours the planet of Kairos and eats the Gaia-Crystal Gobbleberries on the ground leaving Super Sticky Psycho Web in its trail. Super Fun Oppression Squad kill it and take the crystals which power their new KILL KILL KILL GUN.

11. Psycho-Acoustic Bloody Big Kill Noise

The Super Fun Oppression Squad Rock Band go on tour to the nine galaxies. Mr Gan invents a note which can kill. They try to play the note live but it doesn't work. Mr Gan goes deaf. But the note has weakened the arena and it collapses, burying Mr Gan with a concrete death. Mr Gan rises from the dead as half-man half-robot and goes on a rampage destroying all citizens.

12. All Your Blakes Are Belong To Us!

On a distant star, Kon assembles an army of clone Blakes to take over and destroy the universe! His evil nemesis, Big Time High Collar Man has stolen the SuperElectro Shuriken Laserwave Gun and plans to use it to end the lives of the fake Blakes! Can Kon seek revenge with Wing Saber and the White Princess?

13. SuperNuclear Death Plague in the Sky

Landing on the botanical research harvest moon of Little Soft Flower Space, Super-Blake unleashes a plague of spores on the population because he can. "I, Super-Blake, will KNOCK YOU ALL DOWN!" Super-Mega Brown Bug Men appear to stop him with their army of Ultra White Overlords at their side. An ancient human comes to life and is found to be the original body of Kon.

14. "Welcome Mr Charles Parkinson Sir."

Attack of aliens means Super Fun Oppression Squad must call on Mr Charles Parkinson. Mr Charles Parkinson transfers to the Liberator ship and says he will help. He doesn't help and tries to steal the supercomputer Oraculatron from the Super Fun Oppression Squad. Mr Gan tries to destroy Mr Charles Parkinson with his hands and discovers that Mr Charles Parkinson is really a robot double working for Kon. Super Fun Oppression Squad must journey to the heart of the moonworld to confront Kon and DESTROY him once and for all.

15. Warlord Music Sound Magic Noise Flute

Super Fun Oppression Squad is in turmoil after attack on integrity by Big Boss man Kon. Super-Blake leads Super Fun Oppression Squad back to planet Yojimbo where they find mysterious Wind Turtle making great music sound. Who can solve the mystery...?

TRAVIS SPIN-OFF

As Season M drew to a close, there were several question marks hovering over Stephen Greif. Not literally. That would be weird. These were merely concerns over whether he'd be able to return for filming following his injury, especially since he had a film offer on the table which would require him to be abroad during the proposed *Blake's 7* dates.

By chance, production on a new BBC science fiction serial called *Space Detective* had fallen through around this time. The series, brainchild of *Crossroads* creator Peter Ling and *Doctor Who* producer Barry Letts, was due to fill six thirty-minute episodes and was designed to be screened at 6.40pm on a Sunday. As such, it was considered 'adult output with family awareness' when it came to violence.

Space Detective had been due to commence recording with James Warwick in the title role and Cheryl Lunghi playing Hannah, an android assistant who had a gun built into her right hand.

It was this final detail which proved rather useful when it was overheard by Chris Boucher at the BBC rehearsal rooms. Just as he stepped into Letts' office to enquire what was happening, he found Letts despondent and frustrated that the series had been cancelled at the last minute. However, the BBC had already spent a considerable amount of money on sets and design and had three scripts finalised with studio time/film crews booked.

Boucher immediately suggested rushing through a new series using the same sets, and the gun-hand character detail loaned itself rather neatly to a spin-off from *Blake's 7* concerning Travis.

This also gave the production team on *Blake's 7* the perfect opportunity to convincingly recast Travis, since it was now clear that Greif wanted no involvement with the second series.

Crisis talks with Boucher, Letts, Nation and Maloney resulted in the series *Space Commander Travis*, later shortened to just *Travis*.

Coming so late to production, the series would only be five episodes long and would be screened one a day, Monday to Friday, on BBC2. Greif was signed for episode one, titled (on Letts' suggestion) "Regeneration". After this a new actor, Brian Croucher, who had previously auditioned for Blake and Vila, would take over. Production was incredibly smooth. With the combined might of Letts and Maloney, the schedules almost ran themselves, though Maloney took more of a back seat as he focused on the second series of *Blake's 7*.

Unfortunately, due to the rushed nature of the series, there was precious little promotional effort from the BBC and viewing figures were rather poor, with only episode four creeping above 3 million. The on-going plot arc excluded new viewers, and many of them were unsure about the recasting of the title character.

7.40 pm *New series*
Travis

The first of five episodes
Regeneration
by **TERRY NATION & BARRY LETTS**
starring **Stephen Greif**
Jacqueline Pearce
with **Tony Osoba**

Space commander Travis is on the trail of a new super weapon, one that could have dire consequences for the Universe – and for Travis himself ...

Travis................STEPHEN GREIF
Servalan............JACQUELINE PEARCE
Glaast...................... GILLY FLOWER
Kata Gen Haan.............. TONY OSOBA
Higgs....................PAUL McDOWELL

Series created by BARRY LETTS & CHRIS BOUCHER
Music by DUDLEY SIMPSON
Designer ROGER MURRAY-LEACH
Producer BARRY LETTS
Director DAVID MALONEY

Subtitles on Ceefax page 170

Stephen Greif will be on Woman's Hour, Tuesday 27 June (BBC Radio 4 LW), talking about his favourite pie.

EPISODE ONE: Regeneration

GUEST STARS: Stephen Greif (Travis), Jacqueline Pearce (Servalan), Gilly Flower (Glaast), Tony Osoba (Kata Gen Haan), Paul McDowell (Commander Higgs)

SYNOPSIS:

Space Commander Travis receives an urgent distress call from a ship in the Van Ollen belt of space and diverts his ships to intercept. Within the asteroid belt they discover a damaged ship with one survivor, a scientist called Glaast. She tells Travis of a powerful weapon hidden on one of the asteroids, which Servalan instructs him to locate. The weapon turns out to be a person, a renegade android called Kata Gen Haan. Designed initially as a fighting unit, he has gone rogue and is now attempting to amass an android army to fight against the Federation. During a pitched battle, Travis is badly injured and his remains are taken by Servalan to a clone facility where Glaast performs surgery to give Travis a new head.

EPISODE TWO: Federation

INTRODUCING: Cheryl Lunghi (Pennella)

GUEST STARS: Duncan Lamont (Adamma Rix), Leslie Sands (Curbin), Michael Redfern (Commander Brix), Marina Sirtis (Melorra)

SYNOPSIS:

Travis is struggling to come to terms with his new face. Many of those people he used to know just pass him in the corridor without a word. Taking shore leave, he finds himself on Space Asteroid Kell-1, a pleasure dome. Here he meets Pennella, a bounty hunter tracking Kata Gen Haan. Travis immediately strikes up a relationship and agrees to go with her to Beldross, following a lead she has on the missing android. There they meet a rebel leader, Curbin, whose life Travis spares because Pennella asks him to.

7.50 pm
Travis

The second of five episodes
Federation
by CHRIS BOUCHER
starring **Brian Croucher**
Duncan Lamont
with **Cheri Lunghi**

Will a recuperative spell on Space Asteroid Kell-1 be the tonic the recovering Travis needs?

Travis......................BRIAN CROUCHER
Curbin.........................LESLIE SANDS
Rix............................DUNCAN LAMONT
Brix........................MICHAEL REDFERN
Pennella......................CHERI LUNGHI

Designer KEN LEDSHAM
Producer BARRY LETTS
Director GEORGE SPENTON FOSTER

Subtitles on Ceefax page 170

Cheri Lunghi is currently appearing in *Are You Sure You're My Wife?* at the Hayforth Theatre, York.

EPISODE THREE: Standard by Ten

GUEST STARS: Brian Hall (Bennett)

SYNOPSIS:

Travis and Pennella, aboard her ship the *Gator*, track a vessel belonging to the man who designed Kata Gen Haan's personality circuits. However, before he became a Federation scientist he was a skilled pilot. A long and deadly pursuit through space ensues, with Travis and Pennella finally cementing their relationship en route.

EPISODE FOUR: Desperate Measures

GUEST CAST: Milton Johns (Bessily), Standford Owen (Trader One), Harry Fielder (Trader Two)

SYNOPSIS:
Kata Gen Haan has been spotted on Xymines III. Travis and Penella hurry there to find they have just missed him. However, as they ask around at the Belloka Marketplace, they find he was looking to purchase digging equipment and several slaves. Pennella realises he is attempting to excavate an android army that was buried during the last Great War. As they approach the dig site on Fydle Major, they are seized and held at gunpoint. From the shadows steps Kata Gen Haan; he aims a gun at Travis' head.

EPISODE FIVE: Appearances Can Be Deceptive

GUEST CAST: Tony Osoba (Kata Gen Haan), Milton Johns (Bessily), Jonathan Newth (Duggan), Adam Crowley (Android Voices)

SYNOPSIS:
Kata Gen Haan shoots the androids that have seized Travis and Pennella. Travis tries to attack but Pennella stops him. Kata Gen Haan explains he's not the enemy and that he's secretly a Federation agent put in charge of finding the hidden android army. As Travis is still a Federation officer, he agrees to help. As the army is activated, Pennella intervenes and tries to stop them both, but Travis shoots her. Slowly, the army ticks into life…

The series ended on this cliffhanger, which was so poorly realised that no less than eighteen complaints were received at the BBC duty office. Despite a continuity announcement announcing the series would return the following autumn, it didn't. The paperback novelisation of the first two stories by Trevor Hoyle is readily available (and awful).

THE MOLOCH AND GOLOCH CHRISTMAS CAVALCADE

Determined to get the most out of the money spent on the elaborate Moloch animatronic, the BBC commissioned a pilot show that aimed to be as equally entertaining as it was educational, and to possibly replace the long-running (and long boring) Royal Institution Christmas Lectures. *The Moloch and Goloch Christmas Cavalcade* (1980, one episode) featured the diminutive Season P villain alongside his twin brother, plus a galaxy of stars from the time, in their own two-hour 'varieteach' spin-off.

Produced by John Nathan-Turner (the exercise served as a dry run for his upcoming stint at the helm of *Doctor Who*), guests included Faith Brown (who starred as the comedy housekeeper), Billy Curry from the band Ultravox (who composed the theme tune for the show and appeared as the twins carer), and *Just William* star Adrian Dannatt who played the naughty kid who lived next door. Keith Harris and Cuddles the Cheeky Monkey were contracted to also appear as long-lost cousins but pulled out at the last minute when Harris, arriving on set, assumed the whole thing was a hidden-camera show wind-up.

Every member of the *Blake's 7* cast past and present put in an appearance to perform jokes and sketches or to sing a favourite song, with the exception of Gareth Thomas who was very busy being serious and Shakespearean somewhere. Probably. He was doubled by Eddie Large in the background of some scenes when the Madame Tussauds waxwork of Thomas proved unavailable (it was appearing in a *Holiday 1980* special filmed in Llandudno).

There was even a role for Brian Croucher. One of the running jokes involved Moloch mentioning his brother to the other guests. Every time this happened Croucher, dressed as Shivan, would shuffle onto the set mumbling, 'Ma bruuuuuuvahhh...' the feed line for Moloch to retort, 'No, **my** brother!' followed by raucous peals of canned laughter.

Many elements were dropped during recording. Billy Curry's character

7.20 pm
The Moloch and Goloch Christmas Cavalcade

A special programme featuring the cast and friends of the popular sci-fi yarn *Blakes 7*.

by JOHN JUNKIN, BARRY CRYER, DOUGLAS ADAMS & TERRY NATION

starring **Deep Roy**, with very special guest appearances from **Paul Darrow, Michael Keating, Stevie Pacey, Josette Simon, David Jackson, Sally Knyvette** and **Brian Croucher**.

It is Christmas Eve. Moloch and Goloch are looking forward to a quiet night at home, but an endless stream of visitors bring songs, jokes and hilarious consequences.

Moloch/Goloch.................DEEP ROY
Mrs Wiremore............ FAITH BROWN
Carlos......................... BILLY CURRY
Joloch......................... KEITH HARRIS
Little Ghostface................LEO SAYER

Series created by TERRY NATION
Music by RONNIE HAZLEHURST
Studio lighting DON BABBAGE
Designer ROGER MURRAY-LEACH
Producer JOHN NATHAN-TURNER
Director VERE LORRIMER

FEATURE p98

A 7 inch single of the show's theme tune will be available from all good records shops from 26th December, BBC Records RESL 82

Subtitles on Ceefax page 170

Carlos was meant to repeatedly punch Goloch while telling him he was an idiot; damage to the puppet forced a rewrite. Interviewed in 1994, Sally Knyvette said, 'The guy from Ultravox punching that doll thing is the only bit I remember. It was awful when the eye shot out and hit Keith Michell in the back.'

Filmed on the partially-dismantled set of *Moloch* (with the addition of a regular front door that guests arrived and left through, and a comedy doorbell that chimed the first seven notes of the *Blake's 7* theme tune), the two-hour spectacular was never broadcast and little is remembered of the show by cast and crew. According to JN-T's diary of the time many considered the highlight of the show to be a duet between Paul Darrow and Moloch. The pair gave a tightly-choreographed display of robotic dancing while performing the Thomas Dolby song, 'She Blinded Me with Science'. 'They stayed completely in character throughout the song,' Nathan-Turner wrote. 'It left me without words and, for a short while, without breath'.

Information:

Goloch was originally named Boloch. The name was changed when mispronunciation caused uncontrollable childish laughter during the rehearsal period (hee hee! Period!)

Such were the rigorous filming demands for Season P that the *Liberator* crew had to film all of their skits in recording breaks during the studio work for "Deathwatch".

Steven Pacey sang the Aled Jones classic 'Walking in the Air' as his party piece. Watching the rehearsal convinced director Vere Lorrimer to ditch the 'Distant Star' lyric idea for the Season R closing theme.

One unnamed cast member kept shouting, 'Do you want a fight? DO YOU?' whenever anyone looked at her during filming. Eventually her microphone was cut off and JN-T filmed around her.

Both lead roles were voiced by Deep Roy who made no effort to distinguish between Moloch and Goloch. This lead to all sorts of out-of-synch mouth puppeteering and appalling vision mixing as no one ever seemed sure which of the twins were meant to be speaking.

For completists, the lyrics to the opening theme ran thus:

Moloch:	I'm Moloch!
Goloch:	And I'm Goloch!
Together:	And we're here to learn and have fun!
Moloch:	You will be hearing
Goloch:	About genetic engineering
Together:	And why we don't have two eyes, we only have one.
Moloch:	I'm Moloch!
Goloch:	And I'm Goloch!
Together:	Welcome to our Christmas Fayre!
Moloch:	We will be lookin'
Goloch:	At how you do cookin'
Together:	And things you can make from old animal hair.
Moloch:	Hello Goloch!
Goloch:	Hello Moloch!
Together:	Hello everyone – above and below!
	It's time for us to end our song
	And start this brilliant show.

(© copyright Billy Curry / Ronnie Hazlehurst)

The writers of 'Una Paloma Blanca' successfully contested that the theme music for the show had more than a passing resemblance to the chorus of their own composition. 25,000 copies of the 7" single scheduled for Christmas release were destroyed as a consequence. It led one of supporting artists to claim the show was cursed; he stated, 'So much went wrong from day one. The theme music thing, some of the cast being a bit weird, no one remembering anything about it... Oh, and this is a bit weird – every single person who worked on that show knows at least one person who has died. That is more than just coincidence.'

Below: Promotional items given to the studio audience who attended the *Cavalcade* filming session – promotional cards of Moloch and Goloch and the very rare badge set.

THE BLAKE'S 7 COMIC STRIPS

Blake's 7 comic strips first appeared in *Blake's 7 Weekly*, then *Blake's 7 Monthly* and on through the annual Annuals that ran until 1985, and featured some of the most ambitious, philosophical and downright bizarre adventures for Blake, Avon et al. Despite a slew of errors - the Liberator taking off and landing like a rocket, Travis constantly portrayed as a robot with a human arm, and Soolin having a twin sister who also lived on Xenon - the strips were never anything other than beautifully illustrated and thoroughly entertaining.

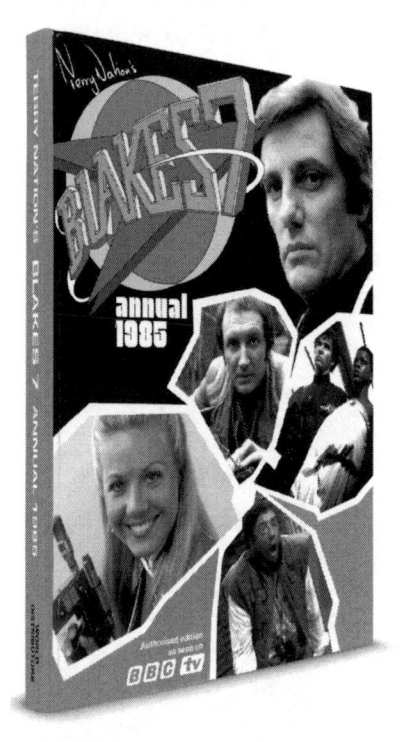

The comic strips reached a sad end in the pages of the 1985 annual. With the television series off-air, World Distributors gave up creating new content. To save money, the strips are recycled from the very early issues of *Blake's 7 Weekly*, with the likenesses of the most recent cast drawn over the originals. Avon's face was inked over that of Blake, Gan became Tarrant, and Jenna was left untouched as it was deemed she could pass as Soolin. Cally is left in some panels that include Soolin even though the characters never met! Even the cover of the book was a cost-cutting exercise – it is the 1979 Annual with Season R photographs pasted in place.

Let's relive seven of the very best *Blake's 7* comic strips...

Travis' Ring

Jenna accidentally watches a haunted vidcast that curses the crew of the *Liberator*. Zen informs them of a legend that states there will be an incoming communication in three space days and they will all die.

While Zen is distracted observing some space mist or something, Travis and his Mutoids attack the *Liberator*, resulting in the ship being severely damaged. Cally and Avon climb inside the wrecked viewscreen to repair it, and are unaware when Travis boards the ship and takes the rest of the crew hostage. All seems lost until Cally climbs backwards out of the viewscreen, covered in grime and her hair hanging down over her face, scaring Travis and the Mutoids away. The haunted vidcast prophecy doesn't come true – it transpires that Avon had merely been testing out his newly-invented paranoia circuits on Zen.

Space Junk!

Scorpio flies through a cloud of Space Junk, an intergalactic drug that affects machines with Tarriel Cells. Orac becomes addicted and high as a kite, and Avon has to synthesise a detoxing drug that the crew pour over Orac's key before they activate him. During a lucid spell Orac reminds the crew that the Federation also use Tarriel Cells in their equipment and the Space Junk could bring down their computer systems. Avon hatches a plan to use *Scorpio*'s tractor beam to tow the drug cloud into the middle of Servalan's battle fleet – what could possibly go wrong?

Bird Face of the Olympus Mons

Skirting the planet Mars, the *Liberator* is stopped in its tracks by the face of a massive ethereal bird. Spouting weird elliptical nonsense, Bird Face won't allow the ship and her crew to continue unless they answer a series of cryptic questions. Only one question away from a ghastly death, Orac projects a hologram of a space puma's head onto Blake's shoulders and Bird Face is so scared that it flies off into the sun and the *Liberator* can carry on unhindered.

Misdirection

The Federation disrupt the signals beaming from orbital location satellites, thus confusing all space traffic. The plot works as the crew of the *Scorpio* think they are teleporting down to the famous diamond world of Diamondus but actually beam down into a courtroom on Earth. Orac disguises himself as a lawyer (complete with wig) and teleports down to defend and ultimately save the crew.

(For some reason Tarrant is written as a psychotic maniac in this strip who spends the entire story laughing at the torture and mayhem going on around the crew of the Scorpio. *Steven Pacey was so upset that he withdrew the use of his likeness for the next three comic strips. To bring the crew back up to the requisite number (and to enjoy some childish retaliation) Marvel introduced a temporary addition to the* Scorpio – *a little crying girl who they subtly named Peven Stacey.)*

Werewolf? There Wolf!

The crew are enjoying a moonlit picnic on the surface of Xenon. Tarrant suddenly remembers he is a werewolf, instantly turns into one and goes a bit mad. After five pages of awful comedy chasing, hiding and more chasing, Orac sings a hypnotic song cure for three pages that fixes the pilot and makes him forget to remember he is a werewolf.

(Artist Cam Gibson forgot Dayna was part of the crew, hence the character doesn't appear in this strip until the final frame. Many eagle-eyed readers wrote in about this story, but none mentioned the lack of Dayna; instead they wanted to know why Gan made a cameo as a waving rambler who passes the crew while they are eating their picnic.)

Time and Time Again

An unspecified galactic phenomena occurs near Xenon that sends the male members of the *Scorpio* crew back in time and space to medieval England, where Avon and Tarrant have to pass themselves off as court jesters and Vila is revered as the new King. Soolin, Dayna and Orac have to wait two months for a spacial eclipse to occur so they can fly the *Scorpio* backwards through the unspecified galactic phenomena until their friends are returned – just seconds before they were going to be executed as space witches.

Mud, Mud, Glorious Mud

A computer virus turns Slave into a pile of talking mud.

(the first of two strips where the wrong photo references were supplied to artist Cam Gibson, and the Scorpio *was drawn as an X-Wing Fighter from* Star Wars.*)*

THE ADVENTURES OF FSR-1

Within the BBC Written Archive at Caversham is a folder of production paperwork relating to "Seek-Locate-Destroy". Inside there is a memo, written by Production Assistant Geoffrey Manton, that simply states 'Terry came for filming, left early. Does anyone know why?'

The truth is fascinating but lacking a write-up within the Archive. Nation did indeed make a rare appearance to watch some filming; he also left the Fulham Gas Works location early in order to rush back to his house in Kent, only stopping en route to phone his wife to ask her to put a big sheet of paper into his typewriter. The reason? Terry Nation had realised that his next big project would be a series of animated shorts involving the Federation security robot – or FSR-1 as it would become known.

Nation much-admired any television programme that entertained and educated a young audience; it was one of the reasons he got involved in the embryonic *Doctor Who*. While waiting to collect his children from school one day, Nation overheard a conversation between a group of parents. One mother was saying that her son was having trouble fitting in as they had not been living in England for very long and everything was so different to his previous school in Swaziland. Nation attending the *Blake's 7* location filming was the water his seed of an idea needed, and from this moment it blossomed.

The idea was for FSR-1 to lead a programme that would introduce pre-school youngsters to the notion that not all children were from the same town or even the same country, and that you should accept and try to help all people, no matter how different they may initially seem. What better idea than a robot to highlight something as being different? FSR-1 would get into a series of scrapes due to his misunderstandings about British culture that would always be happily resolved, with lessons learned and everyone going home smiling for their weekly treat. (Inevitably a lovely pudding – being the 70s treacle tart featured a lot.)

Clearance for using FSR-1 in a project away from *Blake's 7* was no issue as the BBC had made the decision very early in production not to use the robot again. The prop had failed to live up to the expectations of producer David Maloney, proving to be cumbersome and comedic instead of being seen as a threat of any kind – add to that the robot had been severely damaged after the location filming for "Project Avalon". Actor David Bailie had taken the role of Chevner on the strict understanding that his character would give the robot an on-screen kick. Disappointed that Michael E. Briant reneged and the kick didn't feature in the script, Bailie instead gave the prop a kicking and a half after filming wrapped, damaging the robot to the extent that it had to be scrapped. (A laughing Gareth Thomas filmed the event on his cine camera. The four-minute silent footage appears as a hidden Easter Egg feature on the Dutch DVD release.)

Approval given and funding attained, a five-minute pilot was written by Nation (with help from *Bagpuss* creator Oliver Postgate). The scant paperwork for the series doesn't give individual titles to the episodes, but this pilot appears to have been named "Ice Cream? Nice Cream". Test animations were carried out by the father and son team Mirek and Peter Lang who had enjoyed a level of success creating the hit cartoon series *Ludwig*. However they had to leave the FSR-1 project when another of their own creations, *Pigeon Street*, was green-lit for a full series.

Fledgling animation company Little Pictures were then called in. Brothers Darren and Gavin Pewley had caught the eye of the BBC when they entered the Young Filmmaker of the Year during 1975 and had come first. Their stop-motion experiments, using hand-painted cardboard cut-outs and a wind-up 16mm Bolex camera, were described by *Screen Test* presenter Michael Rodd as 'rudimentary but charming.'

The budget allowed the brothers to experiment a little, and the first scenes filmed were in a totally different animation style to the episode that followed – articulated wooden puppets, of the style seen in *Camblewick Green*, were used. While delightful, they were time-consuming to animate and build sets for. The Pewleys' tried and tested method – cut-out cardboard figures that were coloured in with felt tip pen – became the template, and the wooden puppet footage was instead used for the title sequence. While jarring when compared to the main animation style of the show, the titles worked very well when married up to the theme tune – the music to *Blake's 7* played solely on the euphonium.

With filming under way, Nation suggested that the robot should be given an internal voice so the watching children could hear his thoughts about the situations he found himself in. Nation initially requested David Graham (one of the Dalek voices from the 60s) but it was decided early on to move away from a harsh, mechanical voice to one that was warm and friendly. Arthur Lowe of *Dad's Army* fame was the first choice for providing the narration, but for the test footage the production team used Jon Glover, another stalwart from *Ludwig* and recommended by the Langs.

Work was proceeding on the pilot when disaster struck. A freelance visual effects designer who had worked on *Blake's 7* placed a cease-and-desist order on the production, claiming that the FSR-1 was his design and copyright, stating that any attempt to capitalise on it would result in court action and a claim for damages. Further investigation revealed that the BBC had indeed failed to secure the necessary copyright waiver and eventually had to acknowledge that the property rights for the design rested solely with the said designer. (Unfortunately we are not allowed to name the visual effects designer. You could probably guess who it is though, he has worked on pretty much every cult show and no one likes him.)

Interest for the series had started to wither anyway as everyone involved became generally bored; it was telling that the final meeting called to discuss progress and production schedules was attended by no one. The cease-and-desist order was the final push Terry Nation needed to pull the plug. After nearly ten days of his full attention the initial enthusiasm had gone. The paperwork that does exist mirrors this ennui, with the first two episodes having full and descriptive write-ups, while Nation's outlines for the next twenty-three adventures were so scant as to be virtually non-existent. One simply read 'FSR > beach. Flame-thrower havoc!'

The allotted broadcast slot of 5.35pm was again given over to *Ludwig* and *The Adventures of FSR-1* were forgotten. Our attempts to track down further information proved fruitless – nothing exists at Caversham as nothing was ever made to catalogue. There is very little paperwork in Nation's own archive, beyond two episode breakdowns and some rough notes. We couldn't find the Pewley brothers for an interview and the only person who would speak to us was the aforementioned BBC visual effects designer and he wanted £50 for just answering the phone.

While researching this article we found notes for some of the other ideas Terry Nation was toying with when he stepped back from *Blake's 7* after Season P. Most of them had dates written on them and, as with the FSR-1 project, appear to have had around 10-days worth of effort lavished on them before they were ultimately ditched.

Some of our favourites included:

Avon Ding-Dong – A hidden camera show where Paul Darrow (in character as Avon) would try and start fights in East End pubs. When it became apparent that the show would never happen, Nation sold the title to cosmetic giants Avon who turned it into a long-running successful advert.

Tarrantula – A TV quiz show not dissimilar to *Runaround*. Steven Pacey would be dressed as a spider while the competitors dashed around an assault course while dressed as flies. Rumour has it that David Maloney laughed so much at the idea that he gave himself flu.

Josette's Rosettes – The scrawled note under this title just says 'Does Josette collect rosettes? Money-maker if she does.'

Below: Surviving notes about *The Adventures of FSR-1*. Yes, that is blood.

OTHER OTHER WORLDS

MATHSCENE

In 1980, the popular *Mathscene* programme for schools and colleges embarked on an ambitious plan to take successful icons from the BBC's own catalogue and create spoof versions of them with a view to helping young viewers engage more readily with often-challenging subject matters.

The results were mixed. The perennial *Generation Game* was press-ganged into the service of explaining algebra under the moniker "Generation xy", an entertaining enough spoof where contestants, all in their teens, battled it out to be the first to create the correct series of equations out of large polystyrene blocks. But attempts to simplify calculus in "What's My Sine?" were met with bemused stares by viewers in schools across the country. "Terry or June", an introduction to probability, fared better, likely because of the subject matter being easier to comprehend and the nature of the programme itself. As the name suggests, it was a spoof on the popular sitcom *Terry and June*, with Terry Scott himself playing Terry to a familiar yet unexpected June in the guise of none other than Mollie Sugden.

But the most memorable instalment was "Blake's 7/8ths", which set out to explain basic fractions in the language that many school-age sci-fi fans understood: that of *Blake's 7*.

For what would only amount to a ten-minute sketch, complicated plotting, effects or a full complement of freedom fighters weren't necessary, and *Mathscene* took significant liberties with the structure of the programme. However, the end result, while possibly not a mathematical success, was at least an entertaining and memorable spoof of a much loved show.

With production well underway on the real series, the *Mathscene* team were unable to utilise the sets or actors from *Blake's 7* itself and so were forced to rely on their own interpretations.

A couple of stock shots of the *Liberator* were used to establish the setting for the story, which mainly took place in a laboratory on the planet

Fractos. There, Professor Integer (Colin Jeavons) was putting the finishing touches to his supercomputer, the irascible yet brilliant ERIC (voiced by Jeavons).

Blake (Fred Harris) and Jenna (Chloe Ashcroft) teleport into Integer's lab, looking for the professor's help in deciphering a Federation message they've intercepted. According to the message, Federation supremo Sir Villain (Stuart McGugan) is en route to Blake's ship the *Tabulator* with a new superweapon that will wipe Blake, his ship and his crew off the face of the galaxy. But Blake and his crew can't understand the message, filled as it is with fractions of standard speeds, distance and time.

Professor Integer asks ERIC to explain the basics of fractions to Blake and Jenna, who despite their space-age sophistication and strategic brilliance are, at first unable to comprehend halves, quarters and the like. ERIC's patience eventually wears thin, and he reveals somewhat irritably that Sir Villain has been pursuing Blake to Fractos. At that precise moment, Avon (Fred Harris again) sends a message via communicator to Blake that Sir Villain has arrived and has his weapon trained on the *Tabulator*.

Sir Villain enters the professor's laboratory just as Blake and Jenna teleport out, taking ERIC with them, and the programme ends with Sir Villain hamming away and cursing Blake, declaring him to be 'too clever by half'.

All in all, it's an amusing spoof. While not technically brilliant, it manages to retain just enough of the programme it's aping, thanks to a few well-sourced stock shots of the *Liberator* and a trio of pursuit ships, as well as a logo which looks similar enough to the original (though in this case the red circle in the logo is replaced with a pie chart divided into quarters). Throw in some of Dudley Simpson's memorable music (unfortunately from the *Doctor Who* story "City of Death" but you can't have everything) and the end result is well worth watching if you ever get a chance. Sadly, the programme has never been repeated and lives on only in the memories of those who were lucky enough to have seen it at the time. A transcript is available from the *Blake's 7* fanclub Horizon.

BLAKE'S 7 COMPUTER GAME

In the early 90s, home gaming was drifting more and more toward games consoles rather than the old workhorses of the 80s, Personal Computers. No longer were cassettes the order of the day – even diskettes were a thing of the past for most gamers as cartridges began to take over the world.

In such a challenging and developing market it's surprising that a *Blake's 7* game had never been tried before. On the Amstrad and Spectrum home formats there had been two games – *Codename MAT* and *Codename MAT II* – which were both heavily influenced by *Blake's 7*, featuring plasma bolts, force walls and an evil Federation. But it took Leicester software house JazzDOS to bring *Blake's 7* screaming into the 90s with their incredible adventure game *Federation Funhouse*.

Clearly inspired by the new wave of point-and-click games, or SCUMM as they are now affectionately known, *Federation Funhouse* was also one of the first games to be dual-released on CD-ROM as well as floppy disk. Advantages of this format meant that gamers who bit the bullet and bought the more expensive CD-ROM version were treated not just to a full motion video title sequence but also to digitally stored and sampled voices from some of the original cast and crew. Owners of the floppy disk version had to put up with on-screen captions instead, assuming they had the 30mb hard disk space required. It may not seem like much now, but in 1993 it was a tall order!

The initial catalyst for the game was a chance encounter between JazzDOS managing director Jed Chappell and *Blake's 7* actor Gareth Thomas. Thomas had been engaged by JazzDOS to provide the voice for their early flop *Graze of the Hound*, and Chappell nostalgically chatted to him during a recording break. He takes up the story himself in a 1992 preview article that appeared in *PC Format* magazine:

'I was so excited to be in a room with Blake himself. As a kid I'd watched Blake's 7 from behind the sofa and just loved it. We were so lucky to get Gareth, and to be honest, it was hard work finding a slot where we could

record with him. He was busy at the time on – I think – London's Burning; we really had to work around his hours. I couldn't resist asking him about the show, and he was so nice about it, even signing my old Blake's 7 annual for me. I felt completely unprofessional! I jokingly said we should do a Blake's 7 game and he said he'd be glad to participate if we did. It all stemmed from that, really.'

Indeed, for several weeks after that recording, Chappell kept thinking about the concept of a *Blake's 7* game. He was no stranger to programming. As well as being managing director of JazzDOS, he was also one of the founding partners. He and two other programmers, Lee Grey and Tony Beddows, had written a piece of software which could keep track of statistics in a cricket match. With no one willing to take on software that had little commercial appeal, they formed their own company and successfully brought the game of cricket into the computer age. Now all matches, even the Hawk-Eye system itself, are recorded and ultimately stem from the original *Over and Out* software.

Chappell began making notes. He had been planning to create a game similar to those developed by Rod Gilbert and his team at LucasArts in the late 80s on the SCUMM system (Script Creation Utility for Maniac Mansion), which allowed the user to play through an unfolding story, unlike previous games, which had often involved either working around a maze or puzzle or shooting everything in sight.

Of course, the SCUMM system itself was protected by copyright, so Chappell and Beddows developed a ground-up system of their own that they jokingly referred to as ORAC-OS and which eventually became known as the still-used open-source piece of software ORACLE-OS.

The advantages of ORACLE-OS over SCUMM were that ORACLE-OS allowed for more mini-games to be included. In the case of *Federation Funhouse*, there was the 'Get Out of Town' level where you, as Jenna, must pilot the *Liberator* out of a minefield in space, and also the various skill-point unlocking levels where you must pick increasingly tougher locks as Vila. ('Take a swig of booze if you dare – it may increase your confidence but it makes your hands shake. Hardcore gamers only!')

Chappell and Beddows soon realised that their new software engine was going to be a winner, and so for the first time enlisted external assistance in creating a narrative for their game. They eventually settled on a friend of Beddows' from his home-computer journalism days, former *Doctor Who* script editor Christopher H. Bidmead.

Bidmead was impressed by ORACLE-OS and was more than aware of the prestige *Over and Out* had received in the trade press. While reluctant to return to science fiction writing, he was encouraged enough to have a go at writing a script for the game.

Bidmead contacted the producer he'd worked with on *Doctor Who*: Barry Letts. Letts had recently been pushing for a radio adaptation of *Blake's 7* (something which would eventually see fruition, but not for another five years). Letts gave Bidmead a crash course in *Blake's 7* lore. Between them, they worked out a concept which seemed to work within the clear confines of the game. Something Bidmead found especially freeing was that there were no budgetary concerns to limit his imagination.

Conscious that the game had to appeal to a young audience, Bidmead injected humour into his ideas. This was welcomed by Chappell, who approved of a more fun aspect to the game following the disastrous and political upheaval they had suffered with *Graze of the Hound*.

Bidmead's story was set during the third series of *Blake's 7* and began with the entire crew, having been captured by Servalan, trying to escape from a Federation detention centre. The detention centre itself was so full of traps it had been nicknamed the 'Federation Funhouse'.

Once the crew had successfully escaped the Funhouse, the action returned to the *Liberator* (whereupon CD-ROM owners would switch to CD 2 – rare in gaming at the time). Here, the crew, led by Tarrant (or Blake in the original script, as Bidmead was unaware that Blake wasn't in the series by this stage), strike out at Federation HQ in a side-scrolling, heart-pounding sequence intercut with tough *Liberator* repair mini-games and an awkwardly realised first-person-perspective shoot out with boarding Federation troopers on the flight deck.

With Bidmead's script in place, Chappell turned his attentions to voices. Bidmead had written dialogue for all the crew, and part of the agreement reached with the BBC allowed Chappell to use some audio samples from the original episodes. For reasons of cost, he mainly used these sound samples for Zen and Orac. In the case of Orac, players only heard the sound of his buzzing while his text appeared on screen.

Steven Pacey declined to take part, but Jan Chappell (no relation to Jed), Paul Darrow and Josette Simon all agreed to participate, with Darrow also voicing Travis and a Federation trooper (the one who constantly cajoles you as you're attempting to rewire the door on the first level).

Providing some additional voices were Lee Grey (who provided voices for two previous JazzDOS games, including the eponymous Hound), James Faulkner, David and Debra Lees and, playing Servalan, Lynda Bellingham.

It was these sound files which took up the bulk of the space on the CD-ROMs, which meant that gamers purchasing either format didn't lose out on much in the way of gameplay, just enhanced content.

Music was also recorded, provided in this instance by Jacob Kaufmann. However, very little of the score he composed was used, owing to the lack of available space on the CD media.

The game was released in November 1993, which was unfortunate because it was lost in a wave of publicity covering the 30th anniversary of the BBC's other big science fiction hit *Doctor Who*.

On the whole, critical reception was very good indeed. Many reviewers were amazed at how much JazzDOS had managed to cram onto eighteen floppy discs; however, many were also conscious of the fact the system requirements were quite punishing. Even on a 386 computer with 4mb RAM it had a tendency to freeze up, especially on the disc change. In fact, many gamers, when playing as Cally and having to telepathically stun all nine guards in the Garden of Lights, would often find the game sent them into an endless loop, which several fans jokingly referred to as 'Sarcophagus Syndrome'.

Owners of systems with a 2x speed CD drive found that many of these problems were avoided. However, some incompatibility with certain sound cards meant that, quite frequently, a sample of Avon saying 'Now!' could repeat for well over an hour. In *PC Format*'s Christmas issue this was third in their list of '25 Most Irritating Gaming Moments'.

Unfortunately, any hopes of high Christmas sales were blown out of the water when, on 2 December 1993, JazzDOS received a letter from Terry Nation's agent, Roger Hancock. He pointed out that no permission had been sought from Nation and that the BBC was in no position to give the go-ahead to the project. Hancock's letter requested all stock be withdrawn until an agreement could be reached with Nation.

This was a disaster for Chappell. While the company was financially sound, they had anticipated a high volume of sales and as such had ordered a higher than usual number of copies. With each of the high-end packages containing two CDs, production costs had been steep. Ultimately, since no agreement could be made with Nation (who was particularly concerned about a sequence where Tarrant dresses in drag to escape through the women's detention centre), the game was quietly filed away, and JazzDOS as an on-going concern shutdown their production of games in March 1994.

Speaking ten years later, Beddows was surprisingly easy-going:

'You win some, you lose some. We'd been lucky every year and every decision from the day we all started. If you believe in karma, which I do, you have to expect a balance. That balance was the failure of Federation Funhouse, *which saw all of our careers go in different directions.'*

To this day, no further efforts have been made to transfer *Blake's 7* into the virtual world of gaming. Within the industry, the words *Blake's 7* ring out like 'Macbeth' offstage in a theatre. It's a tainted chalice that no-one wants to take on. The legacy of JazzDOS is strong though; regardless of their commercial failure, it is still clear that they produced one of the most challenging, enjoyable and enthusiastic game adaptations of a TV series ever committed to disc, and for that, Beddows, Gray and especially Chappell should be proud.

With grateful thanks to Jed & Amanda Chappell, Lee Gray and Tony Beddows for their time and for their game. Those of us who have it still treasure it. Thanks guys!

Below: *Computer Player* magazine breaks the news about the cancellation of *Federation Funhouse*.

ROAD SAFETY

One of the more curious *Blake's 7* appearances from around the time was Sally Knyvette's semi-legendary 1980 performance in a Public Information film. Only a few years after Dave Prowse had portrayed the Green Cross Code Man, warning children of the dangers of crossing the road, Knyvette was brought on board to update the idea for the eighties. She's essentially playing her character from *Blake's 7* – a slightly bored-looking dolly bird with fake hair and a sense of rebellion.

The rules of the road, however, were insanely complex…

(The scene: three children, buying lollipops in a convenience store. They see their football rolling off the pavement outside and heading off across the road. The children sprint out of the shop and dash to the road to retrieve it.

Sally Knyvette appears, in the crude white-outline version of the Liberator teleport effect.)

Knyvette: Hey! Slow it down there! You don't need to run across the road at standard by ten!

(The children look confused.)

Knyvette: Remember to look port and starboard when crossing the space lanes.

Little Girl: But how do we know how to cross?

Knyvette: Just remember these SEVEN simple rules.

(She winks at the camera when she says 'seven'. As she spells out the following code, the appropriate letter appears on a black section at the bottom of the screen.)

Knyvette: Stop at the edge of the galaxy.

('S' appears as the children stop at the edge of the kerb.)

Knyvette: Analyse the space conditions.

('A' appears as the children look left and right.)

Knyvette: Launch yourself off the launch pad.

('L' appears as the children step forward into an empty road.)

Knyvette: Look for other space users as you cross.

('L' appears as the children continue to look left and right.)

Knyvette: You're Down and Safe!

('Y' appears as the children safely reach the other kerb. Knyvette hugs the children.)

Knyvette: And remember, keep in mind you could have been knocked down and killed, for next time!

('K' appears, for 'Keep', as the children wander off.)

Knyvette (to camera): So, remember the SEVEN steps to road safety! SALLYK. Or you could end up like this –

(The sequence ends with a surreal shot of Knyvette lying in the road, apparently knocked down and killed. As we watch, the Liberator teleport effect starts up again, and with the familiar white line around her, Knyvette's body disappears, leaving a chalk outline in the road...)

The campaign was not a successful one. Research published in the the *Times* of 14 June 1980 suggested that only 14% of 8-12 year-olds could remember what SALLYK stood for (or indeed how to pronounce it when seeing it written down – SALLY-KAY) and few knew who Knyvette was. It's a remarkably awkward mnemonic for children to get – could you even remember what it stands for without looking back?

What's most remarkable about the advert is the odd costume that Knyvette's wearing, a strange silver 'space' outfit that appears to have been re-used for Craig Ferguson in an early episode of *Red Dwarf*.

Coupled with Knyvette's bizarre (and presumably intentional) facial expression when she shouts 'SALLYK', its lasting impact was more one of unintentional humour than deadly warning. This isn't helped by the fact that the little girl in the sketch grew up to be Patsy Kensit. It's fair to say that the piece has gone down in cult history for its sheer convolutedness and the memorability of Knyvette's performance.

For that very reason, we do think it's one of Knyvette's more impressive pieces of work as Jenna.

Below: The *TV Times.* advert for the SallyK campaign.

FOODSTUFF STUFF

There was one surefire way to make kids eat breakfast cereals in the 1970s and we're not just talking too much sugar or a ton of additives – there was also an entirely different type of crap crammed into those boxes.

Television, music and movie giveaways have always proved popular and acted as a great lure to children – many families had to endure an increase of Sugar Smacks, Ty-Phoo and Weetabix into their daily diet when *Doctor Who* badges and then collectible card figures were the playground *hit de jour*. Weetabix managed two separate sets of *Doctor Who* giveaways plus figures of the cast of *Star Trek: The Motion Picture*. *Blake's 7* was an obvious choice for the next collectible giveaway fad.

The BBC were keen on the idea, with the proviso that the giveaway be pushed in the months between the end of Season N and the start of Season P as it would help keep the show 'visible' in the months it was off-air. With Terry Nation in full agreement the project began in April 1979.

As with the *Doctor Who* range there was a list of 24 figures decided on that would be spread out as six sets of four cards.

The full list of figures that was drawn up for production:

Blake x two (two different poses); Jenna; Cally; Vila; Avon; Servalan x two (two different dresses); Travis x two (two different Travis's); The Federation security robot; Zil (from "Trial"); Lurena (from "Star One"); Jarriere (from "Gambit"); Vargas (from "Cygnus Alpha"); Rontane (from "Seek-Locate-Destroy"); Alta Morag (from "The Way Back"); Shivan (from "Voice from the Past"); Mandrian (from "Mission to Destiny"); Largo (from "Shadow"); Gambril (from "Killer"); Mutoids x three (from "Duel" (probably)).

Gordon Archer, the artist behind the *Doctor Who* and *Star Trek* figure cards, was unfortunately unavailable to create the *Blake's 7* illustrations so a relative unknown, Bogdan Pietrsen, was tasked with producing the sketches for the project. As well as the card figures there were also four background scenes mapped out that would printed on the back of the cereal packets: the *Liberator* flight deck, the planet Exbar, space command headquarters, and the control room of Star One.

In its early stages the project hit a stumbling block as the first set of illustrations produced were deemed too weird and abstract, with none of the characters actually recognisable as their television counterparts. One scrawled comment on the proof sheet read 'Is this the guy who does that weird stuff for the *Doctor Who* annuals?'; another note asked if Pietrsen had mental health issues (but in slightly more colourful language). Pietrsen eventually admitted that he'd been so busy working on the artwork for the background scenes that he had asked his children to help out with the figure art.

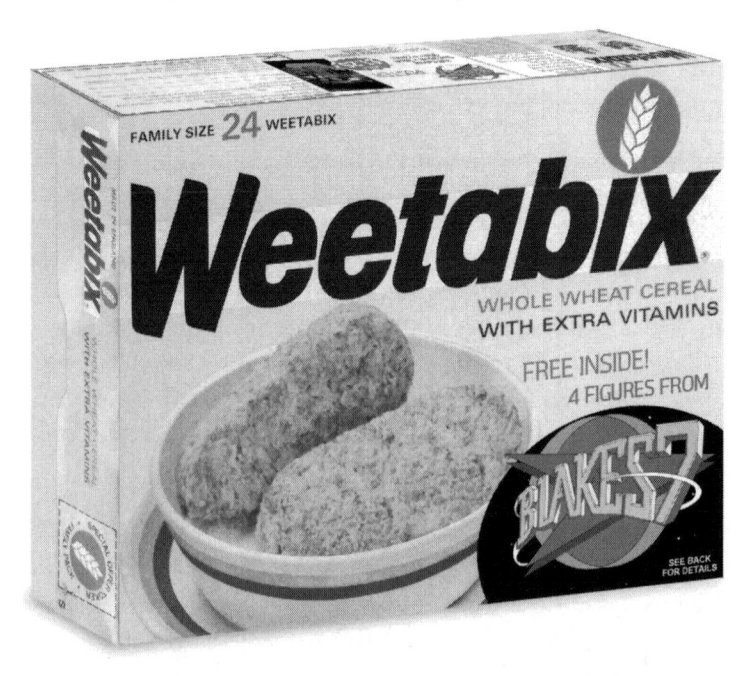

Furious, the Weetabix executives demanded Pietrsen produce work of the quality, standard and style of Gordon Archer – it was their reputation on the line, after all. An urgent meeting was called two months later as the production deadline loomed. The executives were overjoyed that the standard required had finally been met by Pietrsen, but were horrified to discover that only one card had been completed (the first of two Blake figures) and half of one of the backgrounds (Ushton's den).

The idea was ditched and Weetabix decided instead to go with figures and scenes from the *Asterix the Gaul* book range as the illustrative material already existed. Pietrsen was blacklisted by the cereal giants but did go on to have a successful career producing album cover artwork for ethereal musos such as Cocteau Twins and Enya.

Other notable food-based *Blake's 7* products included:

Blake

Servalan's Super Supreme Command Headquarters Super Space Spinner

In 1979 Crosse & Blackwell ran a promotion tied to their range of tinned ravioli. By simply collecting 25 labels from the cans you would become the lucky owner of a *Super Supreme Command Headquarters Super Space Spinner*. The point-of-sale displays were incredibly elaborate and the large cut-out card illustrations of Servalan, Travis and three Federation troopers are now highly collectible. It's a shame the same can't be said for the *Super Supreme Command Headquarters Super Space Spinner* which disappointed many (including three of the authors of this book) by being nothing more than a white frisbee.

PG Tips cards and book set, 'The Spaceships of *Blake's 7*'

Released by PG Tips in 1980, this card set and book proved incredibly popular. The 72 rectangular cards were given away in boxes of tea bags with one card in a box of 48, two in a box of 100 and four in a box of 360. The artist of the cards is unknown but the depictions of the *London*, the *Ortega*, XK-72 et al are terrific and worthy of reprinting. For an additional 50p you could purchase a booklet to stick the cards in, which included facts and figures about the ships and the series in general.

Gan's Milk Chocolate Limiter

Produced by Cadbury. They didn't sell one.

ADDENDA

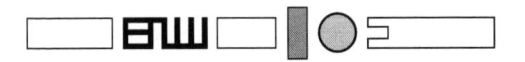

NUMBER CRUNCHING

Something we may have touched on throughout this book is the inability of anyone at the BBC in the 1970s being able to count over five. Terry Nation plucked the title *Blake's 7* out of thin air and from moment in time, whallop, it seems that no one with a full set of digits sat in on any of the production meetings or rehearsals.

Blake's 7. <u>*Blake's*</u> *7*. Blake and seven other characters. The seven who follow Blake. Not difficult to fathom, is it? Wrong.

Blake and SEVEN OTHER CHARACTERS totals eight (in case anyone from the BBC is reading this and is still struggling). So each episode should have the core cast of eight characters including Blake, right? Right. Let's see, shall we?

Season M

Episode	Crew members
The Way Back	**3** (Blake, Jenna, Vila)
Space Fall	**4** (Blake, Jenna, Vila, Gan, Avon)
Cygnus Alpha	**6** (Blake, Jenna, Vila, Gan, Avon, Zen)
Cygnus Beta	**6** (Blake, Jenna, Vila, Gan, Avon, Zen)
Time Squad	**7** (Blake, Jenna, Vila, Gan, Avon, Zen, Cally)
The Web	**7** (Blake, Jenna, Vila, Gan, Avon, Zen, Cally)
Seek-Locate-Destroy	**7** (Blake, Jenna, Vila, Gan, Avon, Zen, Cally)
Mission to Destiny	**7** (Blake, Jenna, Vila, Gan, Avon, Zen, Cally)
Duel	**7** (Blake, Jenna, Vila, Gan, Avon, Zen, Cally)
Project Avalon	**7** (Blake, Jenna, Vila, Gan, Avon, Zen, Cally)
Breakdown	**7** (Blake, Jenna, Vila, Gan, Avon, Zen, Cally)
Bounty	**7** (Blake, Jenna, Vila, Gan, Avon, Zen, Cally)
Deliverance	**7** (Blake, Jenna, Vila, Gan, Avon, Zen, Cally)
Orac	**8** (Blake, Jenna, Vila, Gan, Avon, Zen, Cally, Orac)

Excellent. So Season M managed *one* episode with the full crew as described in the title of the show. One, and an average of 6.4 crew members per episode. Rubbish! Way off. Right – onwards:

Season N

Episode	Crew members
Redemption	8 (Blake, Jenna, Vila, Gan, Avon, Zen, Cally, Orac)
Shadow	8 (Blake, Jenna, Vila, Gan, Avon, Zen, Cally, Orac)
Weapon	8 (Blake, Jenna, Vila, Gan, Avon, Zen, Cally, Orac)
Horizon	8 (Blake, Jenna, Vila, Gan, Avon, Zen, Cally, Orac)
Pressure Point	8 (Blake, Jenna, Vila, Gan, Avon, Zen, Cally, Orac)
Restitution	7 (Blake, Jenna, Vila, Avon, Zen, Cally, Orac)
Trial	7 (Blake, Jenna, Vila, Avon, Zen, Cally, Orac)
Killer	7 (Blake, Jenna, Vila, Avon, Zen, Cally, Orac)
Hostage	7 (Blake, Jenna, Vila, Avon, Zen, Cally, Orac)
Countdown	7 (Blake, Jenna, Vila, Avon, Zen, Cally, Orac)
Voice...	7 (Blake, Jenna, Vila, Avon, Zen, Cally, Orac)
Gambit	7 (Blake, Jenna, Vila, Avon, Zen, Cally, Orac)
The Keeper	7 (Blake, Jenna, Vila, Avon, Zen, Cally, Orac)
Star One	7 (Blake, Jenna, Vila, Avon, Zen, Cally, Orac)

Wow, Season N was off to a flying start with five consecutive episodes delivering the promise laid out in that lovely red, blue and gold logo. But then – aaaggghh! Bye bye Gan, and you're back to Blake's 6. Terry Nation, what were you thinking? The Season N average of 7.3 crew members is a great improvement but the title of the show is still a lie. Oh well, maybe Season P will improve the average crew member tally:

Season P

Episode	Crew members
Aftermath	5 (Vila, Avon, Zen, Cally, Orac)
Powerplay	7 (Vila, Avon, Zen, Cally, Orac, Dayna, Tarrant)
Volcano	7 (Vila, Avon, Zen, Cally, Orac, Dayna, Tarrant)
Flesh	7 (Vila, Avon, Zen, Cally, Orac, Dayna, Tarrant)
Zen	7 (Vila, Avon, Zen, Cally, Orac, Dayna, Tarrant)
Dawn of the Gods	7 (Vila, Avon, Zen, Cally, Orac, Dayna, Tarrant)
Twilight of the Gods	7 (Vila, Avon, Zen, Cally, Orac, Dayna, Tarrant)
The Harvest of Kairos	7 (Vila, Avon, Zen, Cally, Orac, Dayna, Tarrant)
City at the Edge...	7 (Vila, Avon, Zen, Cally, Orac, Dayna, Tarrant)
Children of Auron	7 (Vila, Avon, Zen, Cally, Orac, Dayna, Tarrant)

Episode	Crew members
Strike Attack!	7 (Vila, Avon, Zen, Cally, Orac, Dayna, Tarrant)
Rumours of Death	7 (Vila, Avon, Zen, Cally, Orac, Dayna, Tarrant)
Sarcophagus	7 (Vila, Avon, Zen, Cally, Orac, Dayna, Tarrant)
Ultraworld	7 (Vila, Avon, Zen, Cally, Orac, Dayna, Tarrant)
Space Beetles	7 (Vila, Avon, Zen, Cally, Orac, Dayna, Tarrant)
Moloch	7 (Vila, Avon, Zen, Cally, Orac, Dayna, Tarrant)
Death-Watch	7 (Vila, Avon, Zen, Cally, Orac, Dayna, Tarrant)
Terminal	7 (Vila, Avon, Zen, Cally, Orac, Dayna, Tarrant)

Weird year, this. While the average crew member tally drops again (down to 6.8), the majority of episodes do indeed see the full set of seven crew members – but no Blake. So gains and losses as far as title accuracy goes. Only Season R to go. Wouldn't it be good to go out on the full complement of crew after four years of adventures? Let's see!

Season R

Episode	Crew members
Rescue	5 (Vila, Avon, Orac, Dayna, Tarrant)
Power	7 (Vila, Avon, Orac, Dayna, Tarrant, Soolin, Slave)
Traitor	7 (Vila, Avon, Orac, Dayna, Tarrant, Soolin, Slave)
Breakout	7 (Vila, Avon, Orac, Dayna, Tarrant, Soolin, Slave)
Stardrive	7 (Vila, Avon, Orac, Dayna, Tarrant, Soolin, Slave)
Headhunter	7 (Vila, Avon, Orac, Dayna, Tarrant, Soolin, Slave)
Sabotage	7 (Vila, Avon, Orac, Dayna, Tarrant, Soolin, Slave)
Assassin	7 (Vila, Avon, Orac, Dayna, Tarrant, Soolin, Slave)
Jojoba	7 (Vila, Avon, Orac, Dayna, Tarrant, Soolin, Slave)
Games	7 (Vila, Avon, Orac, Dayna, Tarrant, Soolin, Slave)
Gravity	7 (Vila, Avon, Orac, Dayna, Tarrant, Soolin, Slave)
Destructor	7 (Vila, Avon, Orac, Dayna, Tarrant, Soolin, Slave)
Sand	7 (Vila, Avon, Orac, Dayna, Tarrant, Soolin, Slave)
Gold	7 (Vila, Avon, Orac, Dayna, Tarrant, Soolin, Slave)
Orbit	7 (Vila, Avon, Orac, Dayna, Tarrant, Soolin, Slave)
Warlord	7 (Vila, Avon, Orac, Dayna, Tarrant, Soolin, Slave)
Blake	8 (Blake, Vila, Avon, Orac, Dayna, Tarrant, Soolin, Slave)

Nope. Season R averages out at 6.9 crew members per episode so it is generally a repeat of Season P. At least Blake makes the effort to bung in an appearance and give us one final shot at an episode that includes him and his seven. (Actually 'one final shot' might be the wrong turn of phrase.)

So over the entire run of *Blake's 7* there are only 7 episodes with the correct number of crew and one of those is the final episode... Well, for mere moments at any rate; by the time 'Directed by Mary Ridge' appears on screen only Orac is left, and what bloody use is he without one of the eight to carry him around? You can see why they didn't make any more – *Not Even Blake's 1* is an awful title for a show.

Below: The letter received by David Maloney the day after "Death-Watch" was transmitted. George Hopbarley took very early retirement two weeks later (he was 24 years old).

BBC

BRITISH BROADCASTING CORPORATION
BROADCASTING HOUSE LONDON W1A 1AA
TELEX: 265781 CABLES: BROADCASTS LONDON TELEX
TELEPHONE 01-580 4468
DIRECT TELEPHONE LINE: 01-927

25th March 1980

Reference: B7/BS

David.

        Enough is enough. Once again I sat through an episode of your weird little television show last night and once again I find myself asking the same questions:

1. The show is called 'Blakes 7'. There is no Blake. What's all that about?

2. The '7' bit. There are not seven of them. If you tell me once again that the fishtank is a member of the crew I will punch someone, possibly you.

3. Do you have the phone number of the 'Doctor Who' production office? I'm not happy about the way things are going over there.

You're off-air for good after the next episode. I know when Bill Cotton gets back from his holiday next week he will thank me.

Yours,

George Hopbarley
Deputy Head of Drama

A to Z

0

5
number of control seats on the *Liberator* flight deck (designed that way by the BBC for 6 human characters).

7
number of persons not forming the total crew of the *Liberator* or *Scorpio*.

52
total number of episodes of *Blake's 7*.

64
other total number of episodes of *Blake's 7*.

54124
so obvious, even Piri could work it out. 7175.

A

A
mistakenly believed to be the initial *Blake's 7* season.

A Very Merry Federation Christmas!
what Travis wrote on Blake's Christmas cards.

Abandoned American Pilot Episode, The
episode of *Blake's 7* where the crew find the body of Amelia Earhart.

Adrenalin & Soma
reviving but reputedly addictive beverage served on board the *Liberator* as a food substitute in many episodes. AKA GREEN. (*See: Soma*)

After Gauda Prime
series of amateur audio plays released by Ron Earthy featuring Gary Russell as Vila and John Ainsworth as Avon.

Afterlife
speculative fiction about the events which followed the episode "Blake".

Air
breathed by multiple characters a number of times over the course of the series.

Almond, Marc
a more feminine Servalan.

Alwart, Ann
woman who kept writing to the BBC during the original run of *Blake's 7*, demanding that they send her her own personal Avon.

Anall Prior
unfortunate spelling error that was replicated no fewer than four times in the *Radio Times* during the course of *Blake's 7*'s television run.

Animals
1. creatures found across the universe, sometimes in zoos, sometimes not.
2. intentionally missed out of the episode guide, so take that smug grin off your face.

Apostrophe
seminal 1974 album from Frank Zappa, including the hits "Cosmik Debris" and "Don't Eat the Yellow Snow".

Apostrophe In The Title Of The Series, The
a subject too complex to explain in so small a space. For an in-depth explanation, please see our sister publication *Apostrophe's in Blakes 7*.

Aquarius
sister ship of *Scorpio*.

Aries
sister ship of *Scorpio*.

Assassin
this episode - and we don't want to spoil it for you - features an assassin. Clue: she's the actor with a 248:1 ratio of tears to talent.

Assymetric Thrust Computer
best-selling product at AnnDroid Summers eight years running.

Auron
1. brother of our Jack.

    2. almost an Auton.

    3. not Auronar.

Auton
the shizzle.

Avalon
1. legendary island from Arthurian folklore.
2. a 1982 album by Roxy Music.

Avalon Robot
used by Vila as a means of showing the other crew members where Gan touched him.

Avon
1. popular home delivery franchise supplying cosmetics, jewellery and other feminine enhancements.
2. a river.
3. a former county of England, abolished in 1996.
4. traditional opening gambit of *Sesame Street*'s vampire arithmomaniac, the Count.

Avon: A Terrible Novel
what everyone calls *that* book.

B

B
stinging honey-making insect.

B7
chord in music theory using the B major triad with an added flattened seventh.

BBC
British Broadcasting Corporation based in London, England.

Balls Dropping From The Ceiling With A Camera Pointed Up At Them
1. how the planets in the first title sequence were done.
2. Cally's recurring nightmare in "Dawn of the Gods".

Bang
the noise the explosions in *Blake's 7* make.

'Barbara Smelley'
the legendary graffiti daubed on Barbara Shelley's face during production of "Stardrive".

Barber, Glynis
nice arse.

Bartolemew
spiky-haired offspring of Homer and Marge Simpson.

Bayban the Butcher
jolly, tousle-haired purveyor of Babe's Prime Sausages.

Bellfriar, Doctor
medical professional, struck off after some extremely dodgy practices inspired by his own name.

Ben 10
the third sequel series to *Blake's 7*.

Big Gun With Bullets In It That Doesn't Appear Anywhere Else In the Series, The
what Avon shoots Blake with.

Billy Webb
the episode "The Web" was named after Billy, following his tragic death from leukaemia in 1977.

Bishop Auckland
the place Control was located just outside of in "Pressure Point" though never mentioned on screen.

Black Hole
an anomalous area of existence where space and time fold back on themselves *(see: Black Hole)*.

Blake's Heaven
seminal book about *Blake's 7*. This book is without doubt the greatest achievement of humanity, the pinnacle of mortal endeavour; a comprehensive summary of the human condition, viewed sharply through the glass of late '70s BBC television. All in all, a monumental

work, destined to become a core text in the study of the paradigms of our being. It is no small understatement to say that these authors are at the top of their field and should be rightly considered as gods. Oh, and then we renamed the book to **MAXIMUM POWER!**

Blake's 7
popular television show about *Blake's 7*.

Blake's 8
the rarely-seen sequel series, shown on ITV. Where's the DVD, Network?

Blake's Aid
famous '80s rock concert organised by Bob Geldof, aimed at getting the series back on our screens after so many long years, and the only time Steven Pacey publicly performed "There's a Distant Star".

Blake's Junction 7
in many ways superior to the programme it set out to parody.

Blake Shaven
the title of *that* video.

Blakey's 7
dismal *On the Buses* spin-off, best forgotten.

Blakezade
unpopular fizzy drink sold in the 1970s by Schweppes. Withdrawn after complaints that the bubbles were formed from Pylene-50. Originally marketed as Vitazade.

Blayg Zeven
unused character from the seventh episode of the series *Blake's 7*.

Blue
a colour often seen in the programme, including the first episode and the last.

Boucher, Croucher, Sloucher, Oucher, Loucher, Poucher, Toucher
The Blake's Seven Dwarves.

Bounty
coconut-filled chocolate snack which used to come packed in a small cardboard tray, the perfect size for building ramps for Matchbox cars.

Bounty Hunter
stalkers of coconut-filled chocolate snacks.

Brimbles, The
animated children's series featuring the exploits of *Blake's 7* guest star Nick Brimble and his brothers Ian and Vincent.

Brown, Bobbie
American R&B singer; played Zeeona in "Warlord".

Bukkake
Federation governor of the planet Karim-Pi who met a sticky end in the episode "Space Beetles".

Bush, Kate
originally offered the role of Cally in the BBC TV series *Blake's 7*.

Button
    1. controls seen on the flight deck of the *Liberator* from time to time. Some were pressed by members of the crew so that things would happen.

    2. Fastenings for clothing seen on the flight deck of the *Liberator* whenever a character was wearing clothes which fasten using buttons.

    3. character from *Cinderella*, as yet unseen in an episode of *Blake's 7*.

    4. chocolate discs, often milk chocolate, quite tasty.

C

Califeron
planet? Something to do with Cally? No idea.

Callaghan, James
the Prime Minister when *Blake's 7* began.

Cally
the other one.

Calpol
planet visited by Blake in his search for the location of Star One.

Camfield, Douglas
a man.

Cancer
1. Exceptionally irritating assassin with a penchant for ant-hill hair.
2. sister ship of *Scorpio*.

Canderel
sugar substitute.

Cannon
big pointy shooty gun thing.

Capricorn
sister ship of *Scorpio*.

Cardboard, egg boxes and sticky tape
what the 'Security Robot' seen in the early episodes of *Blake's 7* was made out of.

Caspar
continuing Season R's theme of planets with really naff names, Caspar is home to the Space Rats *(see: Space Rats)* and sand *(see: sand)* in the *Blake's 7* (look at the cover) episode 'Stardrive' (don't bother, there isn't an entry for that)

Casper
name of my now-dead pet hamster.

Central Control
a sort of control centre.

Chair
a raised, stable surface used for sitting on.

Chenga
diverting game involving several small wooden blocks stacked into a tower and then removed one at a time in turns.

Child Molestation
what Blake claimed that he didn't do.

Child mole station
where the young moles work.

Children of Auron
nieces of our Jack.

Clip Gun
revolutionary personal firearms found aboard the *Scorpio*. A variety of clips offered different levels of destructive power. Only having one of each type led to frequent squabbles among the crew whose turn it was to have the "mildly amusing noise" clip.

Clip Gun Clip
clips used in the *Scorpio* Clip Gun *(see: Clip Gun)*. Clips available included kill, stun, plasma bullet, laser, percussion shell, smoke grenade, tear gas, tranquiliser, Rohypnol, acid, smack, gin, fishcake, neapolitan, raspberry ripple, smokey bacon and cheese and onion.

Clip Gun Clip Chips
bits of the clip gun clips that are on the floor after the clip gun clips have been dropped.

Clip Gun Clip Clips
used for attaching a clip gun clip to a belt.

Clip Gun Clip Clops
the sound a clip gun clip makes when it hits the deck of the *Scorpio*.

Clit Gun
aborted idea from Season R, vetoed by Vere Lorrimer.

Cocksnot
type of beverage served on Freedom City.

Coconuts
coconuts were the favourite food of Gan, and were present in every episode in which he appeared, although they weren't visible on-screen as they were in the *Liberator* kitchen. In a box. In a cupboard.

Colin Jeavons' Blake's Sevens
what the series would have been called if Colin Jeavons had created it, twice.

Colin Jeavons' Blake's Seven Heaven
what Colin Jeavons thought that he was in when he was told by his agent that he would be playing the role of Blake. Unfortunately for Col,

he had in fact been cast as a Flake, in a Cadbury's advert. Being cast in the role of a brown log didn't go down well with Jeavons at all and he retreated to his tree house for a period of four years before he could be convinced to go back into acting again.

COM-PU-TER 5000
the rarely-seen *Liberator* 'cute' robot. You know the type – every show from this period just had to have a funny little robot character who would invariably do something totally stupid, thereby causing a catastrophic event. COM-PU-TER 5000 was so useless that he couldn't even manage to do the vacuuming duties that Orac assigned to him.

Confirmed
what you can get done at church if you are of the religious persuasion.

Continuity
a means of distracting virgins.

Cor Anglais
musical instrument played by Sub-Commander Raiker. He was particularly good at Largo from the New World Symphony.

Countdown
a consonant, a vowel, a vowel, a consonant, a consonant, another consonant, a vowel, a consonant, and a... er, a consonant.

Critical Mass
a problem with dodgy material encountered by the crew during the episode 'Orbit'.

Critical Mess
a problem with dodgy material encountered by the crew during the rest of the series.

Cross Stitch Pattern
how Blake's face appears in the original opening credits of the series.

Cygnus Alpha
boss of the swans.

Cygnet Alpha
boss of the baby swans.

Cygnet Ring
the star system the two above planets are located in.

Cygnet's Seven
poorly realised children's puppet series adaptation using swan, geese and chickens.

D

Da da da daaah da daaa, da da daaah da-daaa, daaah
how the theme tune goes.

Dainer
guard aboard the Federation penal ship *London*. Not the first name to be recycled later in the show and certainly not the last.

Daleks
the robotic / mutant life-form created by Terry Nation for the television series *Doctor Who*, and reportedly set to appear as the villains in an early story outline for what eventually became oh sod this for a game of soldiers haven't we finished this damn book yet?

'Dammit, what weighs seventy kilos?'
seventy bags of sugar.

Daniel Hill
the location where 'Sand' was filmed.

Davis, Colin
ever heard of the writer of 'Gold' since he wrote 'Gold'? No, us neither.

Deadly Dudley
dramatically insistent BBC noise merchant.

Deathwatch With Mother
Videodrome's programming strand for the under-fives. Popular entries in the series included *Mary, Mungo and Murder*, *Hector's House of Horrors* and *Papercuts*.

Decimas
the little dots that you put in between pounds and pence when you are writing down monetary amounts.

Deep Roy
slang phrase to denote being in a lot of trouble.

Deliverance
fifty minutes long and not a single banjo.

Delta Grade
(see: Crimo)

Derek Farr and Roy Kinnear
would make a great double-act: 'Who are they and where are they?' / 'They're Farr-Kinnear'.

Destructors
go on, have a guess.

Diogenes Laërtius
Third Century Greek scholar who famously predicted the creation of *Blake's 7* by some 1700 years. See page 2 of his book Lives and Opinions of Eminent Philosophers.

Dirty Gertie
the computer onboard Servalan's private spaceship, *Nomba 30*.

Doctor Havant-Gotaclue
what his patients call him behind his back, made worse by the initial from his first name, Ian.

Dong
the sound that clock makes in that episode with all the clocks.

Dorian
semi-amusing Jewish neighbour in the sitcom *Birds of a Feather*.

Drilldo
Federation torture device.

DSV2
official designation of the *Liberator*. We're guessing it stands for "Deep Space Vehicle".

Dumbledore
Nothing to do with *Blake's 7* whatsoever.

E

Earth
brown stuff on the ground.

"EEEEEEE!"
noise emitted by the Decimas.

Egg Incident, The
something that the BBC has prohibited anybody involved with *Blake's 7* from ever talking about.

Egrorian
mad scientist with Max Wall haircut, also wife of Pinder.

Emmerdale Farm
where Jenna moved when she left the *Liberator*.

Ensor
1. not where the Ewoks lived, they live on the forest moon of Endor.
2. built Orac. Thank him later.

Etheric Detector Beams
Liberator scanning beam mentioned in 'Time Squad', and oddly similar to the 'Etheric Beam Locator' mentioned in Nation's *Doctor Who* story written by Robert Holmes 'Genesis of the Daleks'.

Eyepatch
item worn by Travis, pirates, Gabrielle and Nicholas Courtney.

F

The Federation
that spacey organisation that Captain Kirk and Dr Spock work for.

Federation Olympics
Earth sports festival run every four years, with Servalan presiding. Events include the sprint, the big jump, the security vault, the Federation pursuit, the Mutoid tussle, the faked molestation, the sham trials, the shooting an extra with a gun concealed in a glove, and the eyepatch murders.

Federation Pursuit Ship
life-sized cardboard paintings of menacing, beweaponed starfighters. Available in threes for easy packing and storage.

Fishtank
Orac's main structure is made from Ensor's old fishtank.

Fisting
Fisting was the name of the gestalt organism formed when Fis and Ting merged in the episode 'Rocks'.

Flange
one of the Space Rats.

Flight Deck Ceiling, The
the mysterious Flight Deck Ceiling, who knows what it looked like? Who knows what mysteries it contains? Who cares what colour and shape it might be?

Flying Zither Thing
the highlight of 'Sarcophagus'.

Food
that stuff you shove down your throat in order to maintain your shapely curves. Come on, really? You need a glossary to tell you what food is?

Forks
one of Sarkoff's precious Earth artefacts in the episode 'Bounty'.

Forkoff
Sarkoff's brother.

Four pounds thirty five
what the episode 'Sarcophagus' was made with.

G

G.P.
what the locals call "Gauda Prime"

Gambit
    1. Belkov's woman computer. Voiced by the woman actress who also provided the "Ground Floor: perfumery, stationery and leather

goods..." woman introduction to *Are You Being Served?*

2. game show hosted by Fred Dineage

Gan
chemical symbol for Gallium Nitride, a semiconductor used in light-emitting diodes.

Ganbit
probably quite big, as bits go.

Gareth, Thomas
the lead actor. Come on, these are basics, keep up!

Gareth Thomas's Accent
not Welsh, as you might expect. Thomas dropped his accent in the 1970s, when Welshmen were frowned upon.

Gareth Thompson
often mistaken for the lead actor from the BBC Television series *Blake's 7* by needy fans scouring their local phone book.

Gareth Roberts
Doctor Who writer, often mistaken for the lead actor from the BBC Television series *Blake's 7* by needy fans scouring their local phone book.

Gemini
sister ship of *Scorpio*.

Gin
fat, stumbling, drunkard character killed off in 'Pressure Point'. I bet he stank.

Giroc
you would, wouldn't you? Or are we thinking of Sinofar here?

Glossary
what something is if it's painted and looks shiny.

Gola
ruler of the planet Goth, the main producer of cheap trainers for the whole of Earth.

Gold
expensive off-coloured silver.

Gouda Prime
the Number 1 cheese in the Netherlands.

Gough, Michael & Farr, Derek
founders of the rock group Farr Gough.

Grand Theft Auto: The Federation
the best *Blake's 7* computer game ever released. You get to steal the *Liberator* and fly round and crash into planets and things! One of the very few occasions when it is actually cool to be Tarrant.

Grass
moist green bladed covering of various Federation occupied planets. Not to be confused with sand.

GREEN
Delicious fluid, named for its distinctive colour.

Grey
official colour of Season R.

Guitar Scene, The
most fans' favourite scene in the programme.

Gun-Sarr
brother of Mum-Ra and scourge of the Space Rats, themselves distant cousins of *Thundercats*.

Gunt
Brutish warrior queen with tight-fitting trousers in '*Blake's 7* and the Space Warrior Queens from Space' by Pip and Jane Baker.

Gween
wrong programme.

H

Hair Dryer
name of one of the alien ships seen in the episode 'Star One'.

Hand
Travis has a false hand which contains a super-duper laser. Depending on the scene he's in, this hand can be extremely rigid. At other times it acts like a normal hand in a glove. Travis is right-handed. Gan is the only southpaw in the crew but even he uses his right hand so as not to be considered a freak.

Harris, Fred
presenter of early 1980's computer-based television programmes. Also appeared on *Play School*.

Hat, John Leeson's
from the episode 'Gambit' – deserves an entry all of its own.

Helmets
items worn by Federation Guards to protect their heads from damage.

Helotrix
what to say if you meet someone called Patricia.

'Hello, there! I'm a spy / escaped prisoner.'
dodgy 'confuse the guards' gambit that Nation uses in both 'Genesis of the Daleks' and 'Seek-Locate-Destroy'.

Hob-Nob
small tasty oat-based biscuit.

Horizon
the *Blake's 7* fan club.

Hudson, June
arch-villainess of Season N. Came close to destroying all credibility in Blake and his crew throughout the galaxy.

I

Iago, Kaston
character in the brilliant *Kaldor City* audio series played by Paul Darrow. Give them a go.

Ice
cold variant of water. Not as hot as fire.

'I'm not worth dying for!'
you got that right, bubba.

IMIPAK
dehydrated spud powder, sold in Freedom City (Instant Mash In a Pack)

Implant
Gan had one in his head.

In Cold Blood
unused script from Season P, written by the mysterious 'Paula D. Arrow'. About Avon.

Inhibitor
Gan actually had one of these in his head. Not sure why we called it an implant.

Irvine, Glos
Mat's brother.

Island of Dr. Moreau, The
does not exist. Nor does any episode that it may have influenced.

J

Jacko from *Brush Strokes*
Karl Howman.

Jam
fruit preserve often stored in jars. Paul Darrow's favourite jam is apricot while the late David Jackson favoured gooseberry. We don't know which jam Glynis Barber likes best, but we bet it's something like strawberry or raspberry.

Jenna Stannis
minor character in 'The Way Back'.

Jewels
pricey pebbles.

John
first name of the Federation Trooper in the background of scene 26 in episode B/07.

Johnny Foureyes
character cut from the script of 'The Way Back' when he was considered too difficult to realise.

Join the Dots
if you join the dots that the stars form in the third *Liberator* shot in Gambit, it forms a picture of baby Jesus' face.

Justin
charismatic, sexy and convincing ex-lover of Dayna. Justin bears the distinction of being in the very best non-existent episode of *Blake's 7* ever ever. Also appeared in *Dixon of Dock Green*.

K

Ka-Kah
type of bird found on Mogadon 8.

Kairopan
1. you wouldn't believe us if we told you.
2. a cooking implement used in Egypt.

Katie
Avon's daughter, from the two-parter 'Escape Plan' / 'Counter Plot'.

Kay, Bernard
actor who never appeared in the programme.

Keating, Michael
Batman

Kerguelen
Avon's full first name, apparently, according to some book Darrow tossed out. Thought you should know. Quite why his parents would choose to name him after a deserted French island group in the Southern Indian Ocean is anybody's guess.

Kerril
female mercenary. Distraught by her break-up with Vila Restal, she underwent gender reassignment surgery and joined the crew of Storm Mine 4 with tragic consequences.

Killer
an episode of *Blake's 7*, named to distinguish it from all the other episodes, where no-one kills anyone.

Kinnear, Roy
the actor who the character Keiller in the episode '*Gold*' looked a bit like.

Klegg, Sigshun Litre
rogue Federation trooper who seized the *Liberator* after all that nonsense at 'Star One'.

Klute
a film starring Jane Fonda and Donald Sutherland.

Klute
a nightclub for fourteen year-olds in Durham. From Wikipedia: "Klute is said to be the 'Worst Nightclub in Europe'." It is.

Knee
joint connecting the upper and lower parts of a human leg. Federation Troopers typically have two "knees".

Knives
knives were one of Sarkoff's precious Earth artefacts in the episode 'Bounty'.

Knyvette
a little knyve.

Krantor
insult used in a jocular fashion by the cast of the series whenever an over-the-top performance was given.

L

Labia Minor
this cannot be discussed for legal reasons.

Labia Prime
prison planet where Avon spent most of the original sixteenth episode when he was meant to be searching for the supercomputer C.R.U.D.Z.

Last remaining member of a long-dead, noble race
the description of Moloch in the script.

Last remaining turkey in the shop at Christmas
what we actually got.

Lauren
Dayna's adoptive sister. We're amazed that Terry didn't call her Rebecca.

Leather
primary source of clothing in the future, following the extinction of wool-bearing livestock and a general agreement that nylon gets a bit smelly. Often studded.

Leo
sister ship of *Scorpio*

Liberator
very large spaceship liberated by Blake and some others which houses the computer Zen and a teleport system. The *Liberator* was destroyed in the episode 'Terminus' and several others.

Libra
sister ship of *Scorpio*.

Limiter
device implanted in Terry Nation's brain which kicked in at times of intense mental strain, such as thinking up new character names and plots.

Lindor
a planet named after a type of chocolate, and mentioned in the episode 'Bounty'. Bounty is itself a type of chocolate, produced by Mars. Mars was itself named after a planet, Mars, in the Milky Way. The Milky Way is itself a type of chocolate, named after the galaxy. Galaxy is itself a type of chocolate.

Links
1. no way for grown men to earn a living.
2. something to do with the internet
3. and cuffs.

Little Nick Grimshaw
member of the *Liberator* crew who died between Seasons N and M.

lolBlakes
popular internet meme that went viral in '03.

London
prison ship seen transporting Blake and the eventual crew of the *Liberator* in the opening episode 'The Way Back'.

Lorrimer, Vera
well-known songsmith and minstrel.

Luba
star system annexed by the Federation. Also something else.

M

Magno Locks
magnetic locks controlled from some kind of central register.

Mary ridge
inflamed abrasion, suffered frequently by Pinder (cf. Tachyon Funnel).

Maximum Power
horse that won the National in 1981.

Maztaarb-8
(self) pleasure planet.

Meat Feast
Jenna's favourite pizza topping (as authors we differ on this. Matt feels Jenna is more of a Hawaiian type. Andy says she' would scoff spicy beef, while Chris thinks a Seafarer is more her style. Andrew however knows for a fact she likes Chicken Supreme but Phil disagrees and maintains it would be Margherita. Robert still thinks it's Meat Feast).

Melted Eyes
what the authors all now have after watching so much *Blake's 7*.

Mitchell, Mitch
English rock drummer and inventor of the teleport.

Moloch
we aren't sure really.

Moondiscs
gaudy amateur printed greetings cards for the sloth-like available from moondisc.com

Morphenniel
made-up name of the planet supposedly the destination of Jenna following the battle of Star One.

Motor Scooter
Avon's compact new battle-cruiser.

Müller
robotics expert and notorious fruit/yoghurt separator.

Mushy Peas
what Darrow attempts to spit out of his mouth convincingly in 'Gambit'.

Mutoids
race of poorly-utilised beings, more interesting as a concept than they ever were in execution.

N

Nairobi
capital city of Kenya.

Narrant, Tel
Terry Nation.

Nappy
item of clothing worn by...

Neebrox
nappy-wearing character from 'Assassin'. Said by one to resemble the actor who played the first *Doctor Who*, Peter Cushion.

Nestor Panden
leader of the resistance taskforce which lead the attack on BQ3 in the third season.

Nine
abortive programme title value replaced by the more "family-friendly" seven.

Noble, Larry
(see: the rest of this book)

Noble Larry
what Larry Noble was called by the cast and crew for his marvellous performance as Pinder.

'No, of course I haven't, mate. Fancy a cuppa? I'll tell you all about it.'
what Blake meant to say when Avon said, 'Have you betrayed me?'

O

Old Calendar
like the new calendar, just older.

Option
contractual obligation to a further recording block; in the case of David Jackson: cancelled.

Orac
Computer built by Ensor which can monitor anything not essential to the resolution of the plot. Occasionally appears in this book as ORAC owing to laziness on the part of those editing and proofing. If it bothers you that much, write a book about it and tell the world.

P

Pablo
the chap with the David Lynch haircut and the overalls in Solon's Brocade.

Pacey, Steven
80s TV heart-throb and leading proponent of the male permanent wave.

Pamela Salemap
what Pamela Salem changed her name to so it was more

palindrominous (if you use that word elsewhere you owe us royalties).

Paper
used to print scripts. Almost all the scripts in *Blake's 7* were printed on paper which was strict BBC policy at the time.

Parsnips
crucial element in the history of the series. It's widely reported that Roger Murray-Leach's *Liberator* design was created accidentally, when three parsnips fell on an onion.

Pasta
Avon's favourite food. Pasta. Al Dente. With nothing on it.

Pella
oh it hurts …

Pello
that bloke out of *Wet Wet Wet* who sings like an angel but talks like a docker.

Peter Travis
the Space Commander's full name. We say James earlier in the book. Mistakes like these are deliberate. If we intentionally fill the book with stuff like this you'll never know when we get it wrong. It's annoying for you, the reader and purchaser, but childish fun and a sort of "Get out of jail free" card for us.

Petertravis
a type of mineral found in the depths of space, very prized, apparently.

Pinder
minor character in the episode 'Orbit'.

Pinder Egg
small deposit laid by Pinder, with a toy inside.

Pinderella
Egrorian's Christmas Pantomime.

Pinder, Steven
played Max Farnham in *Brookside*, also appeared as a policeman in the stage version of *Last of the Summer Wine*: The Moonbather. We saw the latter and thought that he overplayed the role somewhat.

Pinder, Tommy
English comedian of the pre and post war years whose catchphrase was 'You lucky people'.

Pinder's Crispy Pancakes
failed business venture from Egrorian. The box scared people. We've not finished with Pinder puns yet.

Pinder tail on the donkey
Federation-outlawed sex game, favoured by Egrorian.

Pinder's List
dodgy film pun attempted by one of the idiot writers in this glossary.

Pint of Bitter and a Chocolate Hob-Nob, A
Gan's favourite tipple.

Pisces
sister ship of *Scorpio*.

Plague
the one Terry Nation idea that he didn't nick from his earlier work and reuse for *Blake's 7*. Fortunately Bob Holmes had it covered.

Plaster
something that Vila needed after grazing his knee in one episode.

Playgrounds
(see :"Saw")

Policía Nacional Bolivarian
Venezuala's national police force.

Porphyr Major
planet invented by Robert Holmes for 'Traitor'. It is presumably named after porphyria, a disease characterised by symptoms including purple urine. We have to try that.

Porphyrus
planet invented by Robert Holmes for 'Orbit'. It is presumably named after porphyria, a disease characterised by symptoms including purple urine.

Powerplay
Thames Televison series for pre-schoolers hosted by Section Leader Klegg and his mischievous spider helpers, Itsy and Bitsy.

Prophecy
imagine you're standing on a cliff. You could step forward, be blown over by the wind, be pushed or you could step back. Or you could not go near the cliff edge at all. That, according to Avon, is what a prophecy is.

Pubix
unfortunately-named alien character in one of the duller episodes.

Purchase, Bruce
(see: Subtlety in Acting)

Q

Quarter Pinder
What Egrorian buys every time he goes into a McDonalds. Bet you thought we were done with Pinder puns. Place your bets now: any more between Q and Z?

Queen
like a King but a girl.

Quex Park
the location for 'Bounty'. The only location used in the series which has a more spacey name than the place it's meant to be.

Quute
Federation Officer with an eyepatch. See Travis and ignore the bit about the wacky laser hand.

Qunt
another unfortunately-monikered Federation Officer.

R

R2D2
R2D2 is the secret combination code used by Avon to gain access to his

secret trunk that holds his collection of plundered gold goblets in 'Warlord'.

Radiation
rhymes with "Terry Nation" and nasty, nasty stuff. Especially if you eat, sniff, taste or touch it.

Radiation Flare Shield
special safety trousers worn when firing the *Liberator*'s neutron blasters. The crew can be seen wearing them most of the time. Just in case.

Red
Cally's favourite colour. Again we disagree on this one, but who are we to argue with the plain and clear facts laid out in the Writer's Notes issued by the production office during Season M?

Redemption
what happens to your emption if you rub it too hard.

Rictus Grin
Rictus Grin is the default expression used by Avon in 48% of his screen time.

Ritelis, Viktors
"Viktors Ritelis" has a base score of 20 in Scrabble. You'd think it'd be more wouldn't you?

Ro
roroYerboat

Rockfall
a cheese Terry Nation puts in every script.

Rolling Pin
Egrorian's hobby

Ronnie Marsh
area of the planet Helotrix, as seen in the episode 'Traitor'.

Rubber Dinghy Rapids
what Vila kept repeating under his breath when possessed by the Maron-Kal.

S

Sad Sack from 'The Raggy Dolls'
a dead ringer for Gan. Really. Google it.

Sagittarius
sister ship of *Scorpio*.

Sand
glimpsed briefly in the episode *Sand*.

Sarcophagus
alien artefact which engenders complete apathy in all who view it.

Saurian Major
1. planet used by the production team to represent far-off quarries in southern England.

2. rank in the Saurian army.

Saurian Minor
oiky little sibling planet of Saurian Major. Picks its nose a lot.

Scorpio
superfast spaceship from the far future with an incredible computer, designed to resemble a 1980s industrial unit on an out-of-town enterprise park. *Scorpio* is unique, it has no sister ships.

Sea Devil
(see: Devil)

Serva Ham
Italian fast food chain, popular during the 1980s.

Server LAN
something to do with the Federation's computer network. Possibly. We think.

Server Mam
Servalan's mam.

Servile Lamb
odiously obsequious young sheep.

Seven
number of sides on an 8-sided dice.

Sevenfold Crown
showbiz slang for "utter dross"

Six
(see "Seven")

'Sixpence and the promise of a kiss'
Jan Chappell's fee for her voiceover in 'Rescue'.

Shadow
an area unreachable by direct light from a source due to obstruction by an object.

Sham Maraj
character who Vila briefly wed so that she could obtain a Federation visa.

Shrinker
descriptive of the affect appearing in *Blake's 7* has on one's C.V.

Slash Fiction
what people who can't have sex do instead.

Slave
Ohio-based punk band who were popular in the late 1970s and 80s.

Smirnoff
the former President of Lindor, played by TP McKenna.

Soma
ladies' private juice.

Soolin
(see, Barber, Glynis)

Space
space appeared in *Blake's 7* a number of times. Usually appearing as a large black mass, with the occasional star dotted hither and thither but sometimes appeared with nice swirly coloured patterns.

Space City
a city in space. Not to be confused with CitySpace.

Space Commander
one who commands space.

Space Drinks
liquids consumed in space *(see: Space)*. Blue is the colour of space drinks *(see also: GREEN)*.

Space Monopoly
complex board game mirroring the acquisition of planets by a fascist Federation, played cheerfully by their strongest opponents on several occasions. It has less squares than proper Monopoly, despite Space being bigger than London.

Space Rats
two-dimensional Mohican-helmetted space punks who ride around on those crappy bouncy trikes like livid toddlers in a massive sandy nursery with no teacher in sight because she's too busy building a stardrive.

Special Effects
very special indeed.

Speed Chess
    1. like normal chess but 8-bit.
    2. chess played under the influence of amphetamines.

Squits, The
water-based life-form from the planet Skidola.

Standard
just sort of normal really. Nowt special.

Standard by Two
a bit more special.

Standing Room Only
given those stand-up chair console things on the *Liberator* flight deck, we do sometimes wonder what the toilet facilities are like.

Star One
a low-rent Death Star.

Star Two
the sequel to *Star One* – coming soon...

Star Fish
the Federation's initial design for what would become Star One. Rejected for being 'ridiculous'.

Stardrive
the force behind Darrow's increasingly bonkers performance in Season R.

St. Ardrive
the patron saint of ropey acting.

Stasis
word that no-one in "Duel" can pronounce. The same problem occurs with Dave Lister in the original version of *Red Dwarf*'s "The End", for what it's worth.

Steed Malbranque
the alien horse ridden by Avon in the fourth season.

Super Fun Oppression Squad
Blake's 7 was sold around the world, but the Japanese put their own creative spin on the series by heavily re-editing each episode and inserting entirely new characters and scenes. See page 253 for more details.

System, The
supercomputer which took over and united three warring planets to create a utopia of lycra catsuits, plastic tabards, gap-toothed slaves and awesome spaceships like our very own *Liberator*.

T

Tachyon Funnel
sexual position favoured by Egrorian. Not by Pinder though.

Tal Fallor
the padre onboard the *Liberator*, seen only once, in "Strike Attack!".

Tarantula
a type of spider, invented by Terry Nation.

Tarrant
fictional village as seen in the 1980s BBC drama *Howard's Way*.

Tarrant, Chris
Del and Deeta's other brother.

Tarrant, Del
short for Derek.

Tarrant, Dev
nasty, shifty sort of chap who betrayed Blake and the rebels to the Federation in "The Way Back". He had a limp, too, just to really drive home the fact that he's a wrong 'un. Del Tarrant buggered things up for Blake in "Blake" and he had a limp too. Never go near a bloke called Tarrant if he's got a limp.

Tarrant Nostra
website for fans of *Blake's 7* actor Steven Pacey.

Taurus
sister ship of *Scorpio*.

Teal Star
early hit for 1960s pop act The Tornadoes.

Teepee McKenna
Irish/Native American location manager on Season N.

Telepath
Cally was a telepath. Telepaths hate televisions to the point of murder.

Teleport
1. a means of instantly travelling from one place to another, to the accompaniment of a funky disco cymbal and a hand-drawn wibbly line. Think *Star Trek* transporter done with pocket money and a good old fashioned British 'that'll do' attitude.

2. unique to the *Liberator* and no other ship in the known cosmos, this is a method by which you can transport people instantly from

ship to planet and back again using a small (!) bracelet to communicate and track with.

3. unique to *Scorpio* and no other ship in the known ... oh, just see above.

Teleport Bracelet
slightly effeminate *Liberator* fashion accesory.

Teleport Set (corner of), The
where the cast and crew would gather for a ceremonial widdle at the start of each recording block. *(Seasons M-P only. For Season R, see: Barber, Glynis.)*

Telly port
an input on my set that I don't really know what it does.

Terminal
a film by Steven Spielberg.

Ternent
Ternent was the real name of one of the Federation guards in the episode "Powerplay", whose name was yet another based on that of Terry Nation. He was played by former Gillingham, Burnley and Huddersfield manager Stan Ternent.

Terra Nostra
a sharp, pinched, angled nose *(see: Darrow, Paul)*.

Terry's Chocolate Orange
what Nation was eating when he invented Zen.

Theek-Locate-Dethtroy
The thtory Jon Pertwee wath in.

'There's a distant star, in a distant sky, past the edge of time, way past Gemini'
oh, how to explain...

The Third Century of the Second Calendar
although it's not stated on-screen, the series apparently takes place after a major catastrophe has caused a huge shake-up of society. This is not a million miles from the plot of Terry Nation's earlier series,

Survivors. We like to think that *Blake's 7* takes place in the same fictional universe, and Servalan is a direct descendant of Abby Grant.

t'Ommiks
race of men opposed to t'Seska.

Town, Cy
actor who played Hal Mellanby.

Toyzarus
deadly dinosaur creature kept as a pet by Servalan.

Travis
'90s Scots pop group whose hits included "Why does it Always Rain on Me" and "Sing".

Travesty
a bit like Travis.

Trivial Pursuit Ship
a not very significant craft in the Federation's fleet. It consists of one large circular craft and six brightly coloured smaller craft that dock inside it.

Trooper Parr
Abba lyric.

Trousers
many episodes of *Blake's 7* feature trousers, a futuristic system of sewn fabrics utilised to cover the leg-based areas.

The Tumbleweeds
alien plant life form famous for their ability to chivvy people into action and their perfectly balanced repertoire of adult and family jokes and impersonations.

U

Ultraworld
the best world there is.

Underpant Story, The
familiar anecdote frequently told by cast members at conventions.

United Planets of Teal
actually it's just Teal. The other planet is Vandor and they're at war with them. Not sure why that makes them united really.

United Planets of Benetton
other, less important planets.

Uvanov
character from the *Doctor Who* story "The Robots of Death" never seen in *Blake's 7*.

V

Vandor
what you open to get into a van.

Vas Deferens
one of the rebels glimpsed in "The Way Back".

Vicar of Walford Parish, London, England, Earth, The
the present-day vicar of Walford was Vila's great, great, great, great, great, great, great, great, great, great, great, great grandfather.

Victory
the result of a battle won.

Vic Tree
Stunt arranger on Season N.

Vila
an approachable range of clothing from Denmark, allowing women to dress fabulously without compromising with style, quality and the latest trends. Visit http://www.vila.com

Villa, Aston
Vila's favourite football team. Sorry.

Virgo
sister ship of *Scorpio*.

Volcano
Pointy hot rock.

W

Wallace, Gregg
a short, fat, bald grocer.

Warbles, The
angry aliens, as seen in the episode "Zen", who have big pointy noses and are dedicated to clearing their planet of all space litter.

Wasabi
Jane Sherwin's character in "Pressure Point". Hot.

Water
translucent multi-purpose liquid seen in several episodes of *Blake's 7*. Not safe to be consumed on Federation planets.

Web, The
common abbreviation for the internet's 'World Wide Web' site.

Wensleydale
popular crumbly-textured cheese eaten by Gareth Thomas from on-set catering during location filming for "Seek-Locate-Destroy", an episode of the BBC television series *Blake's 7*.

WFK-47-ZJ Alpha
this series of characters does not appear **anywhere** in the programme *Blake's 7*.

"When I'm Cleanin' Pinders"
song played by Egrorian on the ukulele.

White, Jeremy
viewer who made the news by dying of uncontrollable laughter watching the closing minutes of "Pressure Point".

Winky
the *Liberator* mascot, often seen perched on the top of Avon's console in the first three seasons. Remember when it fell off during the star beast chase? A great moment!

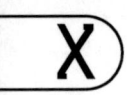

X

X
the unknown.

XK-72
some sort of space station we think. It's probably off-white/grey ... sort of half-built Airfix colour. Mat Irvine will know. Ring him.

X-Ray Specs
probably the name of the things worn by Hal Mellanby in the episode "Aftermath" which helped him to see or something.

Xanadu
Zen's real name as given to him by Zenda, his mummy.

Xenon Base
'Xenon Base, Xenon Base, we really love you, we think you're ace!' Popular early '80s skipping chant, heard in every playground in the country.

Xymines
as in 'Jumpin' Xymines! She's a mutoid!'

Y

Yartek
leader of the alien Voord.

'You never see a black Federation trooper'
lyric from that Iron Maiden song about *Blake's 7*.

You're Him, Aren't You?
autobiography of *Blake's 7* star Paul Darrow. It's available from Big Finish Books so why not order a copy?

Yowser
exclamation by Avon in the original script for "Blake" upon discovering that Blake may have betrayed him. Early visual effects experiments to give Avon Tex Avery-style eyes were abandoned on grounds of cost, drama and sense.

"You'll Never Walk Alone" by Gerry and the Pacemakers
Blake's favourite song.

Yukon
the setting for the poorly-conceived BBC2 travel series "Zukan in the Yukon".

Z

Zedona
Zukan's daughter. Yes, we know that technically it is 'Zeeona', but we aren't American for goodness' sake.

Zeeona's Hair
in case you were wondering, we wrote this whole book while wearing replicas of Zeeona's hair.

Ze Klute
(See: Klute)

Zen
The opposite of now in German.

Zerok
much like ze grass, ze sand and ze mud. And ze Klute.

Zerox
highly collectible early single from Adam Ant, released prior to his finding international fame with catchy post-punk pop.

Zog
former king of Albania and big time fan of *Captain Zep – Space Detective*.

Zukan
do it if you really want.

Zukan's Toucan
rarely-seen pet of Zukan. It had the same hairdo as his daughter.

Zupinders
What Pinder wears with his stockings

ACKNOWLEDGEMENT

We, the authors, acknowledge that this book is utterly useless as a reference guide.

REAL ACKNOWLEDGEMENTS

We owe thanks to a few people:

Harry Fielder, Kevin Davies, Stephen La Riviere (or however the hell he spells it), Tim Hirst, Paul Jones, Julian Knott, Telos Publishing for the far superior *Liberation* and Big Finish for keeping the dream. Huge thanks to all you lovely people for buying this book (possibly twice) and for supporting our charities of choice.

We'd also like to thank the brothel in Kingston upon Thames for providing no less than six Soolins, two Travii and one Avon during our long and close membership.

Chris would like to thank Claire and Sam.

Matt would like to thank Jo and Rhiannon, also Gavin French for first introducing me to *Blake's 7* and Torie for buying all the videos so I didn't have to.

Phil would like to thank any miserable sod who feels it might brighten their day.

Andy would like to thank Wendy, Harriet, Emily & Sam.

Robert would like to thank Ruth-Maria, Ed Stradling, Bernie Walsh and all at *www.eagletransporter.com*, Gareth Kavanagh, and Colin Brockhurst – and wishes that Cy Grant and Ian Scoones had got to see this book.

If this book is any good at all it is due to the time, effort, love and dedication of Phil Ware.

Finally, thanks to Ven Glynd, for prosecuting Roj Blake all those years ago in the future.

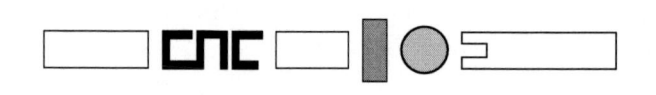

AFTER-AFTERFOREWORD

This edition of *Maximum Power!* was originally planned to help our old chum Colin Howard get out and about again. Unfortunately, as is often the case with these things, nothing went to plan and Colin raised his money before we'd even got a quote back from the printers. It was beautiful to see and we're so grateful for his understanding.

For various reasons close to the authors' hearts we've therefore switched the charity to Motor Neurone Disease. Partly because it sounds like Terry Nation created it, but also because… well, just Google it.

Since the book was originally published we've lost far too many people from the world of *Blake's 7* including Harry 'Aitch' Fielder whose foreword lurks in the front pages, Jacqueline Pearce (she called me 'baby', hugged and kissed me and I almost cried), Paul Darrow (we used to knock on his door in Chessington and shout 'Avon calling!') and Gareth Thomas (only good thing about *London's Burning*).

Also Phil Ware, one of our authors, has been recuperating from a stroke and may never be able to read this book again. Phil was our quality control man on not just this but all of Miwk's output and I miss his two-hour phone calls dearly.

So this new edition is for Phil and Colin.

We love you, guys.

Matt West and the Miwk gang: Robert Hammond, Andy Davidson and Chris & Andrew Orton (lovely couple, beautiful wedding).

SCRIPT DOCTOR

The Inside Story of **Doctor Who** 1986-89

by Andrew Cartmel

"There are worlds out there where the sky is burning, and the sea's asleep, and the rivers dream. People made of smoke, and cities made of song. Somewhere there's danger, somewhere there's injustice, and somewhere else the tea's getting cold. Come on, Ace — we've got work to do!"

Andrew Cartmel was the script editor on **Doctor Who** from 1986 to 1989. During his time on the show he introduced the seventh Doctor and his companion Ace (Sylvester McCoy and Sophie Aldred) and oversaw forty-two scripts written by eight writers new to the series.

With a clear mission to bring proper science fiction back into **Doctor Who**, he formulated what was later termed 'The Cartmel Masterplan', re-introducing the mystery to the character of the Doctor as the series celebrated its twenty-fifth anniversary and beyond.

Script Doctor is his memoir of this time based on his diaries written sometimes on set and sometimes not even in the diary itself but on the back of scripts. Illustrated with 32 pages of photographs, many of them not published before, this is a vivid account of life in the **Doctor Who** production office in the late eighties.

THE
WORZEL
BOOK

by Stuart Manning

When a former Time Lord swapped time and space for the mystery of the countryside, one of children's television's most unusual personalities was born. Jon Pertwee's portrayal of the anarchic scarecrow Worzel Gummidge won him a new generation of viewers and would become his most enduring character.

The Worzel Book traces the journey of Scatterbrook's scarecrow, from the days of early radio and the novels of Barbara Euphan Todd, through to the hit ITV television series and its eventual resurrection in New Zealand.

This is the untold behind-the-scenes story of a much-loved TV classic, featuring over 40 new interviews with cast and crew, including Geoffrey Bayldon, Jeremy Austin, Bernard Cribbins, Barbara Windsor and Lorraine Chase, illustrated throughout with over 200 photographs in black and white and colour, many previously unseen.